IS IT REAL WHEN IT DOESN'T WORK?

Doug Murren
and
Barb Shurin

THOMAS NELSON PUBLISHERS

Nashville

To the family of believers
at Eastside Foursquare Church

Published in Nashville, Tennessee, by Thomas Nelson, Inc., and
distributed in Canada by Lawson Falle, Ltd., Cambridge,
Ontario.

Unless otherwise noted, Scripture quotations are from the NEW
KING JAMES VERSION of the Bible. Copyright © 1979, 1980,
1982, Thomas Nelson, Inc., Publishers.

Scripture quotations noted NIV are from the Holy Bible: New
International Version. Copyright © 1973, 1978, 1984 by the
International Bible Society. Used by permission of Zondervan
Bible Publishers.

Library of Congress Cataloging-in-Publication Data

Murren, Doug, 1951–
    Is it real when it doesn't work? / Doug Murren and Barb
      Shurin.
      p.   cm.
    Includes bibliographical references.
    ISBN 0-8407-7472-9
    1. Christian life—1960– 2. Murren, Doug, 1951–
      I. Shurin,
Barb. II. Title.
BV4501.2.M88 1990
248—dc20   90–38076
                                          CIP

Printed in the United States of America
1 2 3 4 5 6 7 — 95 94 93 92 91 90

Contents

Introduction

I have only one problem with "formula Christianity": It doesn't work!

Events like sitting in the burn ward of a local hospital, talking to the lone survivor of a helicopter crash, have totally shattered for me all formulas for being a Christian. In that crash a young woman had lost her entire family in just one, dark moment; her husband and two children were snuffed out, just like that.

As I sat in her hospital room, gazing down at her on the "swing" bed on which she rotated to allow her blood to circulate more freely to the charred, pain-filled tissues of her skin, I began to speak with her. She was a Christian.

Her oft-spoken question to me over the three weeks that we prayed together was "Why did this happen to me? I love God." Her only prayer request was "Pray that I'll die, Pastor."

She did eventually die after three weeks of total agony. Because I trust in the sovereignty of God, however, I know that His purposes prevailed in her life. She was angry, bewildered, perhaps even bitter. I have to admit that her question was contagious and landed squarely in the hearts of all those who came to minister to her.

When I walked through a Haitian orphanage hospital, I could find no Christian formulas working that day, either. In fact, I couldn't even eat later. My vision had locked onto the sad, sobering picture of the distended bodies of children suffering from extreme malnutrition. My heart choked on the thought that their parents had actually given them up, hoping that someone would feed them; they could leave these fragile, precious lives to chance.

Large tumors hung from the children's arms and legs; mucus from tuberculosis trickled down their small faces. Forty or fifty kids grabbed my legs, literally climbing on top of one another, trying to be held by me. My heart ached for them.

Why them, God? Why not me, instead?

I also faced the agony of holding my little girl in the middle of the night, trying to comfort her as she cried and whimpered after major surgery. Raissa had been born prematurely. As with many premature babies, the oxygen supply had been cut off too long from her brain, leaving her a victim of cerebral palsy. To allow her more mobility, skilled surgeons had totally remade her hips. The painkiller the doctor gave her seemed to have little effect. Neither could my wife and I find any balm to help ease the pain in our own hearts that awful night. We could only pray, "God, please heal her."

I found no formula Christianity that held up under this test, either. However, God never left us that traumatic night.

Though formula Christianity is an ever-present temptation, it never works. Actually, Christianity isn't even a creed. Christianity is a *relationship* with Jesus Christ. It is in this relationship with Christ that life finds its meaning and a sense of calmness in the face of turmoil and unpredictable pain.

Pragmatic Americans have allowed their religions to invade and interfere with their faith in Christ. Their "religion of the good life" is the competitive god to reality.

We would believe—if formula Christianity worked. *Technique* has become the faith of our time, however. We're in an age of doubting Thomases. "I won't believe, unless I see His hands and feet," Thomas said emphatically. We're in the same category: If it works, great! If it works, you are great, but it *must* work for me!

As a pastor, I've seen people lose their faith because of this kind of thinking. Now, don't get me wrong. In my short life, I've also seen a few miracles. In fact, I thoroughly believe in miracles. I know, without a doubt, that they occur today, just as they did in Christ's time. They're occurring right now as I write this. In fact, some of you reading this may have experienced miracles in your own lives.

But I don't think miracles come when we need them the most. At least, from my own perspective, they have never come when I thought I needed them the most.

Chapter 1 of Luke has a beautiful story about a priest and his wife, Zacharias and Elisabeth. The Bible says that they served the Lord faithfully, with sincerity of heart and with intensity of spirit. In his enigmatic way, Luke says that they were without a child. In addition, they were aged beyond the years of even expecting a child; yet, Zacharias was still found at the Lord's altar. It was at that altar that the Lord told him that he would receive a son.

Their son, John the Baptist, came very late in life when it was more difficult for them to enjoy a child. The formulas had failed for Zacharias and Elisabeth. The text even suggests that, perhaps, this topic of conversation was something the people of their day could not quite understand. Back then, couples "automatically" had children when they married, so Zacharias and Elisabeth must have had something innately wrong with them because they had no child. Yet, God knew when He wanted them to have a child. It did fit a formula, but not humanity's formula.

I have given a series of messages to my congregation from the book of Peter. As we worked through this book, both the congregation and my family began to experience a lot of help with and freedom from our frustrations with Christian formulas that had failed. First Peter was written by the apostle Peter—the first "rock" of Christ's church, the great, first elder of the church—and this book is addressed to a group of people for whom the usual Christian formulas hadn't been working either.

It was written to a group of dispersed Christians who had been forced to flee their homes and relatives. They had become refugees from their own homeland, a Christian *Diaspora,* the scattering of believers when Roman persecution reached Jerusalem in the early decades of the church, during the reign of Nero.

Most Bible scholars believe that this book of letters contains the last sermons that Peter ever wrote or preached. He was writing them to believers whose lives, families, and vocations had been disrupted, not in spite of their faith, but *because* of it. Economic and political conditions and pressures continued to hammer on the spiritual lives of Peter's friends.

He was greatly concerned for their welfare—and rightly so.

Would this flock lose their faith in the face of its apparent failure to work for them? Would they assume that God was now against them (an even worse problem)? These were certainly possibilities in the light of current events.

As we worked through this series on 1 Peter, I could imagine this age-old prophet grieving that, in his absence, his flock would buckle under this severe persecution. Peter knew he had to address the inexplicable: Why do Christians suffer? For that matter, why does anyone suffer? Especially, why do people suffer when they are seemingly doing right? If this young faith was to be God's final act on earth, why wasn't it bringing the easy life to its followers?

With great joy, a friend recently exclaimed to me: "Pastor Doug, my children are now attending the best school in Seattle! It was God all the way!"

At the time, I rejoiced with him. The next morning, however, a puzzling thought leaped into my mind while I was showering: What if it had been God's will for them to be in the *worst* school in Seattle, for whatever reason? Would we still have praised the Lord? Probably not. In America, particularly, I think we're committed to the comfortable—that is, the gospel of luxury, the faith of the expedient, and, sometimes, even the idea that God is the tool to get us what we really want.

The book of 1 Peter helped me to sort my way through many of these questions. I also confronted my own penchant for formulas—formulas that would insulate me from the need for relationships—formulas that would help me to avoid the painful and unwelcome in life. I have concluded that none of these is ultimately avoidable to a believer.

I'm not sure I can offer a solid philosophy about pain and suffering. Others with better minds and more time have done, and can do, that. But, on the flip side, I'm a pastor. I'm still concerned that the people I love and shepherd do not lose their faith in Jesus over misdirected Christian formulas.

The apostle Peter was attempting to answer the most difficult question in the Christian faith: Is Christianity real, even when it isn't working? Let's find out.

Chapter 1

Chosen by God
(1 Peter 1:1–2)

Peter, an apostle of Jesus Christ, To the pilgrims of the Dispersion in Pontus, Galatia, Cappadocia, Asia, and Bithynia, elect according to the foreknowledge of God the Father, in sanctification of the Spirit, for obedience and sprinkling of the blood of Jesus Christ. (1 Peter 1:1–2)

We all like to be chosen, for there's something very special about being chosen. Every girl in junior high loves to show off her "going steady" ring. That cheap little circle of metal around her ring finger speaks volumes about her being approved of and accepted by her "dreamboat" boyfriend.

I know I like to be chosen. I liked it back in junior high school when I was picked right after Todd Zorenson or Dave Black for the baseball team. Though I didn't match up to their athletic prowess, being chosen right after their names were called meant a great deal to me all the same.

Yes, we all like to be chosen. One day in Rome (or perhaps it was Babylon), the great apostle Peter wrote to a group of Christians to remind them that *they* were chosen too. He also reminded them that their being "called" by God was the very reason for their being Christians. Peter desired to impress on all his Christian friends that God had voted for them, that they were chosen by God.

All of us, from time to time, need to be jarred into facing the reality of being called by God. Humanism, on the other hand, tends to creep into our thinking concerning Christianity. It can come in a variety of forms, but usually has us believing that the whole idea was ours, not God's.

Toward the end of the nineteenth century, Alfred Nobel, a

Swedish chemist, awoke one morning to read the startling news of his own obituary in the local newspaper! That was stunning enough, but as he read, here's what it said: "Alfred Nobel, the inventor of dynamite, who died yesterday, devised a way for more people to be killed in a war than ever before, and he died a very rich man."

Actually, it was Alfred's older brother who had died, not Alfred himself. When the newspaper reporter heard that a Nobel had died, he wrongly assumed that it was Alfred, so the reporter took it upon himself to write an epitaph for Alfred.

Right then and there, Nobel decided that if that was how others perceived him to be, then he needed to change the direction of his life before he did actually die. He decided that he would much prefer to be known for something more edifying than having developed a device to kill more people than ever before and for having amassed a fortune because of it.

Of course, we all know that Alfred then initiated the Nobel Prize for Peace. He is now known as a pacifist who developed honors and awards for scientists and writers who foster and motivate civilization toward peace. Nobel may have rightly felt that "every man ought to have the chance to correct his epitaph in midstream and write a new one."

The book of 1 Peter challenges the dispersed church of Jesus Christ to remember that the very foundation of their faith is the fact that God voted for them. At this writing, the believers were facing terrible times and tough-to-handle problems. From its introduction to the end, this letter is filled with encouragement and exhortation that the believers should pause to consider their epitaphs. It was essential to Peter that each would have an epitaph befitting him or her as a believer—an epitaph that would glorify God.

Throughout, 1 Peter isolates four distinct ways in which God calls us to fulfill our purpose in life:

- holiness in the marketplace,
- holiness in our families,
- holiness in our relationships with others, and
- holiness in our future.

Nihilism (the belief that there is no meaning or purpose in existence) is one of the great diseases of our time. The street gangs in the 1980s exhibited its presence in their songs and lifestyle. A recent movie about the Vietnam War echoed this belief through the statement repeatedly spoken by soldiers on the war-torn hillsides of Vietnam: "It don't mean nothin'."

I honestly believe that the pandemic use of illegal, mind- and body-destroying drugs in our culture is nothing more than the manifestation of nihilism. It's a given: People cannot live without meaning and purpose! This senseless, meaningless philosophy has pervaded our society for a long time. After all, we figure, if we really have evolved from a one-celled animal or have grown out of some bump on a log, then what does it matter how we play out our lives?

The times we most need to be reminded of our call by God are when things aren't working out for us. Peter evidently felt the same way, for he painstakingly reminded his flock, who were facing the tortures of persecution and the agony of separation from loved ones, that they had been called by God.

The entire book of 1 Peter is designed to direct its readers to refocus the meaning of their lives, as well as to encourage them to believe and hold onto the fact that the ability to fulfill our purpose on this planet for the number of years allotted to us is not just a possibility, but a *promise*—even in the most treacherous times.

HISTORICAL BACKGROUND

The conditions that precipitated Peter's letter to the believers are found in this historical context: It all began on that fateful day of July 19, A.D. 64, in Rome, when Nero, the self-serving, lunatic emperor, put his own city to the torch. Singlehandedly, he literally turned Rome into a raging inferno!

It was already common court knowledge that he hated Rome's architectural layout. The inner-city streets were narrow and twisting; the wooden structures were dilapidated. It became an increasing embarrassment to him when foreign dignitaries journeyed to Rome.

Nero and his architects had designed and constructed a model of a new, symmetrical Rome, but he reasoned that his all-consuming ambition would never be realized, unless some stroke of fate somehow demolished the inner city. So, on that hot summer night, half-demented Nero decided to help fate along: He torched Rome! The historical account of this catastrophic event states that when the fire died out in places, Nero actually sent men out to set it ablaze again!

Though it was never really proved, it was, nevertheless, common knowledge that Nero had started the terrible conflagration that wiped out Rome's inner city and snuffed out hundreds of innocent lives. Out of Rome's charred remains, the phrase "Nero fiddled while Rome burned" was coined. Incensed Roman senators and citizens alike railed against Nero, demanding retribution.

Under this political pressure, Nero, being the coward that he was, looked for a scapegoat, and the Christians conveniently played into his hands. As Nero had some knowledge of "those who followed the teachings of one Christus," having been informed by his spies that the followers of the Way were looking for another city, he decided that the Christians would be the perfect ploy to take the heat off himself.

Nero screeched, "The Christians did it! They're to blame for this outrage! They have destroyed our beloved Rome so they could build another city for themselves. They must be severely punished! Soldiers, arrest the Christians and throw them in the dungeon!"

Having his soldiers arrest the Christians en masse at their meeting places, Nero not only lent credence to his monstrous lie, but also cleverly and diabolically got the Roman senators and citizens off his back. This marked the beginning of the Christians' hiding and meeting in the catacombs under the city—the approximate time when 1 Peter was written.

In those horrifying times, Christians were herded like cattle into the Colosseum and other sports arenas throughout the Roman Empire, where half-starved, ravenous lions were turned loose to chase, catch, and devour alive the hapless Christians! Evil Nero and the bloodthirsty Roman spectators, who cheered and jeered the wholesale slaughter of the Christians in a carnival-like atmosphere, thought this was great sport.

But it didn't stop there. Christians were also blamed for many natural tragedies. Any excuse was used to persecute them. Enough evidence has surfaced over the centuries to prove that these horrible, macabre events actually happened. It is known also that Christians were arrested by Nero's henchmen, dipped in vats of oil, and tied to stakes in Nero's gardens, where they were mercilessly ignited as torches to light the evening festivities Nero staged for his guests! The anguished screams and wails of the poor, tortured, dying Christians delighted the barbaric appetites of Nero and his guests. It was to this group of persecuted believers, facing these kinds of trials and tortures, that Peter addressed his concern and encouragement.

Peter's heart was moved to challenge his severely persecuted believers to refocus their lives. What had been a fairly secure environment for Christ's church for almost sixty-five years now became a dangerous environment. Except for the occasional, moderate harassment by nonbelieving Jews, Christians had experienced little or no interference in their worship. As the church became stronger and its ranks swelled, Jewish persecution abated. Then Nero commenced his personal vendetta against them, and Christians became fair game for one and all.

Imitating Nero's demented lead, his appointed governors, stationed in the outposts of the Roman Empire, perpetrated even more atrocities against Christians. For instance, whenever a natural disaster (such as an earthquake or a local flood) occurred, affecting that area's economy, the local governor would claim: "The atheists (Christians were called atheists) have brought this disaster upon us! They have made our gods angry because they live here. We must rid ourselves of them for bringing the judgment of our gods upon us!"

Consequently, in Asia Minor and other regions of the Roman Empire, thousands of Christians were regularly rounded up, tortured, and murdered mercilessly. These tactics of local governors curried favor with the central government in Rome, advanced their political careers, and assured their continuance in office.

Though Christianity was originally a *religio licitus* (legal/permitted religion) and was initially considered by Roman law to be under the canopy of the Jewish faith because Christians first met in synagogues, it was no longer safe from persecution from Nero's time onward. When Christianity was declared illegal in A.D. 112, persecutions of Christians escalated in both frequency and severity.

Imagine, if you will, the possibility of the church of Jesus Christ being blamed today for a severe economic downturn. Then visualize your beloved children, family members, and yourself being arrested, having animal hides sewn to your bodies, being herded into a local arena, and facing wild, half-starved animals turned loose on you. It would certainly make altar calls a lot tougher, wouldn't it?

The gist of the dialogue between the believers and Peter was "Okay, so we've been called by God, and we have a destiny to fulfill. So why does it appear as though God is now against us? If we have been pleasing to God up to now, why are our lives suddenly being threatened? Why are we being arrested, tortured, and thrown to wild animals?" Fair questions.

Peter's original name was Simon. In Matthew 16:18, Jesus gave him the new name of Peter, which we all know means "a rock" in Greek. While the disciples sat around a campfire with Jesus one evening, eating fish and roasting marshmallows (or something like that), Jesus started a conversation with them.

Jesus asked, "Hey, guys, who do people say I am?"

Several disciples said together, "Well, Jesus, some say You're Elijah . . . Elisha . . . Jeremiah the prophet . . . Elisha returned."

Jesus said, "That's great, fellas! Good input, but who do *you* say I am?"

Peter answered, "You are the Christ, the Son of the living God."

Jesus said, "You're right, Peter, but there's no way that you figured that out all by yourself."

Right then and there, the other disciples took a vote and decided that Peter wasn't smart enough to figure out that revelation on his own. They concluded that God the Father had revealed this astounding information to Peter.

Jesus said, "Bless you, Simon Barjona. You will no longer be called Simon, but you will be called Peter hereafter."

Simon, formerly a wishy-washy person, had now become "a rock." It's a beautiful illustration of our Lord's moving beyond the obvious. Our calling by Christ allows us to do this also, just as it did Peter.

We think we're so cool and astute when we state an observation that "Harry is an obnoxious, prideful believer." But Jesus never stays within the obvious. He moves beyond that, because He realizes that our being called by Him establishes for us a new identity in Him.

Jesus continued, "Upon this 'rock' (you, Peter) I will build my church, and the gates of hell shall not prevail against it. And I will give you the keys to the kingdom of heaven. Because of the words that came out of your mouth this morning, the world will never be the same."

Hearing that, Peter got pretty excited. But what was Jesus doing? He was simply predicting Peter's potential. Later on, in that same chapter, however, Peter doesn't quite measure up to his potential.

Jesus then announced, "Okay, guys, now I must go to Jerusalem, be crucified, and be raised on the third day."

Peter: "Hey, wait a minute, Jesus! I don't get that. That's a bad plan! It doesn't make sense! I mean, we don't come out looking so good, you know, when our leader gets killed. That's not the way to go, Lord."

Angrily, Jesus whirled around and confronted Peter: "Cool it, Peter! Zip your lip! Get behind me, Satan, because you're offending me!"

Christ was really saying, "You're not fulfilling your potential, Pete. In fact, you're now being influenced by Satan, and this offends Me."

Of course, Peter was quite perplexed by Christ's sudden anger. Who wouldn't be? Several weeks later, during the night of Christ's betrayal, Peter's potential slipped a bit more, when he denied knowing the Lord three times.

Wouldn't you hate to have your epitaph put you down when

you finish your life? I know I would hate to have someone write an epitaph like this for me: "Doug Murren had a lot of potential. . . ." That's something you say to someone just to be kind. Doug Murren had a lot of potential, but he sure didn't do much with it, did he?

What fascinates me about Peter's introduction to this book is that he uses his new name boldly—"a rock," the name Jesus chose for him. Notice that he did not introduce himself as *the* apostle or *the* one whom Jesus chose to build His church on. He simply said that he was *an* apostle.

Because he desired to point out that the believers were called to fulfill a distinct and very wonderful purpose, Peter referred to himself by his apostolic name. Peter finally fulfilled the potential for which he was chosen by Christ. I think that's pretty exciting and commendable. He's become Peter the Rock, sharing his Christ-given stability with the faltering band of believers who faced unimaginable suffering.

Shortly after this writing, Peter was crucified upside down, somewhere near Rome. Refusing to be crucified in the same manner as his beloved Christ, Peter pled with the Roman soldiers to crucify him upside down, saying: "I am not worthy to be crucified as my Lord was." History conjectures that his death occurred in A.D. 64.

Peter has become a window for everyone to look into the wonder of God's calling upon his or her life, a window that challenges us to allow Peter to become "Everyman" for us. Peter discovered that Christ's purposes were not found in him alone, but in how he cooperated with the other apostles and how they fit their lives together for Christ's glory.

Our purposes are never found alone, but are found in community. When we work together, a lot of the missing pieces fall into place. When standing alone, we can feel as though the entire world has fallen on our shoulders, but when standing with others, the load is then shared and becomes less burdensome and more tolerable. We also become recipients of some of the greatest resources that God would share with us when we work in community with others.

Perspective is important, especially when we are facing torturous times. It's important to remember always that the kingdom of God does not ride on our shoulders alone, but is shared with Jesus. Each of us is but a small piece of the puzzle.

BELONGING: KEY TO SURVIVAL

When the crushing times of crises, breakdowns in relationships, and lost dreams come upon us, there is nothing more important than a sense of belonging. Peter did not state that he was the apostle, but "an" apostle of Jesus Christ. The genitive form here literally suggests possession, that Peter *belonged* to Jesus Christ.

A recent issue of *Psychology Today* contained an article about social scientists who have discovered a new kind of depression, which they call the "boomer blues." They have determined that the "boomer generation" (forty-two and younger) is the most depressed generation in modern social history. One of the correlates presented is that a woman of this generation has a 30 percent chance of experiencing a serious bout of deep depression in her mid-thirties, contrasted with her grandmother, who had only a 3 percent chance. They also discovered that the same generation (my generation, incidentally) is the most self-centered one in modern times!

One conclusion these social scientists reached was that the boomer generation has forgotten that they can experience a natural "high" by helping others—that is, doing something that benefits others more than it does themselves.

Belonging to a church or organization, for instance, allows us to move into being other-centered. Myopia (nearsightedness/lack of foresight), on the other hand, has a way of amplifying our agonies and isolation when we're in the midst of turmoil.

Though this postulation of these social scientists contains some merit, I don't agree with them totally. As a number of us have ruefully experienced, helping others can at times be empty and unrewarding. Conversely, *true fulfillment comes from living a Christ-centered life!* Peter said that he was an apostle of Jesus Christ because he lived his life with Christ as his core and center.

In other words, believers have discovered that their greatest potential is realized when they put Christ right in the middle of all they do. He shows them how to fit together with other believers to bring about God's purposes for their lives.

GOD VOTED FOR YOU

Large, impressive theological words have never meant much to me. Terms like *election, being chosen,* and *set apart* mystify me. While thumbing through some old books in my library, I found in one the statement: "God voted for you."

Think about that a moment. We do make a difference in the world around us, because God voted for us! We are God's elect, God's chosen ones.

As humans, we are all approval-seekers looking for someone to approve of us. Whether being chosen to play in a junior high baseball game, as a date for the senior prom, or being elected to a board of directors, we all desire and seek approval.

How do we know God voted for us? We know through His Son, Jesus Christ.

Bob is a successful businessman who rose rapidly through the ranks of a burgeoning new computer programming firm. As he sat on the edge of my office couch, he nervously stroked his hair back. His eyes were dark and sunken from lack of sleep.

When he had sat down, I could tell that he was on the ragged edge of a nervous breakdown. Being a he-man sort of guy, tears didn't come easily to him, but on this particular night, they streamed down his face.

Bob began, "Doug, I don't know if God is real anymore. Do you know about Sue and me? Do you know that she's left me for another man?"

Leaning forward, I mustered my compassion and asked gently, "Bob, what makes you think that?"

"Well, if all this Christian stuff is real, and if God is really on my side and I am really chosen by Him, then all this bad stuff wouldn't happen!"

"And why do you say that?" Perplexed, I wondered how a man like Bob had managed to lose the strong faith he'd had just a year before. Granted, the turmoil of a yearlong hassle in his relationship with Sue had definitely brought a lot of wear and tear, but I never expected Bob to lose his faith or that I'd see him in such a state of despair.

"God can't possibly be for me, Doug." He began to sob uncontrollably. "He couldn't be real, or I must have done something to displease Him. I know I haven't been the best husband in the world, but I do love Jesus, and I prayed and prayed that He would help me. I guess I'm just the unlucky sort. I've been that way all my life."

Though I tried to stop him, he wouldn't be interrupted. When Bob finished, I took his hand and reviewed the basis of Christianity.

"Bob, God made one foolproof statement to you by sending you His Son, Jesus Christ. God chose you by giving you His Son. He called your name and revealed His Son to you. He said, once and for all, that you've got His vote!"

Bob had held the faulty premise that he could determine whether he was chosen by God or not by how well his life was going. The failure of this faulty formula will bring the strongest of faiths crashing down to the ground.

By writing his letter, Peter wanted to make certain that the believers of his day knew and understood thoroughly that they were, in fact, chosen by God—in spite of Emperor Nero's crushing blows on them.

JUST PASSING THROUGH: STRANGERS IN THE WORLD

I'm glad that Peter didn't call us "strange people," though he did call us "strangers." Ultimately, we have to realize that, as Christians, we will never be 100 percent fulfilled or satisfied in our lives here on earth, because we're created in such a way that we don't feel entirely at home here.

I think that we Christians have difficulty in grasping the concept that the world will never be perfect until Jesus returns. We will neither realize our full calling nor receive a total explanation for everything we've experienced (or will experience) until He returns.

Have you ever visited a foreign country in which the people speak another language? I've visited several such countries.

Immediately upon my arrival, I was at a disadvantage because I couldn't order food, read the street signs, or ask directions. I didn't belong because I couldn't speak the language. This creates a terrible feeling of isolation and loneliness.

I've been in the backwoods of Poland with three other Americans when our vehicle broke down. It was a horrifying feeling for us, because we were unable to communicate with those who drove by to explain our predicament.

Several people drove by in the hot July sun, which set a couple of hours later. Through the night we sat huddled in the car. Finally, when morning came, a police officer came along, and we were able, through sign language, to make him understand that we needed help. The Poles are warm, good-hearted people, and they did their best to make us feel at home, but we still knew we didn't belong because we couldn't speak their language.

I don't think God ever intends for us to get completely comfortable down here. Because we have become Christians, we are now strangers on earth. We're awaiting the creation of a new world while we continue in His will to contribute our most and give our best to this age. We won't always fit in, but that's okay. In the meantime, we can smile about our predicament when we remember that God chose us. So the next time something doesn't make sense to you, remember: It's not supposed to, because you don't really belong here.

Ultimately, our final purpose will not be on earth, but with Christ when he returns! It follows, then, that much of what will finally make sense to us and bring meaning to our lives is yet to appear. Therefore, never feel that whatever happens in the years allotted to you is the final curtain. We will have eons to discover the true meaning of Christ's blessings in our lives.

BLOOM WHERE YOU ARE PLANTED

"Scattered throughout Pontus, Galatia, Cappadocia, Asia, and Bithynia." (1 Peter 1:1, paraphrased)

The believers of Peter's day lived in real locations with real addresses, the same as you and I . Most of them had fled Jerusalem in the Christian Diaspora, leaving the apostles to repopulate the church there.

In verse 1, Peter names specific locations to which these Jewish believers had relocated. It's interesting to note that the land mass comprising these cities and/or states has the limited circumference of approximately three hundred miles, whereas today believers live all over the world. These sites of dispersion (relocation) were places of identification to Peter. I believe that what Peter was asking his faltering band of believers to do was to bloom where they were planted!

Now, as tempting as it might appear, the myth about greener pastures is just that—a myth. It is actually wrong. Some typical thoughts that roll through Christian minds are:

- I just *know* God would really use me if I were in Europe . . . if I were in Africa . . . if I were somewhere else but here.
- If I could just work for that other company, nothing would hold me back! Man, I'd be dynamite!
- If I had just married Clem (Hortense) instead of Clyde (Minerva), I just *know* I'd be a super Christian!
- And so the wishful thoughts go on *ad infinitum, ad nauseum.*

Probably the strongest, greener-pasture myth is "what might have been." A prime example of this myth occurred in my own life.

Not so long ago, I received a call from the pastor of a church of another denomination in another state, asking whether I would consider moving. He offered me a church in the sun and a house on the beach! Wow!

Now, don't get me wrong. I love Seattle, but occasionally, our gloomy, rainy winters get to me. It had been a particularly hard week for me, and it seemed as though nothing was going right. We had experienced several staff changes and surprises. I had also received several letters from people, complaining that they didn't like various parts of our services. In the midst of all this I was feeling just a tad unappreciated. I told the caller that I would get back to him shortly.

I phoned home, excitement evident in my voice. "Hey, Deb, someone just called and offered me a large church in sunny California with a house right on the beach! It sure sounds good! Even though we're pretty committed here, I thought I should at least call you about it and get your opinion. What do you think, Hon?"

Debbie answered, "No, we don't want a house on the beach, Doug. We want to be where God wants us."

"Sure, Deb. Of course, we do," I responded almost half-heartedly, my enthusiasm draining away.

Then Debbie said something wise, which has stuck with me since, "Doug, we can do everything we're supposed to do and be who we're supposed to be right here as well as anywhere else."

I knew she was right, and that penetrating reality will linger with me for years to come.

I recently learned an interesting fact. I believe it's one of the reasons the church in America is so wounded and hurting today. What I learned is that most pastors move every two years! Does that surprise you? It certainly did me.

A long pastorate is considered to be four years. Yet, we have clear evidence that if pastors stay at least seven to ten years, the effectiveness of their ministry accelerates phenomenally!

And so it follows that blooming where you are planted seems to be the best way to go. Wherever you work and wherever you live, you can be enabled by Christ's Holy Spirit to carry out God's purposes in that job or place. Consequently, whomever you're married to, whatever your kids are like, and whatever job you have, you can leave your mark for God. You can make a difference right there!

GOD KNOWS YOUR ADDRESS

". . . the elect, according to the foreknowledge of God the Father, through sanctification of the Spirit." (1 Peter 1:2, paraphrased)

Foreknowledge is a tricky word to understand. It actually derives from the word *prognosis,* meaning "before knowledge." That is, God knew before you knew. God's prognosis is what we're all about. Others may say:

- You're going to be a loser.
- You're never going to amount to anything.
- You're never going to succeed at anything.
- You're never going to do anything worthwhile.

However, God's prognosis for you is the only one worth listening to!

I enjoy some of the writings of John Naisbitt. In *Megatrends,* Naisbitt predicts that by the year 2000 the middle class will be larger and richer, and that the English language will literally dominate the entire business world—even more so than it does now. Further, he predicts:

- That art and literature will enjoy a renaissance unequaled by any other in history;
- That the welfare state will come to an end;
- That there will be a decline in population in the major cities; and
- That business and culture will be dispersed to the multitudes in metropolitan areas around the United States. New York, Los Angeles, and other major cities will no longer be the center of everything.

And here's another of Naisbitt's predictions that does not sound like heaven to me at all: By the year 2000, personal communications will have advanced on such a worldwide scale that everyone will have a phone number! In other words, from the moment of your birth, you will be given a phone number and handed a phone! Does that sound like hell, or what? It certainly sounds like that to me. No, thank you! I won't take one. In fact, it reminds me of a cartoon I once saw—you know, the usual, beatnik-looking guy standing on a corner holding a sign: "Repent, or the world will never end!"

God has a better prognosis than that for all of us. When I think about what I'd like on my gravestone, this very simple, yet profound, statement comes to mind: "This man loved Jesus Christ." I believe that is God's prognosis for us all.

As Christians, we are being set apart by the Holy Spirit to obey God. In the Holy Spirit's vernacular, "to obey" simply means "to hear." The Holy Spirit makes us able to hear God's prognosis for us in Christ and to ensure that this prediction is fulfilled by obediently paying attention to His will and following through on it.

One of the primary signs indicating our being filled with the Spirit is that we really start caring about people who are lost and don't know Jesus. Jesus said that would be one of the first phenomena to happen when His Spirit came upon His church, that we would "preach the gospel in Jerusalem, in all Judea, in Samaria, and in the uttermost parts of the world" (Acts 1:8*b*, paraphrased). Because the Holy Spirit fills you, God's prognosis for your life is that you will have a heart for the world and that, as the Spirit is allowed to work in you, you will always be able to fulfill a sense of purpose in your life.

Obedience is a scary word for me. It has set up many negative alarms. I suppose this came from growing up around ultraconservative people, who spoke so often about "how hard it is to obey Jesus."

If you look at 1 Peter 1:2, the way *obedience* is used is to mean "promise." It declares that, by the blood of Jesus, we will obey Him, because without Jesus' blood none of us can possibly obey God. It takes the freeing dynamic of the blood of Jesus to enable us to obey God fully. Christ's blood sets us free to obey.

I have a friend named Ollie, who is a finish carpenter. He was raised by an immigrant family from Scandinavia and had a very hard life when he was growing up. Ollie always wanted to be a doctor. I found this out one day when we walked around the site of our present church building.

I inquired, "Ollie, do you have any kids?"

"Oh, yes, pastor. We have two daughters and one son, the doctor. We raised him to be a Christian and to be a doctor. I always wanted to be a doctor myself, but as the son of an immigrant, I just couldn't afford medical school. We just kept telling him what he was. We never ran his life, you know, but we just referred to him as 'our son, the doctor.' That was our prognosis for him."

Ollie's rosy cheeks blushed with pride as he related this to me. His story caught my attention. It was their *prognosis* for their son's life, which they repeated over and over to him.

Likewise, obedience to the blood of Jesus allows us to hear

God's prognosis for our lives in the middle of any situation! Many voices in the world speak negativism, perhaps even deliberate, harmful statements to throw us off the track. But the blood of Jesus allows us to enter the throne room of grace, with our ears wide open to hear what God has to say about us instead. God's prognosis for us is that we have hope and a future in Christ.

A few weeks ago, something happened to me that a pastor generally just hopes will happen. After a service one Sunday morning, a young woman in her twenties greeted me and said, "Pastor Doug, it's great to see you again!"

Now, I didn't have the slightest idea who she was, but not wanting to disappoint her, I faked an answer: "Hi. It's great to see you too. I haven't seen you in a long time. By the way, who are you?" Honesty prevailed at this point.

"Well, you probably don't remember me, pastor, but you and Debbie led me to Jesus in your kitchen about five or six years ago. Shortly after that, I met and married a young man, and now we're both pastors. I heard that you were going to be preaching here today, so I just had to come and see you. We've had some hard times, but you and Debbie have really influenced us and helped us to get through them, even though you didn't know it. When we hit those hard times, we'd just say to each other, 'What would Pastor Doug and Debbie do in this situation?'"

When she finished, I exclaimed, "Oh, God help you! Don't do that! Ask what Jesus would do, not what I would do!"

At the same time that I was shocked by her statement, I was very touched by the unknowing way Debbie and I had been able to influence this young couple. I couldn't think of any significant time that we had ever talked with this couple. I've concluded, however, that in addition to taking large steps of obedience, we need to take the simple little steps of obedience as well. As we become sensitive to hear God through the blood of Jesus, it becomes easier for us to take these obedient, smaller steps. Perhaps it is these smaller steps on which the kingdom is built. Perhaps this is where our destiny and meaning are really found.

There can be error in the gargantuan formula that says, "If I make this stupendous sacrifice or undertake this large project, I am really doing God's will." I'm utterly convinced that that's not the way it happens. I believe that the small steps of obedience bring us to a total fruition of God's will in our lives.

PRAYER

Jesus, we love You, and we pray that Your Holy Spirit will be confirmed in our lives today to remind us that we are chosen and called by You. Lead us away from the false formula that says Your pleasure is discovered by how well things are going for us, or that Your displeasure is discovered by how bad things are going for us. Please deliver us from the formula that says that if we will do the extraordinary, the stupendous, the gargantuan, then we will find Your will. Help us to obey You each day in the little steps of obedience. Help us to bloom where we are planted. Lead us away from the formula that says that the will of God is for us in another place.

Chapter 2

Is Christianity Real?
(1 Peter 1:3–12)

*Blessed be the God and Father of our Lord Jesus Christ,
who according to His abundant mercy has begotten us
again to a living hope through the resurrection of Jesus
Christ from the dead, to an inheritance incorruptible and
undefiled and that does not fade away, reserved in heaven
for you, who are kept by the power of God through faith for
salvation ready to be revealed in the last time. In this you
greatly rejoice, though now for a little while, if need be,
you have been grieved by various trials, that the genuineness of your faith, being much more precious than
gold that perishes, though it is tested by fire, may be found
to praise, honor, and glory at the revelation of Jesus
Christ, whom having not seen, you love. Though now you
do not see Him, yet believing, you rejoice with joy inexpressible and full of glory, receiving the end of your faith—the
salvation of your souls. Of this salvation the prophets have
inquired and searched diligently, who prophesied of the
grace that would come to you, searching what, or what
manner of time, the Spirit of Christ who was in them was
indicating when He testified beforehand the sufferings of
Christ and the glories that would follow. To them it was
revealed that, not to themselves, but to us they were ministering the things which now have been reported to you
through those who have preached the gospel to you by the
Holy Spirit sent from heaven—things which angels desire
to look into. (1 Peter 1:3–12)*

One day, a young woman named Susan called me, sobbing.
Hardly able to understand her, I said, "Susan, calm down and
tell me your problem."

Between sobs, Susan told me about leading a friend to Christ a year earlier. Her friend had called her to announce that she was terminally ill. The caller had other problems as well. Her son was showing signs of becoming a juvenile delinquent. Compounded with her serious illness and her problem son, Susan's friend had just received the heartrending news that her husband was considering leaving her for another woman!

Susan had boldly shared the gospel with her friend, claiming that if she would accept Jesus Christ, she would most likely be healed, her son would turn his life around overnight, and her marriage would be saved.

Through her sobs, Susan blurted out to me, "God has failed me, pastor!"

Now, I had to admit, with the kind of offer Susan had given her friend, who could refuse coming to Jesus? It was certainly a good sales pitch for salvation. But is it true?

"Pastor, my friend refuses to remain a Christian. She called me back, bitterly angry. Not only is she still diagnosed as being terminal, but her son is now in prison, and her husband, who filed for divorce this week, has now moved in with the other woman!"

I responded the only way I knew: "I'm really sorry to hear that, Susan."

I searched frantically for a pastoral tone and words that would comfort her, all the while clutching the phone as the wheels in my mind groped for some pearl of wisdom. But before I could answer, Susan harshly interrupted my train of thought.

"Pastor, if that's your Jesus, you can take Him and keep Him!"

I suppose many of us have been in the same unfortunate position as Susan found herself, making promises for God that He, perhaps, doesn't intend to keep.

We can never accuse the apostle Peter of this, however. He flatly told the people he pastored and loved that they could expect trouble. In fact, Christianity wasn't really designed to keep us out of trouble, according to his letter to the dispersed Christians.

Now, this message will strike three tendencies that creep

into every one of our hearts, because we are human. One is the belief that God is more interested in our comfort than anything else. Let's label it the "materialistic well-being view." This can be threatened by any statement Peter made that suggests God isn't interested in making sure that our comfort zones are thick and plush.

The second group will have trouble with this section of Scripture also. They are what I call the "ultra-optimist" or the "hyperfaith" people. The reason they struggle with the idea that God may not be gung-ho for the comfort path is that they believe we simply need more faith. This group claims that if we have more faith, we will, of course, have fewer and smaller problems. It's an inviting formula, I admit, but is it true?

The third group, who ought to take care when reading this section, are those whom I call the "perpetual whiners." They are quite willing to claim that God has, in fact, given them a rougher road than anybody else.

These three tendencies can be tempered by a simple insight into the mind of God, which Peter desires to share with his flock and with us.

Now remember, Peter was writing to a group of dispersed Christians, probably thousands of them. Just try to imagine Sister Ruth or Brother Nicodemus hiding in some hovel with other believers and reading this letter from the apostle Peter.

It wasn't an easy thing to be a Christian at that time. The group to whom Peter was writing had not only seen terrible things happen to their loved ones and friends, but also they had fled their homes and had lost all that they had known in life. They had to leave behind grandchildren, grandparents, businesses, and vocations. All of this gives rise to several questions in our hearts:

- Is Christianity real when it doesn't work?
- Where is God when I need Him?
- Am I really called?
- Do I have a purpose in life, even though my life doesn't look like it right now?

"Blessed *be* the God and Father of our Lord Jesus Christ"

(1 Peter 1:3a). Peter began the body of his letter with the doxology, a call to worship, and a prayer.

Perhaps what he suggested by this is that we should not discuss our problems, our sufferings, or life's trials until we pause for a moment to praise and give thanks to God.

Perhaps the first question we should ask is "Who?" not "Why?" Worship is an effective way for believers to focus on life through God's Word. We can't really get our lives into focus unless we're worshipers of God first. Life doesn't make much sense for believers or nonbelievers unless we are committed to being worshipers first. So God puts us into focus right away.

Peter declared boldly: "Blessed be the God and Father of our Lord Jesus Christ!" It is worshipers who have the truest insights concerning life, and worshipers are candidates who can gain insights into the power for living!

THE REAL YOU IS NEVER IN JEOPARDY

. . . to an inheritance incorruptible and undefiled and that does not fade away, reserved in heaven for you, who are kept by the power of God through faith for salvation ready to be revealed in the last time. (1 Peter 1:4–5)

Peter brought exciting news to his Christian friends in the catacombs and in the hovels of retreat in various parts of Asia Minor.

He declared: "You will outlive every problem you have! Remember this: Whatever comes down, the real you will never be in jeopardy! The real you cannot be destroyed!"

One of my favorite writers in the twentieth century, who is a great writer and biographer, is Aleksandr Solzhenitsyn. In one of his essays he told about discovering what he believed to be the greatest of the powers he had over Gulag. He declared that the Soviets could take away his job, they could destroy his manuscripts, they could even take his family and his health, but they could never kill the real Solzhenitsyn!

At one point, while undergoing interrogation by and harassment from the KGB authorities, he decided that he would no longer fear Gulag. He could then smile, sneer, and mockingly have inner joy, despite the claws and angry faces of the KGB. He steadfastly determined that he would *not* become who they wanted him to be. At that point he became an indestructible person. He found that faith in Christ was the source of his indomitable character.

Solzhenitsyn's newfound stance so frustrated and infuriated the KGB that eventually they had no choice but to release him from prison because they could not break him; they could not destroy him. Solzhenitsyn knew that his real person could not be tampered with.

Peter gave us the key for living victoriously through pain and trouble by using three simple phrases to describe God's promise, which is ours to claim:

- an inheritance, incorruptible and undefiled,
- does not fade away,
- but is reserved in heaven for you.

In other words, *there isn't a problem of any kind that you or I will ever have that we won't outlive.* You name it—you can outlive it, because Christ is in your life!

Peter was telling his friends in the Diaspora that they could never actually be harmed. This unalterable fact still holds true today. We may be fed to wild tigers, but our real persona can't be touched. We may lose all that we own, but by our faith in Christ, He promises that our real selves will never be destroyed. Isn't that great?

Because Christ arose from the dead and was resurrected, His indomitable life fills all believers. That is, we are all "come-back artists"—and everyone loves a come-back story. The Christian resurrection of life means that we can *never* be kept down. We will outlive anything!

Now, some of you may not realize that this is the heart of Christianity. Some of you, perhaps, think that something else is the core of our faith. Not so. As fine as some of our Christian institutions may be, and as well-developed as our creed and doctrines may become, nevertheless, the resurrection of Jesus from the dead is the cornerstone—the very core—of all our experiences in Him. Because Jesus Christ could not be kept dead and His tomb was empty, we cannot be destroyed!

THE END ISN'T REALLY THE END

The fact that the end (death) is not really the end is the basis of our hope. Christians can't be kept down because we're filled with the resurrection of Jesus. We always have the hope of a new beginning. When all else collapses, we know that the end isn't really the end. That's what Peter said to his dispersed flock. Remember: We each have an inheritance that possesses a quality that can never be destroyed, regardless of what happens to us.

Your distress may be a disease. This disease may eventually take your life on earth, but *no disease can destroy the real you*. Some of us may lose our homes, but our real selves can never be tampered with because our real home is reserved for us in heavenly places with Christ.

I know this sounds like pie-in-the-sky Christianity, but I believe that is what Peter was saying, that this world will not make sense within the limited confines of our world of just five senses. Scientific formulations and observations cannot equitably answer the human spirit's cry to the big question "Why?" Peter's response never bothers to answer the "why," but simply says "who" and then begins to tell us "what." This inheritance, which we can count on and to which Peter referred, has three eternal, remarkable qualities to it.

1. *Our Inheritance Is Noncorrodible*

We can never be in jeopardy because our lives are noncorrodible. The Greek word used here for *noncorrodible* means "it doesn't perish." In the Puget Sound region, if the undersides of cars aren't undercoated, they rust out. The salt on the roads and the salt water spray both take their toll and will cause the sturdiest of metals to flake away. So when we buy cars in this area, we have them undercoated with an anticorrosive to prevent salt and other destructive forces from breaking down the car's metal frame and doors.

Our lives have a noncorrodible quality; they've been under-coated, so to speak, because of Jesus' life in us. The world's destructive splashings will never succeed in eating away our real selves.

This term for "never corrode" was also used in a military context to describe an impenetrable city. If a vanguard force couldn't make their way into a city, then it was considered im-perishable. Peter thus reassured his flock that enemy attacks would never make it into their lives, because their lives were impenetrable and noncorrodible. It doesn't matter what's going on around us. You and I own something; we have an inheritance in Jesus that is noncorrodible. It will not experience oxidation; it won't rust; it won't crumble; and it is incorruptible.

2. Our Inheritance Is Undefiled

Our inheritance will never be polluted. It will never change in its very makeup. It cannot be chemically tampered with.

The word *spoil* is related to the word *fermentation*. Have you ever bought natural apple juice or made it without preserva-tives, let it sit out for several days, and then tried to drink it? It's sickening because it has turned to vinegar. Fermentation also occurs in packaged meats. I once tore a package of meat open, but left it at the back of the fridge for a couple of weeks— forgotten. When I finally pulled it out, it had turned green and had begun to grow the basis for penicillin. Peter stated that our Christian lives will never spoil like that. Because Christ is in our lives, our real selves will never ferment, nor will they ever rot.

That means that, as hard as worldly pressures may come upon your life, your true self cannot become polluted. The real you cannot be composed of a mixture that would be destruc-tive. The basic makeup of the real you can never be changed.

3. Our Inheritance Will Never Fade

Have you ever experienced the joy of owning an oriental car-pet that you unknowingly placed partly in the scorching sun and partly in the shade—for months on end—without realizing you'd left part of it in the sunlight? If you have, you probably realized that you now have a two-tone carpet.

I collect magazine and newspaper articles for future sermons and put them in various office filing trays. I used to know which tray was which, but now that I've collected so many articles, I have to wedge them in wherever they will fit, hoping that someday I'll sort them out and set up a proper filing system.

Some of these articles are next to a window where the sun beats down on them. As you know, newspapers turn yellow in a matter of weeks, so articles that once had rosy, cheery faces in the pictures now show green-faced, Martian-like people.

The Greek word Peter used for *fade* describes that same process, a process where the heat and sun have taken their toll on an object and have changed its color. But as hot as the heat may be turned up in our lives, we're never going to change. We will never fade. There will never be any two-toned Christians. You and I will not be affected by the world's scorching sun on our tested lives.

Our lives are protected, and the real part of us is tamper proof. We have something in heaven that will never be in jeopardy, and that real part of us understands this.

In this you greatly rejoice, though now for a little while, if need be, you have been grieved by various trials, that the genuineness of your faith, *being* much more precious than gold that perishes, though it is tested by fire, may be found to praise, honor, and glory at the revelation of Jesus Christ. (1 Peter 1:6–7)

In your anguish, have you ever cried out that you just can't take it anymore? Well, don't look to Peter for comfort or sympathy. He doesn't offer any, but basically says: "Buck up! You can take it. Hang in there."

Occasionally, some of us have had a bad hour; some of us have had a bad day. Now and then, I meet someone who has had a bad week. And on rare occasions some of us have had a bad life.

Thus, to put Peter's theology in the language of the 1990s, he's simply saying: "Life is hard, then you die. So don't worry. Be happy in the meantime."

Most of us are not overly endowed with perspective. Putting your life in perspective, whatever you suffer, is a great gift that God can give you. When our daughter, Raissa, was born two months prematurely, she died three times in two days! Soon after, she was diagnosed with cerebral palsy. Now, at the age of thirteen, she's a dynamo, filled with intelligence, a zest for living, and a hunger for God. Praise the Lord!

I still remember entering the hospital accounting office to make arrangements to pay Raissa's enormous bill of $17,000 for her six-week stay. I had just finished at Seattle Pacific University and was beginning a new ministry. We had no medical insurance—something no one should be without today. By today's standards, $17,000 doesn't seem like a giant hospital bill, but it seemed insurmountable to us in 1976, with one toddler and a newborn. In addition, her yearly medical upkeep and several corrective surgeries over the next few years amounted to thousands of dollars more. As a result, we faced many years of tremendous medical costs.

Nervously, I glanced at the hospital accountant as he pushed his large black-rimmed glasses up his nose and leaned back in his chair, which squeaked multiple cries for oil under the press of his weight.

"How much can you pay, Mr. Murren?" he asked.

Gulping from embarrassment, I responded honestly, "Well, this is only our first year pastoring, so we can afford about $5 a week."

I'll never forget the look on his face. It was as though lightning had struck. I could visualize the wheels turning as he mentally calculated $5 a week into that $17,000 bill.

Recovering from his initial shock, he grinned and said,: "Well, Mr. Murren, I think we can help you out. Let's start off here."

Reaching into his large desk, he pulled out a stack of grant forms. Along with our payments of $5 a week, he thought we could get quite a bit of help from grants and that we just might be able to work things out in our lifetime. We both laughed at the seeming impossibility of the task that stretched out before us.

I also remember another day, eight years later, when my wife, Debbie, with a hint of exultation in her voice, asked, "Guess what, Doug?"

"What, Hon? Is our phone bill a little larger than we expected again?"

"No. I put the last payment on Raissa in the mail today!"

That was really exciting! Believe me, it wasn't much fun paying on that hospital bill all those years. Eventually, we were able to pay a little more than $5 a week. But in a very real way I'm glad we went through that period of hardship and deprivation because it brought perspective into our lives. I do believe that we came to understand some things we wouldn't have otherwise, and I think we know Jesus a lot better for this experience.

It would have been a greater help, however, if we had had the amount of perspective at the beginning of that journey that we acquired by the end of it. I believe this is what Peter is challenging us with: to launch out into the Holy Spirit's arena and allow Him to give us His perspective on life's matters—a perspective from an eternal position. The Holy Spirit is able to look from the end back, and He excitedly anticipates the process of our becoming. Whatever we suffer, it isn't going to last forever.

Peter invited the people he loved to gain that perspective as well. Like Peter's friends, we are invited to look at ourselves as though we are precious gold.

For example, when a refiner puts ore into a hot furnace, the ore is broken down until it comes closer and closer to being pure gold or silver. Ultimately, the refiner knows the point at which the metal has been refined enough, when he can look into the crucible and see his reflection in the metal and when no ore ripples are left in it. The metallurgist of Peter's day, along with most of the people in his time, would have recognized the ore-refining process. When the refiner's reflection could be seen in the gold or silver, the process was complete. Likewise, it is the Holy Spirit's pleasurable gaze into our lives on which we are to focus.

I don't know many people who have signed up voluntarily for the subject of Suffering 101. Of course, the way life is arranged, in its abnormal and fallen state, I'm sure we've all been drafted into that hard course in life.

THE REAL YOU WILL NEVER GET WORSE . . . JUST BETTER

[Christ,] whom having not seen you love. Though now you do not see *Him*, yet believing, you rejoice with joy inexpressible and full of glory, receiving the end of your faith—the salvation of *your* souls. Of this salvation the prophets have inquired and searched diligently, who prophesied of the grace *that would come* to you, searching what, or what manner of time, the Spirit of Christ who was in them was indicating when He testified beforehand the sufferings of Christ and the glories that would follow. To them it was revealed that, not to themselves, but to us they were ministering the things which now have been reported to you through those who have preached the gospel to you by the Holy Spirit sent from heaven—things which angels desire to look into. (1 Peter 1:8–12)

Not only is your life never in jeopardy, but also you will outlive and always overcome any trouble that comes your way. That is the true you.

The belief of humanity in general, which is addicted to hedonism, is that God was created to be our butler in heaven, pouring copious blessings upon us. The "gospel of the luxuriant" may not fit into God's scheme. However, our true inner self knows that we will overcome, with the Holy Spirit's help, whatever the obstacle or challenge we may face. We will not get worse; His promise is that we will get better.

Even though His work isn't usually evident, God is always at work in our lives. Here's what I perceive to be Peter's line of logic: Though today's believers have never seen Christ personally, we still love Him. Then, why is it so difficult for us to believe—when we have trials, trouble, suffering, and tribulation—that in the midst of our problems God is at work, even though it doesn't look like it? If we truly believe in Christ and love the One we haven't seen, isn't it just as easy to believe that He's at work in our lives in ways that aren't immediately visible to us?

When I started pastoring seventeen years ago, I erroneously thought a pastor was supposed to be an "answer man." Now, though I don't know yet what I'm going to know when I'm finished pastoring, I really don't think it's going to be much of anything. At the rate I'm going, I might know half of what I did when I started.

So what Peter was trying to have us understand is that God is at work, even though we can't see Him. To those persecution-torn believers of the first century—and to us today—Peter stated: If we can believe in Christ to save us, then we can just as easily believe that He is at work in our present circumstances, even when it doesn't look like it!

I'm convinced that the worst question any suffering Christian can ask is "Why?" It won't help to ask that, because God will never answer that question. The prophets, Peter said, told us about the grace we would experience in troubled times. However, the prophets didn't have the foggiest notion of what they were talking about because they were in the dark. What God was up to was so marvelous that they couldn't begin to grasp it.

Even the angels want to inquire into what God is doing with you and me. They can't understand it either and are perplexed by the whole matter. If the angels can't figure it out, we puny humans shouldn't even try. Instead, we must by faith accept the fact that Christ is at work in our lives, even though it may not look like it.

Recently, a young woman who had been diagnosed as having terminal cancer visited me. She was, naturally, quite fearful and was beginning to doubt God, even to the point of losing her faith. We discussed her situation at length. Another day, another time, I would have searched my mind for a simplistic explanation. But having held the hands of numerous dying people has hampered my outpouring of "wisdom" in such instances.

This was her story: In her late thirties she had finally found a man she loved, but now it looked as though she would have only fifteen to eighteen months to live. Grabbing my hand with her trembling hands, she began to talk.

"Pastor, I'm losing my faith. I can't possibly believe that God would tease me like this. My whole life, I've looked for someone who would love and care for me. Now that I've found him, I'm going to die!"

I answered, "Under the circumstances, don't you think it

would be quite normal to have your faith threatened? I'm so pleased that you came to see me today, but I really don't know what to tell you. I do know that Christ isn't demanding that you have more faith now. He's simply asking that you realize that He is present in your suffering. My heart really goes out to you, and I know our church is with you during this time. However, as I sit here, I know that you may very well die, and I think we both need to talk about that. I can't even pretend to know how it must feel to be in your situation, but I do know that God is at work in your life right now."

I reached out to take her other hand, and we began to pray together. She was quite relieved to know that God wasn't going to require more from her than she was able to give.

Just two weeks earlier, I had sat in a hospital room and prayed for a young girl from our congregation who was slowly dying of terminal cancer. She was now but a skeleton of her former self, whom we knew and loved; yet, her eyes still glistened, and delight was still heard in her German accent. Even on her deathbed, she was still a charmer.

Her nurses injected her with morphine regularly to ease her pain. Several of us shared the last few moments of her short life.

Looking into her eyes as I prayed with her, I said: "The real you understands that your body has just simply given up, but this disease doesn't touch the real you."

Through her morphine, pain-filled stupor she winked at me as she replied, "Yes, pastor, the real me belongs to Jesus!"

After I shared this poignant story with the young woman in my office, I said, "The real you that Jesus is making is larger than this whole issue, simply because Christ is in you, and God is at work in you."

I'm still praying for this young woman, and though it appears on the surface that God isn't doing anything for her, I know that He is. She's a wonderful woman who has sought God all her life.

I get very angry with diseases. This young woman is so capable and such a blessing to many; yet, our assurance is that God is at work in her, even in her darkness and a shortage of answers. By the time we finished praying, I saw the indomitable character of Jesus Christ rise up in her. Her real self now reflected Him.

Now, don't get me wrong. I thoroughly believe in contending for healing. In fact, I've had the joy of seeing many people healed. By the same token, if I were diagnosed as having a serious illness, I would have it confirmed by two more doctors. Then I would have someone anoint me with oil and pray for me, but I wouldn't tell anyone else. Why? Because, being a pastor, I'm certain our congregation would over-bombard heaven with prayers for me. As it is, my phone goes into overtime. The third action I would take would be to fight that disease with everything in me, by whatever means available, for as long as it would take, for I believe that this is the will of God in such matters.

If, by some strange happenstance, these efforts didn't work, I would still know the entire time that the real Doug was never in jeopardy, that I would be getting better, and that, because my life is kept in Jesus Christ, it will never fade.

We all believe, I'm sure, that the Lord wants us to have good health, prosperity, and success; and that He never objects to our blessings, but is delighted when we are prosperous believers. But I don't believe that success and prosperity are the essential promises of the gospel. In fact, according to the Scriptures, we who are blessed have been allowed to be because God felt that He could trust us to be good stewards of His resources and would express and extend His blessing and love to those less fortunate.

What God does object to, however, is our having great wealth and being inconsiderate of the poor. He does object to our having good health and not thanking Him.

Conversely, I know people who are apparently doing everything right, yet are not prospering, are not in good health, and are not successful. I strongly disagree with those who say that if you tithe to God, He will bless everything you do. And those TV preachers who promise that God will give their donors $10 back for every $1 given to them anger me, for these are not true promises. We cannot presume to claim or to promise that God will do something; that is God's decision alone.

Now, don't get me wrong. I most certainly do believe in tithing. And I believe that our Lord is a giving Lord Who challenges us to share in His character. But I do not believe that we'll get richer and have perfect health or be successful because we tithe. I do believe that we can certainly count on becoming richer in character. Paul made it clear that we should be on the lookout, that when we sow abundantly, we will reap abundantly.

I think Peter's great concern here (and every pastor's) is that this message—the certainty of God's victory over evil, no matter what the signs—might cause us to become nonfighters. We most certainly do need to contend for our world and turn it right-side up. By nature, I'm a fighter, and I desire that everyone in the church be a fighter.

So I think Peter was saying: "Hang in there, kids, with the certainty that the Lord will be present in your lives." I appreciate the fact that Peter did not say, "Try harder, kids. Believe more; believe harder." Instead, he said, "Rest in Jesus and the guaranteed quality of what we've been given in Him."

I don't think we believers mean to, but, sometimes, we present Christianity to our friends when they are in a place of great need. One day at school, a fat seventh-grader turned out for track. By some mistake, he was put in the line-up for the 800-meter race. He ran as hard as he could. His face got red, he was puffing like a steam engine, his heart was pounding against his chest, and he was about half a lap behind the field.

Suddenly, a middle-aged woman ran out onto the track, yelling, "Run, Johnny! You've gotta run faster!"

The fat kid gave her a withering look, as if to say, "Look, Mom, I'm just a fat little seventh-grader. I don't even want to be out here in the first place, but I'm running as fast as I can, so stop saying: Run faster; run faster!"

I guess we all feel that way sometimes. We're doing our best, but it's not enough. And sometimes it's okay to be a fat little kid who's doing the best he can.

If you will notice, Peter didn't give his flock a long agenda or a lot of exhortation. He just said, "Remember Jesus Christ in Whom you believe, and everything will turn out okay because He's with you."

In summary, Peter's introduction shepherded a heart pulsating with concern for the believers assigned to his charge, and he urged them (and us) to remember these truths:

- That the real you is never in jeopardy;
- That there is no problem you won't outlive;
- That if you can believe in an unseen God, you can also believe in His unseen workings;
- That you are not going to rust, be polluted, or change color; and
- That God does not offer you easy answers, but He does give you a new perspective.

Chapter 3

Upstream in a Downstream World
(1 Peter 1:13–21)

*Therefore gird up the loins of your mind, be sober, and rest
your hope fully upon the grace that is to be brought to you
at the revelation of Jesus Christ; as obedient children, not
conforming yourselves to the former lusts, as in your igno-
rance; but as He who called you is holy, you also be holy
in all your conduct, because it is written: "Be holy, for I
am holy." And if you call on the Father, who without par-
tiality judges according to each one's work, conduct yourselves throughout the time of your sojourning here in fear;
knowing that you were not redeemed with corruptible
things, like silver or gold, from your aimless conduct received by tradition from your fathers, but with the precious
blood of Christ, as of a lamb without blemish and without
spot. He indeed was foreordained before the foundation of
the world, but was manifest in these last times for you who
through Him believe in God, who raised Him from the
dead and gave Him glory, so that your faith and hope are
in God. (1 Peter 1:13–21)*

Pressure is a way of life in America. One of the greatest pressures of Christians in our time is how to stick to our convictions
when everything appears to be working against us.

Basic to the Christian belief is the fact that this world is abnormal. Since the fall of our ancestors, Adam and Eve, we've
lived in a far less than perfect world. Yes, Eden has disappeared. Small wonder, then, that things don't go as they ought.

Some of the pressures we face are called "temptations."

Temptations arise from within and without to misshape us. Other pressures are to conform to world views and values that are contrary to what we've committed our lives to in Christ, those cultural fancies that attempt to forge us into images other than those God has determined for us.

The Christian is to stand *in*, not outside, the world, right in the middle of the world. That's right! Jesus was careful to pray, in John 17, that we would *not* be taken out of this world, but would stand undaunted in the middle of it and its pressures. The quality of being able to live in this world, yet allowing ourselves to be shaped from the inside out by God, is *holiness*.

Have you ever faced times or challenges that made it really difficult to be a Christian? Have there been times when you'd like to cash it all in and call it quits? You're not alone.

The good news is that God has given us a gift to help us stand in undaunted and indomitable strength by the power of His Spirit, amid the forces that would misshape us. Holiness is God's gift to help us stick to our convictions when everything is working against us.

"Just as He Who called you is holy, so be holy in all you do, for it is written: 'Be holy because I am holy.'" (1 Peter 1:15–16, paraphrased)

In this context, the word *holiness* is used mainly in ethical, behavioral terms. In the entirety of the Bible, the Greek words *hagios* and *kadosh* have as much to do with the distinct difference in quality between God and humans as it has to do with behavior. In most Christian settings, we tend to emphasize behavior when talking about holiness. The Bible actually gives far greater weight to the definition than it would give to a qualitative definition. Being holy is a quality of life that God possesses. It's a quality of life that isn't shaped by the events or the course of the world, but is a quality that stands outside, separated.

To be holy or sanctified means to be separated for the Lord's purposes, to be able to stand in His power and strength outside the pressures while in the middle of them. This is the incredible working of the Holy Spirit. God's Holy Spirit gives us standing power when everything is falling apart around us.

Because God is always at the edge of any hassles we're facing, His power can be appropriated into our realm, for He is never weakened or affected in His holiness by whatever happens to us.

As a pastor, I've had the privilege of counseling many people facing horrendous circumstances. At times, I couldn't imagine how I would withstand some of the crises I've seen other people face. Because we tend to be very subjective, it's easy, in the face of pain, loss, and suffering, to feel that God has somehow become indifferent.

The American "god of the good life" flees in the face of less-than-optimal circumstances. Yet, our God of the Bible lives in the middle of crises with as much dignity and conviction-strengthening as in the best of times.

I think that this is the whole point of the book of Job—one that his would-be comforters would be unable to grasp. In Job's loss, God wasn't affected at all. I think this is the discovery Job finally came to, when God asked Job where he was when God created the heavens and the earth. The strong point that the Lord wanted to get across was that no matter what Job was experiencing, God had never changed. Neither had what God thought about Job changed—that is, crises didn't affect the unchanging God.

Living in the reality of God's unchangeability is living in holiness. This requires consistent thinking about the Lord. After all, we are but a reflection of the God Whom we worship and believe in.

James Michener shares in his novel *The Source* a fascinating story of a Canaanite tribesman named Urbaal. In this story, Urbaal and his wife, Timna, are visited by the priests of their pagan Canaanite faith. They are asked to submit their firstborn son to be sacrificed in worship of their god, Makor. It would have been blasphemous for Urbaal and Timna to refuse to surrender their infant son to the arms of this child-consuming god of the Canaanites. With great anguish, they gave up their son.

As Timna watched in horror her son being consumed by the fire, the tribesmen stood around the altar of the high priest to choose who would spend a week with the new prostitute priestess. Their fertility gods demanded that one man be chosen from the village to live with this cult prostitute priestess for a week. Because his first son had been offered as a sacrifice to Makor, Urbaal was a candidate in the election. When his name was drawn, Timna was emotionally crushed by the obvious delight on Urbaal's face.

As she turned and walked away from the scene when her husband departed to live with the priestess for the week, she could not hold back her anguish over the sight of their only baby son being consumed in the fire of the pagan idol. Timna made a profound statement: "He would have been a very different man if he had had a different god" (p. 148).

The true God we worship comes out in our times of pain and suffering. Peter was most concerned that those under the pressures of his time would be holy—set apart—in the understanding of Who their God was.

God remains distinctly holy and all-powerful in His character, and His power is always available. The message here is that we are called to share in God's distinctive life qualities in a world that always works against them.

This means standing against the pressures of a downstream world. It also means walking in the paths that the Lord has provided for us.

Not far from where I live, near beautiful Stevens Pass, just before the quaint little town of Leavenworth, Washington, there is a fish ladder that spans the breadth of the Wenatchee River. During spawning times, one can drive right up to the edge of the fish ladder to observe large chinook and coho salmon attempting to leap the waterfall, approximately ten to fifteen feet high. The salmon will leap and leap to the point of exhaustion, trying to get up over the falls. Eventually, they discover that, just to the left, there is a fish ladder that helps to escort them up and around the force of the falls, over which they could never have leaped.

People love to watch them struggle as they repeatedly hurl themselves forward in their attempts to leap over the crest of rushing water. They struggle to get over this way, ignoring the ladder that the Department of Fisheries has provided for them to help them circumvent the strong current.

Likewise, holiness is walking in the pathway provided by the Lord to help us circumvent the forces and currents that work against us. When you are suffering, here is something to remember: Stick to God's way. The temptations are always great, in the face of loss, to swap God's plan for another, but attempting to face the forces and pressures of the world on your own won't work.

Holiness also describes the process of Christian transformation. We are made different. We are made to be separate. Peter called his followers (and us also) to live in the quality of life that was given to us when we received Christ.

When my wife and I first moved to Kirkland, where we presently pastor, we didn't have much money. We planned to pioneer a church with a small group of people. In fact, we started with ten people in our living room. To be able to manage our dreams, we found a house we could rent, with the agreement that we would do some renovation work on it.

The backyard of this old rundown, two-bedroom house contained a swimming pool that hadn't been cleaned in at least six or eight years! The algae was so thick that anyone could walk on the water.

The first thing I did was to call a pool service. When the pool man showed up, he was as shocked as I was by the condition of the pool. He had a great laugh when I told him that I had begun to empty all the water out, only to discover that I was flooding our neighbor's house.

He said, "Son, you never empty the water out of the pool. You simply change it."

We got in with nets and scooped out all the algae, broken limbs, drowned rats, and even a bat. Once we got most of the debris cleared off the top, we spotted an opossum three to four feet down. As we scooped it up with the net, its decayed body spread throughout the water. What a sickening sight!

We put new filters in the water pump, added chlorine and some startup chemicals, and then fired up the pump. After several days, the water began to clear. When it did, I jumped into the pool to scrub the sides, as the pool man had instructed. Within seven to eight days, the water became crystal clear.

There was only one problem: I could never get my wife to go into that pool. Each time I tried, she'd say, "You won't catch me swimming in 'possum soup."

No matter how I tried to convince her that the water was now clean and pure, she said that it was still the same water. I have to admit that swallowing that water from time to time did make me remember the 'possum that fell apart that first day.

We're just like that pool. The water was the same water, but it was cleansed. The elements that would make the water unclean with their contagions were being destroyed by the presence of the outside element, chlorine.

Likewise, holiness is the quality of God's life that lives in us to keep us pure and clean. Outside His presence we don't stay holy. God's presence in our lives allows us to withstand the corrosive pressures of this world. Facing pressures in times of suffering is an essential skill for all believers.

Every parent has probably given his or her child a lecture or two on facing peer pressure. Yet, even as adults, we have to face peer pressure, especially when life isn't going well.

One of the studies I enjoy, which can have different approaches, is usually done in upper level psychology classes. It's a fun exercise, and it's a great trick to play on a friend too.

Here's the game plan: The class secretly chooses one student who will *not* be told what the class is doing that day. The professor then puts a simple mathematical equation on the blackboard or states some historical fact that everyone knows. For example, the professor puts $9 \times 9 = ?$ on the board and asks for the answer.

A student who knows the game answers, "It's 87, professor." Everyone knows, of course, that it's 81.

The professor then asks, "How many *agree* with that answer?"

All the students, except the unenlightened one, raise their hands in agreement.

The professor says, "That's correct. Now, how many *believe* that the answer is 87?"

Again, all but the one student raise their hands in agreement. Eventually, most of the time, the one person who is not in on the game plan will agree that the answer is 87. Though she or he knows that the answer is 81, peer pressure makes the person say it's 87. This exercise demonstrates that, for some reason, we are all highly susceptible, as humans, to bankrupt and to abandon our convictions under that kind of pressure.

Peter cautioned his followers that they, as Christians, would never find their true destiny unless they were capable of working against peer pressure. In other words, *we are to be people who swim upstream in a downstream world.* By our distinctive characteristics and quality of living, we are to stand out from the crowd with the message of Jesus.

FOUR PRACTICAL LESSONS FOR SWIMMING UPSTREAM

Peter gave us four practical steps to take so that we won't evade our convictions or give in to our anticonvictions. These four practical ways will help us to stick to what we know to be true and right.

Be Prepared in Your Mind

"Therefore gird up the loins of your mind . . ." (1 Peter 1:13). If you're going to stick to your convictions when everything is working against you, you need to set your attitude square and straight. Now, when the New Testament uses the term *mind,* it does not primarily mean the gray matter in your skull. It refers to your "attitudinal center." Peter said, "Gird up your mind"—that is, prepare your mind; get your mind right; get your mind on course.

Keeping your mind right is vital for thriving in a time of suffering. To be a believer is to let your mind be right, to set your mind on the right course—that is, the course that's lined up with the mind of Christ.

Peter instructed the Christians of his time and our time to keep their minds alert. Don't go to sleep in this world. You can't afford it. Think judiciously about all the input that comes your way. Don't just swallow everything hook, line, and sinker. Get your attitude set up right, especially when life is progressing less than optimally.

I've heard it said that 80 percent of any task depends on a

person's attitude before beginning it. For example, if you're going to be a successful salesperson, 80 percent of your task is having the right attitude before you make your first call. Or if you're going to be a believer, a Christian, you have to get your attitude straight. A Christlike attitude sets the tone for all your thoughts, words, and actions. So put your mind in the right place.

I recently found an interesting article in a business magazine. Someone actually conducted a study as to why customers stopped patronizing a business and moved to a competitor. This is what he found:

- 1 percent had died (a legitimate reason, I suppose);
- 3 percent had moved away (also reasonable);
- 5 percent left because of friendships or other loyalties. They knew someone on the competitor's staff or started their own business (understandable reasons as well);
- 9 percent were drawn away by competition (regrettable, but a factor in the American business system);
- 14 percent left because the business's product had become substandard (also understandable);
- 68 percent left because of the crummy attitude of the company's employees! Customers stopped patronizing this business because they were treated rudely or indifferently by the employees.

So if you intend to stick to your convictions, you should prepare your mind by setting your attitude straight. Successful living in life begins with a Christlike attitude. It begins with an attitude that is shaped from the inside out, rather than from the outside in. Holiness requires an alertness, which begins at the attitudinal center of our lives.

Be Sober

Here, Peter was talking about our will. By that, he meant that we should be in command of ourselves. We know that being sober means not being under the influence of foreign substances. Being sober is avoiding the unruly influences that surround us. Being sober means controlling our will from the inside out. We all know that it is unlawful to drink while driving. It is also very dangerous to have a loss of control while Christianizing.

The Bible states clearly that before we met Christ we were under the influence of principalities, powers, and what the Bible refers to as "the world," meaning the course of human culture and human attitudes. Principalities and powers have to do with those unseen spiritual influences that attempt to set the course of humanity on destruction by establishing pervasive and unholy attitudes.

Another way of putting it is that before we came to Christ we were extremely outer-directed. That is, we were controlled by peers, by worldly fads, and by cultural mentalities. The apostle John referred to this as the "spirit of this age." The book of Revelation mentions "prevailing mentalities," as though they were personalities that actually shaped the world's culture.

When we come to Christ, we become inner-directed. We no longer decide the course of our lives by outward pressures. I've discovered that people, in modern concepts of discipleship, often confuse discipleship with being outer-directed persons. True discipleship offers skills and abilities that allow learners to become inner-directed.

True discipleship is teaching and training in Christian thinking. This kind of Christian thinking leads one to self-control, which is one of the fruits of the Spirit.

Christ did not come to dominate people, but to return to us our human dignity and self-control. We can't mature as outer-directed people; rather we need to be inner-directed.

We need to watch for this in our children. During the seventeen years that I've pastored, I've discovered that some children from great Christian homes have a difficult time facing up to peer pressure. However, children who, perhaps, didn't have as much Christian focus in their homes have an easier time making a choice for Christ and living according to His pattern in the face of these pressures.

Why? I've talked to educators about this. They have confirmed the idea that in a strictly Christian environment persons are often socialized rather than converted—that is, they continue to be outer-directed rather than inner-directed. To be discipled in this fashion does not lead to maturity, for your life decisions are being made by outward pressures—what the Jones family has and what the pastor thinks.

You must have inner convictions, be inner-directed, and be in control of yourself. If you don't, when rough times come, you won't have the fortitude to stand up to them.

Morris was the production manager of a local factory that made components for public address sound systems for rock bands. He came to me with a great dilemma. Business wasn't going well, and his marriage was going bad. His job was also in jeopardy. If he lost that, he feared he would not be able to regain the romance he and his wife once had in their marriage. Production was lagging, and he was unable to meet the rigorous demands of his company, especially with the Christmas season coming on. He became particularly tempted to fudge on his weekly report figures.

Tearfully, Morris told me: "Pastor, I don't understand it. The pressure got to me, and I began lying to my boss. I knew I'd get caught eventually, and I don't even know why I attempted it. I just wasn't willing to run the risk of losing my wife."

I listened intently with a great deal of compassion. Here was a strong, successful man who earned close to six figures a year. He'd been caught in the grips of the pressure to perform. This pressure always destroys because it is never productive. I could identify with his problem, as I too had been pressured many times in my life to conform to outward expectations rather than do what I knew was right.

Interrupting my thoughts, Morris continued: "I just don't understand it, Pastor. I'm afraid I'm going to lose my job now, all because I gave in to the pressure to lie, the pressure to disobey God. What can I do?"

After a long conversation, we prayed, and he recommitted himself to Christ's resources to stand under the pressures of his day. When it looked as though he was going to lose all that he loved, he had resorted to almost any means—even means unnatural to him—in order to protect himself.

We also discussed the fact that God had never changed in the middle of Morris's crisis, that God would remain forever the same. His character is set. He is unchangeable. He is holy. We prayed that Morris would draw upon the resources of his unchanging God—that is, in the middle of his crisis he would be able to level with his boss.

Morris's situation is not unlike the problems of the believers to whom Peter was writing. Peter's message comes out strong: Be in control. Don't give in to outer pressures.

The term *sober,* or *self-control,* in the original language of Peter's letter portrays for us the best description of "one who will stand in the face of a crumbling world," in the authoritative life of Jesus. Being self-controlled is simply controlling yourself.

Be ready to control yourself. Don't give that control to any force or person! Get your mind ready; get it right. Line up your attitude with your convictions.

The believer who is prepared to stand up with an alert mind in the middle of a crisis will come out with greater strength and more profound fruit, along with a greater understanding about what makes for life.

Set Your Heart in Hope

Peter urged: "Rest your hope fully upon the grace that is to be brought to you at the revelation of Jesus Christ" (1 Peter 1:13). In other words, have an optimistic attitude, because Christ will be revealed. When He is revealed, you will have sound justification for having been optimistic about your life.

I believe that another translation of *hope* will have to be devised in the next two or three decades, because in our culture we have virtually obliterated its true meaning. Originally, this word did not contain the element of uncertainty that it does today. Here are some of today's examples:

"Do you think it will rain tomorrow?"

"I hope not."

"Doug, do you think you have enough gas to get to the church this morning?"

"I hope so."

"Gee, I hope Jesus is real. If not, I'm sunk."

These examples carry a definite ring of uncertainty. *Hope,* as used in the New Testament, possesses an intrinsic, definite tone of certainty to it. To "set your hope" means that you can, without any doubt or hesitation, trust Jesus with your future. So be an optimist! If you're an optimist, you'll have a better than even chance of sticking to your convictions! But if you're a pessimist, you'll buckle every time, because the quality of what you are trusting isn't worth leaning on. It has no substance. Therefore, be an optimist!

I like the story about Joe Louis, the heavyweight boxing champ from 1937–1949, when he fought Two-Ton Tony Galento.

In the second round of the fight, Tony kayoed Joe, knocking him down. Joe stayed down for only 1½ counts, scrambled to his feet, and traded punches until the end of the round.

The guys in his corner were yelling, "Joe, stay down! Stay down! Get your equilibrium back! Get your legs back!"

When Joe walked back to his corner after the round, his handlers chewed him out, "Joe, you had ten counts. Why did you get back up so soon?"

Joe grinned and said, "I didn't want to give him that much rest."

Joe Louis went on to win the match—because he was an optimist.

And that's what Peter essentially said: "Set your mind to be hopeful and positive. Be an optimist."

If you're facing a crisis, you can trust Jesus with your future. Being hopeful is maintaining a conviction in the face of a crisis. He can be trusted.

Don't Trust Your Impulses

Watch out for your impulses, especially at a time of loss or crisis. They will get you in trouble more often than not.

Peter put it this way: "Do not conform to your evil desires." The Greek word Peter used for *desire* also translates as "impulses." Particularly, don't trust your sexual impulses to guide you. I can tell you, with great pain in my heart, that untold numbers of people have been deceived and snared into participating in premarital sex and extramarital affairs, believing it was right simply because it felt good to gratify their impulses. Watch out for your impulses. Don't trust them because they'll let you down every time.

Ron Rearick (nicknamed Iceman) and I, while preparing a videotape for teenagers about sexual integrity, researched a number of aspects on this subject. We discovered something quite surprising. The people who are preparing a new sex manual, because of the AIDS epidemic, have arrived at a most incredible conclusion: They're now suggesting that it might possibly be a good idea not to give in to your sexual impulses outside of marriage. Surprising, isn't it? What wisdom!

It then follows that if you're going to stick to your convictions, you had better not trust your impulses, because they will shape and manipulate you in wrong directions. The buying impulse, the eating impulse, the drinking impulse, the gambling impulse, and the sexual impulse should not direct your life.

Recently a specialist on sexual addictions addressed our staff. We made it an educational afternoon. One of the staff members asked the specialist what was usually the trigger point for someone inclined toward sexual deviancy.

Leaning forward over the chair in front of him, the specialist replied: "Extraordinary stress. Most of us believe, in our time of excessive stress, that people in the past who had inclinations toward addictive sexual behavior didn't give in to it as readily. However, in our present time, extraordinary stressful living seems to bring out the very worst that is lurking around in most of us."

We were all shocked. Quite a discussion followed about what stress really means: pressure. The word *pressure* itself means "to draw tight," like stretching a rubber band just short of its breaking point.

Peter found that in times of intense struggle, pain, and agony our impulses can begin to speak to us. They can sound very beneficent. But if not checked and run through the rigors of our convictions, they can deceive us. Impulses can make us feel very good about some things that are very wrong. They are not trustworthy.

Under pressure, we begin to ask ourselves whether Christianity is really real. Or, perhaps, we give in to a past bondage by saying, "But I need this right now."

I spoke the other day with a very successful businessman in our community. At one time in his life, he had been a cocaine addict. He was offered cocaine by some of his employees, after he had become a Christian and been drug-free for several years. He accepted the cocaine, and his addiction kicked in again.

Embarrassed even to discuss the matter with me, he told me, "I don't know why, but I just felt I owed it to myself to have a moment's relief."

The tragedy was that this started him on a six-month cocaine binge. His habit cost as high as $300–400 a week before his wife discovered it. Pressure had caused him to lean on a past impulse, in this case his susceptibility to substance abuse.

Because he began to believe that God was distanced from him, he lost the hope of believing that his future was bright and strong. He had given in to an impulse that was destroying his life.

How do we face these pressures?

- With a sober mind;
- With direction and self-control;
- Being a hope-filled, optimistic person; and
- Being aware that in times of stress and loss, once conquered, old bondages and impulses will surface to try to regain control.

Following these four simple steps will help us to make sure that when pressures numb us at times to the spiritual reality of Christ, we will not buckle.

Peter concluded that what ought to motivate us in the right direction is that we will have to face God and be judged. That is not a popular idea in our time. However, it is true; we will all give an account. This ought to motivate us.

All believers will face God in what is called the "believer's judgment" (*bema* in Greek). Because Christians have accepted Christ, we have already passed the "great white throne of judgment," and our names are now in the "Lamb's Book of Life."

Even in our suffering, we have something to look forward to. We may, in fact, be rewarded with a greater capacity to be Christlike when we see our Lord face to face.

Peter urged his scattered church to be motivated for good, because they would all give an account of their lives. I don't think we would want to ask anything less of ourselves. God will ask some hard questions, I am sure. It won't matter who caught you at something in life, because people can't see into your mind or your heart, but God can.

Another reason we are to be motivated, as Peter concluded, is that we are never to forget how precious the gift of Jesus is. Peter reminds us that the reason it is so important that we obey Christ is that the gift of life He gave us is inexpressibly valuable! It is absolutely precious because Christ was without spot or blemish, the perfect lamb. God sent His very best to you, so obey Him because of the inestimable value of what He has done in you.

Here is a true story to draw attention to this point. Not long ago, my friend Ron Rearick and my wife conspired to play a trick on me. Debbie knows that I don't care for jewelry for myself. In fact, I don't even wear a watch. My reasons aren't based on ethics or my value system. It just bothers me, that's all. I don't like anything on my wrist, and I have a hang-up about jewelry.

I have often joked about preachers who wear Rolex watches. Even more distasteful to me is a diamond tie clip. I don't have a problem with anyone being blessed with money to buy jewelry, but I do think that we need to be responsible with whatever resources God has blessed us with. Now, if you have a Rolex, don't worry about it. It's fine with me.

Well, Ron brought a watch to me with the Rolex name on it. He said it came from the publishers who bought our manuscript for a movie we had written together. He even had a picture of this watch to convince me that it was worth $10,000. Initially, I didn't believe him. But he was persuasive enough that I eventually believed that the picture was of the same watch that he had placed in my hand.

Ron said, "Here, Doug, I brought you this watch from the publishers. They wanted you to have it."

I replied, "No-o-o-o-o way! So this is worth $10,000, huh? Wow! But I can't wear it. I have made fun of preachers who wear these things. No, I'm not going to wear it. . . ." I finally put it on and admired it.

Ron said, "Okay, then I'll just take it back and tell them you didn't want it."

I said, "Well, maybe I should just store it away in a safety deposit box."

Ron said, "Yeah, that would be great! Go ahead and take it."

So I took that beautiful watch home to show it to my family. When I flipped the box open to show them, they all acted so impressed—for about one minute. Then they all exploded into laughter.

They had caught me. My whole family was in on the joke. The watch was actually an imitation that someone had made to look like a Rolex. It was a fine watch in its own right, worth about $60—a far cry from $10,000, however. I certainly treated it a lot differently when I realized it was an imitation.

The point is that it's all in our heads. If we don't realize what a precious gift Christ is, exalt and worship Him above all else, value Him as highly as God the Father does, if we devalue Christ in our lives, then we will not have the power to withstand the forces of this world when they challenge us to compromise our convictions.

When the pressure is on, it is time to remember that we are swimming upstream. Going upstream in a downstream world can be done only by putting the right price tag on Christ and making certain the price tag matches the value of those we love around us, and that we haven't overvalued the goods of this world.

Yes, it is real, and it does work—even when the pressure is on.

Chapter 4

Keeping Your Friends Through Pain
(1 Peter 1:22—2:3)

We have all met the porcupine individuals. They are the ones who are unusually difficult to get along with.

I was invited to speak at a weekend college retreat, which a large number of students attended. It was my privilege to meet with the leaders and representatives from the congregations that were involved in this conference. This group of ten to twelve people included one of these thorny porcupine spirits.

Sharon complained about the length of the meetings and the topics to be addressed. She complained about the kinds of social activities being offered. She complained about the food, about the beds, and about everything.

It is amazing how much contact you can have with people during a four-day retreat when you're working with a small group of people. When Sharon walked into the room, her body language and facial expression automatically alienated everyone, for she gave the impression that she was deliberately trying to make everyone an enemy. If our conclusions were right, she was being successful—none of us could stand her.

On the third evening of the retreat, I shared a message about the love of God, just a simple message about how love works. We read together through 1 Corinthians 13, and I used a number of illustrations on what it was like to be a father. As I expected, Sharon approached me after the meeting, but this time with tears showing in her eyes.

Somewhat reproachfully, she said, "Doug, how do you expect me to understand love when you talk about it from the perspective of a father? Don't you know that not all of us here have had a positive experience with our fathers? In fact, there are dozens of us who have not, and you have seriously hurt us tonight."

I decided to take advantage of this slightly open door as an opportunity to help Sharon to understand that there was a loving Father Who did specifically love her. I asked her some questions about her own father. It seems that he had abandoned her mother and the family when Sharon was small, and she hardly remembered him. All she knew was that she and the other three children had struggled greatly as their mother attempted to acquire a skill to provide for them. Even when her father was with them, they had very little to live on, because he was an alcoholic.

I finally gathered the courage to ask her a question: "Sharon, do you realize that you are difficult to get along with?"

Shocked that I would be so blunt and brash, she countered, "And who are *you* to ask a question like that?"

My response was slow in coming. When I caught my breath, I replied, "I am someone who cares a great deal about you. Could it be that in your own pain you are alienating and shutting off everyone else, just in case we might let you down too?"

Sharon broke into sobs. As we continued our conversation, one of the leaders of the college retreat joined us, and we were both able to share with Sharon. It became evident that Sharon had been living a self-fulfilling prophecy that made certain that others would reject her. In her own hurt, she worked to alienate everyone she possibly could to remain "safe." There are lots of Sharons in our world.

In the times when it looks as though our lives aren't working and the promises aren't coming true, it becomes quite easy for us to lash out at those who do, and could, mean the most to us. Peter addressed the reality of our need for one another and gave us a pathway to make sure that we don't isolate ourselves. In those moments of deep hurt, we badly need one another.

Since you have purified your souls in obeying the truth through the Spirit in sincere love of the brethren, love one another fervently with a pure heart, having been born again, not of corruptible seed but incorruptible, through the word of God which lives and abides forever, because

"All flesh is as grass,
and all the glory of man
as the flower of the grass.
The grass withers,
and its flower falls away,
but the word of the LORD
endures forever."

Now this is the word which by the gospel was preached to you. Therefore, laying aside all malice, all guile, hypocrisy, envy, and all evil speaking, as newborn babes, desire the pure milk of the word, that you may grow thereby, if indeed you have tasted that the Lord *is* gracious. (1 Peter 1:22—2:3)

As a pastor, I'm gradually learning to listen to the hearts of others. For instance, the other day, I received a letter from a young man who had just been released from prison: "I can't believe you all won't let me escape my past. You promised me love, acceptance, and forgiveness; and yet, you and your staff refuse, in any way, to recognize me or allow me to be a part of the church because I was in prison."

He went on to accuse me of being hypocritical—another Jim Bakker or Jimmy Swaggart. That's not exactly the kind of affirmation a pastor looks for. What is startling about his letter is that none of us even knew he had a criminal record! The poor fellow, for some reason unknown to me, had felt rejected by our church.

I have to confess that my first reaction to this letter was anger. I wanted to boot him out, but this is Christ's church—not mine. One of the first things you learn as a pastor is that you don't get to choose the people you have been called to shepherd.

After a pause to refocus my thinking and ten minutes of prayer, I decided to call this hurting young man and listen to his heart, for his letter revealed more than just angry words on the page. He had obviously suffered severely in his lifetime. Because he had evidently felt rejected all his life, he had developed what is called a self-fulfilling prophecy. That is, if he wasn't rejected deliberately, then the twisted mechanism in his psyche made certain that he felt rejected.

I placed the call, and a delightful conversation followed. He was quite surprised to hear from me. He became broken in his spirit, and he wept when I told him that we had had no idea he had been in prison and were glad he had started attending our church.

This young man blurted out a sad story. He had twice been sold by his mother to someone else and had been raised in the ghetto, usually in a drug-infested environment. We both decided that he had evidently come to feel "at home" with rejection, so at home with this feeling, in fact, that he would purposely set up situations where he could confirm his faulty belief that he didn't deserve acceptance by others.

We then prayed together, and I'm delighted to report that this young man is working through his insecurities and the agonizing pain of rejection he had suffered for so long. I have told his story only to point out that all of us, in our own pain, generally reach out to hurt others.

Several months ago, Debbie, the kids, and I drove to a shopping mall in which the parking lot used cement dividers for cars to park against. Upon returning to the car after shopping, I was negotiating intensely with my kids about something. Forgetting that I'd parked in front of one of these blocks, I put the engine in drive gear instead of reverse. The car lunged forward, up over the block, and became high-centered on it.

Embarrassed, I said accusingly, "Now, look at what you made me do, Debbie! And if you kids wouldn't make so much noise when I'm driving, these things wouldn't happen!"

Ignoring my stern tone, they all cracked up. Their hilarity became contagious. Acknowledging, finally, that I was out of order, I laughed too. They all knew the *real* problem. I was trying to blame them for my own mistake.

Here again is an illustration of our human tendency to look for a scapegoat when things go badly for us. Unfortunately, scapegoats are often those we love the most. Apparently, pain causes us to sacrifice our relationships more readily than does any other human experience. When we're to blame, we generally shift our blame to someone else. And if we can't do that adequately, we then make it as miserable as possible for others to take the heat off ourselves.

That is what Peter suggested to that group of suffering believers: "Watch out! Just because you're hurting, don't neglect or evade your call as a Christian community to be led by the Word that was preached to you."

> Therefore, rid yourselves of all malice, deceit, hypocrisy, envy, and every kind of slanderous talk. Like new babies, crave spiritual milk so that you may grow up in your salvation. (1 Peter 2:1-2, paraphrased)

This is a pragmatic section of Scripture. It's pretty hard to miss Peter's point. He flat-out says: "No matter how bad life gets, you should still express love to one another. Don't sacrifice your relationships, no matter what pressures you're facing."

Mark Twain once said: "It isn't the passages of Scripture I don't understand that bother me. It's the ones I *do* understand that give me the most trouble" (emphasis added).

ONE OF THE GREAT IDEAS

The other day I picked up a great book with a fascinating title: *Seven Ideas That Have Changed the Universe*. It covers such subjects as the theory of relativity, Newton's theory of cause and effect in the universe, and quantum physics. It's a wonderful and interesting book, though I'm not convinced that those ideas have really changed the universe. It's true that we did determine how the universe works through these discoveries, but I don't think we have done much changing.

Conversely, Peter here presents a concept that is continually changing our planet on a daily basis. It's the great idea that Jesus taught us: love! When we were spiritually born again, we received an imperishable seed that releases in us God's supernatural capacity to love others and to have a heart for the world. In fact, the primary evidence that we are born again is that we not only have the capacity to love, but also are determined to release that love to others!

The distinguishing mark of Christianity is that we love one

another. Christianity is not built on the soundness of a philosophy or on the impeccability of Christian character. It is built on the God-given, supernatural capacity to be truly feeling, caring, loving people!

Love is filled with supernatural provision. Love is a life-style that has been characterized and modeled by Jesus. Love is a possibility for *all* humans. Love is not only possible, but also essential during pain and trouble.

Real love is an art, a skill that must be released continually to be effective. In other words, it is not our job to try to love others, but to position ourselves in a place where love is uninterrupted. Those who are born again and become Christians receive an imperishable seed from God, which creates the miraculous ability to love others.

You're no doubt gradually discovering, as I am, that being a Christian is not necessarily doing the right thing. Rather, it more often involves our not doing or saying things that would stop Jesus' life from occurring in us.

Recently, church-growth experts asked me to list ten steps to help a church to grow. My conclusion was that there are none. Frankly, I really don't know what makes a church grow. I'm not certain that anyone really knows what we should do to make churches grow. I suppose there are some who might know, but I'm not one of them.

I do know, however, that there are plenty of wrong actions and attitudes that will stop church growth. It follows, then, that if you eliminate that which stops love, that interrupts the miracle of love working, you'll then love people the way Christ loves people! This miracle of working love is the cement that binds us together and promotes church growth.

This is the point that Peter was making. He told of the kinds of things that impede love, the kinds of things we're all most susceptible to when we are hurting within. He wanted us to love one another fervently with pure hearts and to feed the miracle.

Love One Another Fervently with a Pure Heart

There can be no duplicity in this kind of love . . . no mixed motives . . . no end to it. It can't be designed to last for only a short term. It can't be designed, like so many of today's products are, to last for about five years and then fall apart.

This kind of love is inexhaustible and possesses a great deal of fervor. Its embers never burn out. Because we become aware that Christ's Holy Spirit within us releases the born-again nature, this love enables us to be outgoing in our love. By "sincere" love, Peter meant: Don't love one another with the hope that you will receive love in return.

Anyone in the "helping" professions knows that helping people with the hope of gaining something in return leads only to agony, frustration, and even bitterness. If you're going to help people so that they will love you because you've made so many wonderful sacrifices for them in the Name of Jesus, forget it. You'll lose your mind and end up quitting because you're burned out.

Sincere love has no strings attached to it, no anticipated returns to be paid. It is *pure*. It is *clean*. You can see right through it. If you set out to love others with the idea of getting love in return, you will become disappointed, embittered, and disillusioned.

That is what Peter referred to. When it gets tough for you, remember that you don't love to get love in return, and you don't love God so that you can get good returns from Him.

The little story that follows aptly illustrates this point. One morning at breakfast, a mother found a bill under her plate from her eight-year-old son, Bradley, which stated:

Mother Owes Bradley

For running errands:	25 cents
For being good:	10 cents
For taking music lessons:	15 cents
For doing extra work:	5 cents
	Total Bill Due: 55 cents

Bradley's mother made no comment after she read his bill, and she said nothing about it all morning. When Bradley sat down to lunch, he found fifty-five cents under his plate, along with her bill.

Bradley Owes Mother

For nursing him through scarlet fever:	00 cents
For being good to Bradley:	00 cents
For clothes, shoes, and toys:	00 cents
For a bike and playroom:	00 cents
For fixing Bradley his meals:	00 cents
Total Bill Due:	Love

The love depicted by the mother in this little story is the kind that Peter talked about: In order to give sincere, unending love toward one another, you can't look for payoffs or expect others to love you back, because you'll be disappointed and disgruntled every time.

Both parents and those in the "helping" professions often end up being the target of anger from those they love or help. It's one of the risks you undertake. If you love people and want to help them, you need to understand thoroughly that those who are hurting will very often lash out and blame you for something they themselves did, for which they need to assume the responsibility. It's just our nature. A great many relationships have been flushed down the proverbial drain at the hands of a wounded or broken heart.

Peter fervently desired his flock to understand that. Because they were facing a hostile world, they needed each other even more than they could ever realize; it was no time for them to quit loving one another. We who are suffering pain and agony in our lives tend to feel that our relationships must not have helped us very much, or we wouldn't be in the mess we're in at the moment.

Peter was telling us not to let go of, not to chase away, and not to run off the very ones we need the most. Instead, love them sincerely and fervently.

To those who would say: "Well, after all, I'm only human. I'm bound to be mean part of the time because I can't be totally loving." Peter countered with: "That excuse won't fly, because you are naturally unable to love outside of Christ. By the same token, you need to realize that, as believers, you're without an excuse, because Christ has imparted a new nature to you that, by its very essence, is loving. Your problem is that you do things that hide that love; you clothe love over. Therefore, because you now have this miraculous capacity to love, get rid of the dirty shirt that covers your love." In the Greek, the word for "get rid of" literally means "take off a dirty shirt."

Peter described the Christian life-style as "ridding ourselves" of those thoughts and attitudes that cover love. He enumerated the five characteristics of malice, guile, hypocrisy, envy, and evil speaking, which betray us when we're not being loving toward others. Initially, these characteristics may sound negative, which is often true about Christianity; it begins with a negative, but then moves to a positive.

The first time I heard about Jesus was from our cleaning man, Ray. He stood on the front porch of our home and talked about Jesus to Mom and me. The essence of what he said was: "Jesus Christ died for your sins. God sent His son to die for you."

Objectively, I know now that that's what he said. But what I thought I heard, after I saw the shock and fear on Mom's face, was: "God hates you, and you're on your way to hell!"

Over the years I've developed a mental exercise to deal with negatives. For instance, whenever I come across negative commands in the Bible, I look for the positive correlative. In our Western mind-set, we tend to get hung up on negatives, rarely moving beyond them. Here are some examples: (1) The correlative of "You shall not steal" is "You shall work hard to earn your own possessions so you will have enough to give away." (2) The correlative of "You shall not kill" is "You shall do that which brings life to others."

When Peter said that expressing malice and desiring to say or do something to hurt someone else is not being loving, he assumed that we would work our way through from the negative to the positive. However, I'm sure we would all have to admit that taking a little nip out of someone else when we ourselves are hurting or disappointed carries a degree of pleasure with it. But when we yield to the dark side of ourselves, Peter stressed, we are feeding the wrong nature. In other words, when we desire to hurt someone deliberately because we're hurting, we stop being loving persons and miracles of God's loving nature at that moment, and the flow of life to us is temporarily interrupted.

Peter listed five easy ways for us to recognize when we're being loving to others. These will also serve as guidelines to tell us when we allow our own pain to destroy both our world and our relationships, which will be so important to us in the future:

1. *When you determine, in your own pain and agony, to say or do the things that will make someone else feel good, you are being loving.* Even when you feel your worst, if you determine to make someone else feel good, you have found a healthy way to overcome your own hurts and agonies.

2. *When you determine not to use deceit or try to manipulate others, you are being loving.* A person who exhibits love creates an atmosphere of trust. The essence of love works only when you are able to tell another person the total, absolute truth, even though it may be embarrassing for you, for love always causes deceit to give way to truth.

3. *When you determine that you will not be hypocritical, you are being loving. Hypocritical* defined is "to put on two faces; to pretend to be someone you're not." Conversely, the positive corollary is to be *nonhypocritical,* "to have a single face."

The word *hypocrite* (to wear a mask) originated from the ancient Greek word for "theater." This was the type of theater in which a lone actor played all the roles, using various masks to express different emotions (happiness, sadness, and so on). For instance, a loving person maintains one face—a loving face. But an unloving person changes faces, based on the circumstances. Thus, to be loving is to rid yourself of masks, to be one way, and not be divided.

The term *hypocrisy* also meant "to contain wax." In the ancient Greek *agora* (marketplace), when a marble statue or bust cracked, the artisan filled the gap with wax and sold it as a top-grade marble sculpture. But if the statue was being transported home on a hot day, the wax would melt, exposing the crack. When smart buyers purchased statues and busts, they had them moved into the sun for a time to determine if any wax melted or could be felt. Hence, a statue or bust containing wax was labeled "hypocritical," while those without wax were labeled "unhypocritical."

So, Peter said that a loving person tells it like it is and doesn't gloss over, cover up, his or her own nature.

Using the analogy of Greek sculpture as a backdrop, Peter urged us not to wax ourselves over, not to be hypocritical, not to be two-faced. Just be the real you.

4. *When you determine that you will not be envious, you are being loving.* The positive correlative to this is that you enjoy seeing others advance ahead of you. What is envy? It is nothing more than jealousy, the brand that wants what another person has.

How do you recognize when you're being loving in this type of circumstance? You get excited and pleased when another person is blessed. You become genuinely enthusiastic when someone else prospers.

I recently counseled a married man who had become involved with a young woman. When he attended one of our services, he surrendered his life to Christ. After the service, he approached me weeping and confessed to me about his affair, which he had just decided to end because Christ was now in his life, and he couldn't continue to live a two-faced life with his wife anymore.

He said, "What I've done is not right. I'm going to face the truth. I'm going to remain devoted to my wife hereafter, if she'll still have me."

Not surprisingly, his wife had suspected his dishonesty all along, but his willingness to expose his dishonesty changed both his life and that of their marriage.

At a subsequent counseling session with him and his wife, I asked, "What caused you to become interested in this younger woman in the first place?"

He replied, "I was angry. I was hurting so bad, I just wanted to hurt my wife. I'm so sorry, Honey. I hope it's possible to work this out."

It wasn't many weeks later that the younger woman in this triangle called me. She wished to remain anonymous and, to this day, I don't know who she was.

This is what she shared with me: "Pastor Doug, a few years ago, I began to attend your church and committed my life to Christ, but I've since fallen away. I recently became involved with a married man, but I know Christ is real, because this man now desires to devote himself to his wife."

After we talked a few more minutes, she resurrendered her life to Christ, and I had the feeling that she would be all right. Love causes us to face our own pain and agony with a maturity that does not want to spread our pain to others.

5. *When you determine to rid yourself of slander, you are being loving.* Slander is the defamation of another's character. If you deliberately make statements to reduce the stature of others (make them look smaller), you are effectively stopping the miracle of love in your own life.

When I feel the most insecure about myself, that's when I'm most tempted—and often give in to this temptation—to make someone else look smaller than I. How about you? Do you ever have that problem? I suppose it's just human nature.

I have discovered that over the years, the longer you're in a group, the more difficult it is to love others. That's really true. In fact, I think that's often why people move from church to church. I suppose you've already discovered that the miracle of love requires cost and attention to face and withstand the rigors of time.

If we believe that our lives fall apart because of some sort of judgment from God, it becomes very difficult for us to live with ourselves. This burden becomes even worse when we live around people who seem to have it all together, who apparently have no problems and are, perhaps, even prospering! That's when the subtle temptation creeps in and the agonizing flaws in our own human nature desire to whittle someone else down. We then deliberately say things that would make the other person appear smaller than we are so we can feel bigger in the face of our pain and disappointments. But slander undermines the kind of relationships that are part of our healing process. That is why Peter was seriously concerned that the believers in his time might, under pressure, become loveless and, therefore, powerless to overcome.

Feeding the Miracle

Peter continued on: "Remember to desire spiritual food, as a newborn baby desires milk, so that you will grow" (1 Peter 2:2, paraphrased).

This miracle of loving must be nurtured or our unloving side will dominate and destroy. Unfortunately, this is the way of the world. Peter, therefore, urged us to develop a desire for the Word of God, which will continue to nurture the loving miracle in us.

Between Sunday morning services, I often drink hot tea to keep my vocal cords limber and alive. One Sunday morning, as I walked by the nursery, I saw a tiny, little guy, about three weeks old, wailing to be fed.

Two women and a man were tending to this baby. Though they should have been able to handle this tiny, screaming baby, they were tripping over one another, not quite sure of what to do.

The baby's wailing seemed to say: "Get my mom out of church! And I mean, right now!"

The baby's attendants seemed to say: "Can't you wait another fifteen minutes? Pastor Doug won't talk very long this morning . . . will he?" Smiling, the three attendants looked at me for confirmation.

But that little guy didn't care. He just went on screaming: "No! Get my mom down here, right now!"

Well, this is the kind of picture Peter had in mind. We are to be driven so strongly to the milk of the Word of God that we will be just like that little wailing baby. No other reading should satisfy us in any way. If we hunger like this for the Word, our loving side will be nurtured.

Here's our challenge: *We are to develop an avarice, a greediness, for the Word of God. And when this Word is received by us as nourishment, we will begin to love!* Peter has a beautiful way of confronting our inability to love with pragmatic, practical instructions:

- Stop saying things that hurt each other.
- Stop saying things that would make another look small.

- Stop being petty.

When under pressure, here are some axioms to live by:

- When you're hurting the most, do something to make someone else feel better.
- Make it a personal project to make others look better than they are.
- Overlook the small annoyances of others.

I am presently reading a book titled *The New Science: Chaos* by James Kleck. In one chapter, he tells the story of Edward Lawrence, a weather forecaster in 1961. At that time, computer programs were just beginning to be used to predict weather.

After Lawrence ran the program through once, he ran it again to obtain the same weather pattern predictions, but decided to intercept it at the midway point to save time. However, instead of using the original figure of .506127, he simply rounded it off to .506 (the equivalent of one flap of a butterfly's wing) and let the program finish its course.

Within minutes, he was astonished to find that the forecast had changed so radically that it was totally different from the previous program! Lawrence had discovered what is now called the "butterfly effect." Now we know why it's so hard to predict weather accurately.

Theoretically and pragmatically, it is conceivable that a South American butterfly, flapping its wings, can actually set in motion a wind turbulence strong enough to affect the courses of tornadoes and hurricanes across North America. Theoretically and pragmatically, a butterfly flapping its wings can likewise alter the entire ecosystem!

Do you see the biblical application of this? *Just one loving act today can set in motion an entire new course for the entire world.*

None of us knows what might happen this week if we were to express the Holy Spirit's love to someone. Even a small act of love and kindness can have far-reaching results. However, our own pain often keeps us from expressing this kind of love.

I believe that finding meaning in the face of our sufferings, disappointments, and discouragements can come to us only when we determine to express love to others!

It is the miracle of love, lived through each one of us, that brings sense to our suffering world, which is apparently falling apart!

Peter knew that the presence of love in the face of pressure brings our suffering into perspective. When I love, I find meaning in my suffering. When I lash out to hurt, I miss the grace found in suffering.

PRAYER

Lord Jesus, we praise You for the miracle of Your Holy Spirit and for the miracle of love that is at work in us. Forgive us for all the things we do and say to stop the miracle of love from occurring. By Your blood, Lord Jesus, we set them aside now, in Your Name. Today, Lord, let us mindfully express the loving nature of Jesus Christ. May our acts of love have an impact on the communities in which we live. Amen.

Chapter 5

Life Is More than Surviving
(1 Peter 2:4–12)

I believe the Bible is "user friendly." Actually, it is really a very simple book to understand.

A second conviction I have about the Bible is just as important to me: It is "life applicable." It's more life applicable than it is theological in its orientation. The Bible gives very little thought to philosophy. It gives, instead, a great deal of concern to practical, how-to living.

As we read through Peter's letter together, we come to realize that it is chock-full of practical wisdom. This wisdom supersedes chapter divisions, which is one of the ideas we will hit along the way. As we touch on the high points, I hope we will discover power that will allow us to stand in the face of an imperfect world. I hope it will allow us to stand, even when our experience in God doesn't seem to stand up to the theology of the "good life."

Peter was very interested in seeing that the church to whom he was writing would not simply settle for survival, but that the people would move from mere survival to dynamic living. The way he accomplished this was to remind them of who they were in Christ.

Coming to Him *as to* a living stone, rejected indeed by men, but chosen by God *and* precious, you also, as living stones, are being built up a spiritual house, a holy priesthood, to offer up spiritual sacrifices acceptable to God through Jesus Christ. Therefore it is also contained in the Scripture,

> *"Behold, I lay in Zion*
> *A chief cornerstone, elect, precious,*
> *And he who believes on Him will by*
> *no means be put to shame."*

Therefore, to you who believe, *He is* precious; but to those who are disobedient,

> *"The stone which the builders rejected*
> *Has become the chief cornerstone,"*

and

> *"A stone of stumbling*
> *And a rock of offense."*

They stumble, being disobedient to the word, to which they also were appointed. But you *are* a chosen generation, a royal priesthood, a holy nation, His own special people, that you may proclaim the praises of Him who called you out of darkness into His marvelous light; who once *were* not a people but *are* now the people of God, who had not obtained mercy but now have obtained mercy. Beloved, I beg *you* as sojourners and pilgrims, abstain from fleshly lusts which war against the soul, having your conduct honorable among the Gentiles, that when they speak against you as evildoers, they may, by *your* good works which they observe, glorify God in the day of visitation. (1 Peter 2:4–12)

I like to ask myself this question regularly: "Doug, are you just surviving or are you really living?"

Peter attempted to impress upon his flock the wonderful plan that God had for them. He wants us also to know the reasons why we have been called to be with God. Understanding the hope of our destiny will help us to succeed and to be motivated in the worst of times.

I think the key word here would be *perspective*. Peter wanted to make certain that the believers, living under excruciating pressures and facing a ghastly experience where it looked as though Christ had failed them, would have a clear perspective—that they were looking up to the high horizons to which God had called them.

Have you discovered, as I have, that enjoying the Lord's blessing depends almost entirely on your own perspective? How I look at life is the binoculars through which I view life. Everything has to do with our own perspective when it comes to experiencing life. Peter's hope was that his people would gain the perspective that would allow them to see Jesus' reasons for their living that kind of life.

As I read through the verses in 1 Peter 2:4–12, I couldn't help but sense the dynamic life that pulsates through this statement, declaring the living nature of those of us who have encountered Christ.

Before World War II, an East Coast liberal named Louis Mumford became gravely concerned about the Appeasers' (a political movement in England and America) being received too positively by the population at large. The Appeasers believed that if the world nations would give in to Hitler's avaricious demand to give him the European nations, they could achieve and maintain peace. Mumford made an interesting observation: "Life is more than just surviving." He also coined the statement: "If there's nothing worth dying for, there's nothing worth living for!"

Christopher Lasch may be familiar to you if you have taken college sociology classes within the last decade. You may even have read his book *The Culture of Narcissism*, which is basically an assessment of our society. In it he said that we are self-oriented—that is, we desire to please and to love only ourselves. His sequel to this book is *The Minimal Self*, in which he postulated the idea that the continual threat of "the bomb" has shifted our culture's basic attitude from developing a life for ourselves to simply surviving through a week.

Maybe you have said to yourself, "If I could just survive this week, I would be happy." Lasch stated that this is a great problem in our society. In fact, present-day thinking shows that there is very little long-term planning beyond five years. A five-year plan used to be considered a very short-term plan. But nowadays, a five-year plan is viewed as a long-long-term plan. In fact, some business consultants advise that the longest you may want to work on a plan is five years. A very short-term society, indeed.

I have recently been advised by my own consultants not to plan ahead more than six months. That is the reality of the speed with which our culture changes. This has some tremendous ramifications. It creates the "hurry-up" syndrome and a sense of being overwhelmed, to the point of simply being satisfied with survival.

Just for fun, I went to a bookstore to look at all the books I could find that used *survive* or *survival* in their titles, to see if we really are as addicted to surviving as Lasch indicated. I found, to my surprise, that we really are. One title was *How to Survive a Bad Marriage*. What a great way to live! Another was *Ten Steps to Parental Survival*. Still another title read *How to Survive the Next Stock Market Crash*. These are hot sellers, by the way.

Peter, like Jesus, said that when we're in the world, when we're under the bondage of the world, of our flesh, and of the devil, we *do* just survive. However, when we're believers, we move from survival to a dynamic life! Though he doesn't outline points one through five on how to move beyond our survival stage, this small section of Scripture nevertheless ought to motivate us and give us some clear-cut ideas so that we are challenged to take hold of some of the resources we have at our disposal to experience Christ's abundant life instead of just surviving.

> As you come to Him, the Living Stone, rejected indeed by men, but chosen by God and precious, you also, as living stones, are being built up a spiritual house, a holy priesthood, to offer up spiritual sacrifices acceptable to God through Jesus Christ.
> (1 Peter 2:4–5, paraphrased)

Our lives are not destructive processes, but constructive ones, because God is building a temple out of each one of our lives. God is also constructing a priestly gift through our lives.

What Peter is saying here is that the world is filled with the processes of death. Death and destruction are synonymous. The devil came to destroy, not to raise up. In fact, one of his names, Abaddon, means "the Destroyer" and "the place of death." One of the characteristic traits of the non-Christian world is that it is psychologically and physically destructive; it's a battle all the way.

You probably remember well the story in 1 Kings 18. Elijah

had just defeated 450 prophets of Baal at their own game. To the astonishment of all Israel, he called down fire from heaven, which consumed a water-soaked sacrifice. Elijah then turned to the people of Israel and told them to choose whom they would serve: Baal or the God Who had consumed Baal's sacrifice with fire. The 450 prophets were struck dead that day by Elijah's sword.

First Kings 19:1 tells us that when Jezebel heard that her prophets had been slain, she sent word to Elijah, through King Ahab, that she would die herself if Elijah didn't die that day. Jezebel's threat caused Elijah to lose his perspective and his nerve and, in losing his nerve, his faith faltered.

Faith is another way of saying, "I like perspective, my viewpoint of reality." There is no greater gift. The Holy Spirit is available to give the gift of faith that will keep our perspective right. Elijah then fell into exaggerations of evil, and he claimed that he was all alone. He told God: "There is no one here but me."

God's reply was, "There are seven thousand others who have not bowed their knees to Baal."

Now, Elijah was never alone, but his skewed perspective made him feel alone in the middle of his crisis. Because of this faulty perspective, he became separated from the support and fellowship of those who were also pursuing God in the face of the false religions that were prevalent at that time in the nation of Israel.

God asked Elijah to go to the mountain. Elijah did so, and his perspective became readjusted after the following events. First, a great wind came, which was so strong that it broke rocks into pieces, but God wasn't in the wind. Then the Lord sent an earthquake. After Elijah bounced off the walls of the cave, he realized that God wasn't in the earthquake either, nor could Elijah find the Lord in the fire that roared about the mountain. He finally heard God in a gentle whisper, which turned his life around to the positive side again.

When Elijah heard that small whisper, his perspective became altered. He then believed that the Lord would multiply. Immediately after that event He anointed Elisha and gave him his mantle and the promise that Elisha would do twice the miracles that Elijah himself had ever done. Elijah's perspective was reshaped in the middle of a life-threatening crisis because God was doing a constructive work in his life.

Our daughter underwent heart surgery when she was just three weeks old to close up the Payton ductus valve in her heart. Back in 1976, this could be accomplished only through surgery. About a year later, this procedure became much simpler and easier by giving preemie babies an injection, which causes the valve to close without surgery. Her premature birth left Raissa with the challenge of coping with cerebral palsy, however. She is now a delightful thirteen-year-old, a wonderful writer with a magnetic personality, who is vitally alive in the Lord and who loves Jesus a great deal.

One afternoon, when I came home from the church office, I walked into the house and was greeted by my wife, Debbie, who had a troubled-mother look on her face—one of those looks that says there's more work ahead. Now, a husband doesn't like to see that look after a hard day's work. After all, pastors rarely like to carry on their pastoral work at home, because home becomes a refuge. When I walked into Raissa's room, instead of my effervescent little girl, I found a solemn, heartbroken little girl.

Stepping through her bedroom door, I asked, "Raissie, what's the matter?"

"Oh, nothing," responded Raissa.

Now, anyone who has hung around a woman of any age for very long knows that when she says "nothing," there's a whole lot wrong.

Walking across the room, I sat down on the bed beside her, wrapped my arms around her, and gently pulled her head to my chest. She began to sob.

"Honey, you can tell Daddy what happened. Did something happen at school?"

"Yes, Daddy," she said, pressing her head against my chest.

"Well, did you get hurt? Did something happen?"

"Clarissa said something," she answered.

"Well, Honey, what did she say?" I asked.

"We were having 'Show and Tell,' and the teacher asked us what we were going to be when we grew up. I said I wanted to be a ballerina and a mamma."

"Well, that's a good plan."

"Yes, but Clarissa spoke up and said I was 'stupid,' that I couldn't even walk right, and no one would want to marry me unless he was retarded because I was handicapped."

Words can't describe the anger that welled up in me as I learned that my own little child had been attacked with such painful words. I was thinking: *Well, who is this Clarissa, anyway? She's in* big *trouble!*

I didn't know what to say. Like other parents, I was searching for more than just a cliché. I really wanted to bring a healing response to my daughter. Finally, in a flash—you know, one of those milliseconds when the Holy Spirit really comes through when we silently cry out to Him—the words came to me.

"You know, Raissie, it really doesn't matter what anyone says about you. You have a long life ahead of you, and you may walk like this your entire life. There will be many people who will make fun of you. There will be many people who will stare at you. So you're going to have to decide right now whom you're going to listen to. Are you going to live your life for everybody else in the world, or are you going to live your life for Jesus?"

I felt her arm tighten around my waist as she replied, "I know Who, Daddy."

"Okay, then. What does Jesus have to say about Raissie today?"

"Jesus says that I'm going to be a ballerina," she answered.

I'll always remember the delight on her face as she looked up with a gleaming smile spreading across her face, now stained with dry tears.

As I walked out of her room, I was quite proud of myself for having responded so well. Of course, in my mind, I thought, *Yes, she'll be a ballerina in heaven.*

It was then that I sensed the Holy Spirit deep inside, sternly rebuking me in a way that only He can: "Don't you understand that every time that little girl walks across the room, it's a dance to Me?"

Jesus is definitely Raissa's audience, and she believes with certainty that God is doing a constructive work in her life. And I believe that that's the only work He can do. The Father, by His very nature, undertakes only constructive building with us, regardless of how life's challenges around us would try to tell us otherwise.

Yes, perspective is the key. Peter said that is the life for which we're ordained. We're to keep a living perspective of ourselves constantly before us.

The second task that Peter acquaints us with in this text is the process of being converted into priests. We each have a priestly call. What do priests do? In this passage, Peter specified that we are priests destined to offer acceptable spiritual sacrifices. We are people whose entire lives are fragrant offerings, praise to God on earth.

Priests also represent God to people and people to God. Wherever we are, we are God-containers. His *shekinah* (divine presence) glory is in us. We don't go somewhere to get that glory, nor do we strive for the experience. It is simply *in* us because Jesus Christ abides in us.

If you're not yet a believer in the Lord Jesus, let me tell you this: It's a totally awesome, exciting experience to walk through life, to be on the freeway, to be at work or at home, and *know* that God is living inside you! No other experience can possibly match it. It's beyond your wildest imagination! It's the ultimate high!

As I gave some thought to the idea about offerings and spiritual sacrifices, I remembered the wedding I'd officiated at a few years ago. They had flowers you wouldn't believe; an incredible variety of gorgeous arrangements filled the room. There was one arrangement that I particularly liked, which I figured cost at least $150–200. It was a real dandy!

As I mingled at the reception and met the family afterward, I observed people loading the flowers into the back of a van. There were so many (I'm not exaggerating), that they had to leave some behind. When they asked me if I wanted any, being the romantic kind of guy that I am, I jumped at the chance to take home the beautiful arrangement I'd admired earlier.

Gently, I put that gorgeous bouquet in my car, drove home,

walked through the door grinning broadly and, with a flourish, gave it to Deb. At first, she was thrilled. She felt romanced, and she was obviously impressed. She smothered me with hugs and kisses. Then she ruined the whole scene.

"Where'd you get them, Doug?"

"Well, they were left over from the wedding today, Deb."

The points I'd gained a moment before were immediately erased off the romance blackboard. I could tell by her eyes that I'd lost all that I'd built up. Why? Because my wife knew they didn't cost me anything. As far as she was concerned, she was an afterthought.

In fact, we have the same discussion over books. When I bring home a book, she invariably asks, "Did the publisher mail this to you?" The other day, when I brought a book home, she asked, "Why did you bring me this?"

I replied honestly: "I already had it, but I was thinking of you."

Over time, I've learned that she is thrilled when I go to a bookstore and take time to pick out a book I know is just right for her. For instance, I recently bought one of Oswald Chambers's devotional books. I knew she'd really like it, so I wrote a nice note, handed it to her, and said: "I love you."

It was great! I was an immediate hero! I've learned gradually that even a small $15 bouquet that I've taken time to pick out for Debbie means a whole lot more to her than a $150 floral arrangement left over from a wedding.

Peter was essentially trying to enlighten us about the same truth here: Don't ever forget the joy we experience when we fulfill our priestly function of offering meaningful sacrifices to God. Acceptable or meaningful, our sacrifices are to express true meaning. The idea is that a sacrifice is supposed to be just that—a sacrifice.

Sometimes in the middle of pain, offering worship to the Lord can be very sacrificial. Emotionally we may feel drained; we may feel battered; we may feel that we have no energy to lift up praises. But it is at these times that worshiping brings us the most freeing power. It may be at these moments, more than any other, that we are operating as true priests who offer up sacrifices that are empowered by a human heart determined to praise the Lord.

Remember who you are. You've probably discovered, as I have, that when you become a worshiper of Jesus, *all* realms of your life move from mere survival to having dynamic meaning, no matter what is going on!

One of my favorite football players is Steve Largent of the Seattle Seahawks. It isn't just his athletic abilities that impress me. His quality of living is also obvious to the entire city. Regularly, Steve gives God credit for what he's accomplished in his life. I'm sure many fans in Seattle wonder, though, how getting the stuffing kicked out of you glorifies God.

As believers, we understand that every one of us also gets broadsided every week by a "linebacker," but that God should still get the glory. We know that, as believers, whatever we do in our lives for God is acceptable worship for Jesus, because each of us is a temple to Him.

Therefore it is also contained in the Scripture,

> *"Behold, I lay in Zion*
> *A chief cornerstone, elect, precious,*
> *And he who believes on Him will by*
> *no means be put to shame."*

Therefore, to you who believe, *He is* precious; but to those who are disobedient,

> *"The stone which the builders rejected*
> *Has become the chief cornerstone,"*

and

> *"A stone of stumbling*
> *And a rock of offense."*

They stumble, being disobedient to the word, to which they also were appointed. (1 Peter 2:6–8)

In other words, there is always a reaction to the Stone, Jesus Christ. What Peter was saying as he explained further the necessity of focus is that focus is a decision called "obedience."

Without focus our lives will become nothing more than survival. They will be mundane and boring if we try to live with Christ as though neutrality were possible with Him.

Let me share an incident on neutrality. Many of us have probably paid multiple visits to airports. The other day I heard a man share a story about leaving a crowded 747 jumbo jet and walking down a narrow corridor with several hundred other passengers. As they headed down the corridor, an electric cart carrying a person with a handicap came toward them, the cart driver beeping the horn and flashing lights as they moved along. He didn't slow down or wait for the crowd at all; he just continued toward the gate at the same pace. People then had to choose whether they would move to the right or to the left. Because the cart driver kept moving at an unstoppable speed, the passengers didn't have a choice; they had to make a decision.

The storyteller said that it was humorous to watch people hesitate for a moment, trying to decide which way to go. Many tried not to decide, but the driver pressed on, forcing them to make a decision anyway. That's the way it is with Christ also. He always forces a decision.

Our perspective is always a decision—for or against. We can choose to see ourselves on a constructive road . . . or a destructive one.

When I was a freshman in college, I attended a symposium on crime and how to solve the crime problem in America. During the presentation, the moderators offered the microphone for student input, asking if anybody had an appropriate contribution to the symposium. Several students shared their views.

One was a Marxist kind of a guy, who went on and on, blaming capitalism for the crime in America. I think you can pick up right away that this was during the latter part of the 1960s. Who could ever have imagined that we would see what has occurred in the late 1980s? The disintegration of Communist nations across the globe has made Communism far less popular than it was at that time.

Eventually, it was my turn to share my two-bits worth. "Well, really, if you're talking about crime, you may as well know that we're all criminals," I declared rather emphatically.

I guess you know that this remark went over really big—like a lead balloon. I could tell by the dirty looks on their faces that the other guys weren't quite as open as I'd imagined them to be. They didn't appreciate my insight.

Having gained their attention, however, I continued, "We all know the Bible is true, but until we're transformed inside, there's no outward change anyway. You can incarcerate us, do anything you want, but ultimately we need the inward transformation through Jesus Christ, which we have to make as readily available as possible."

Now this is how stupid and naïve I was. I thought everyone would pat me on the back and say, "Hey, Doug, way to go! That was a great contribution you made to our discussion today. In fact, let's explore that some more."

Instead, everybody booed me, and a guy at the back of the room stood up and shouted, "Sit down and shut up, you fanatic!"

Everybody echoed, "Yeah, yeah!"

Chagrined, I returned to my chair and sat down. After that, they all acted as though I hadn't spoken. The symposium continued, and a fine discussion followed. For several weeks after that, when the other kids saw me, they'd sit on the other side of the room or laugh and say, "There's that fanatic again."

I learned something from that experience. Jesus is *not* neutral. Jesus, the only true Christ, will ultimately elicit some kind of positive response or negative reaction. We will finally find life when we determine that we will no longer try to live with Christ on the basis of neutrality.

About two years later, a guy walked up to me at the church where I was on staff at the time and asked, "Do you remember me?"

"No, should I?" I responded."

"Well, then, do you remember when you stood up at the crime symposium and told people about Jesus Christ?"

"I'll never forget it," I said.

"Well, do you remember the guy at the back of the room, who stood up and told you to sit down and shut up?"

"Yeah," I replied.

"Well, I'm that guy. I've now accepted Christ!"

Christ's name has never been neutral. His name always elicits either a loving response or a violent reaction from our hearts and minds. To those hearts who have chosen to follow Christ, His name resonates the understanding of the precious gift the Father has sent to us through His Son.

We know that when it came time for God to make a supreme sacrifice, He did not look around for heaven's bargain. He chose His most precious gift—His own perfect Son—to be sacrificed for our sins. There is no one better than Jesus, even in heaven. God gave Jesus up willingly, without any grudge. Now, doesn't that cause you to stand to your feet and shout, cheer, and rejoice in the Lord Jesus?

Why would God send His most precious gift in heaven to us and not complete the task He has called us to accomplish? I believe this is the subtle question behind Peter's statement. The Christian perspective understands that God always finishes what He starts. He has begun building us. He will continue. Even though pain, suffering, and less-than-optimal circumstances often make it look as though our lives are broken down, if God is living in our hearts, the process will always be constructive.

> But you *are* a chosen generation, a royal priesthood, a holy nation, His own special people, that you may proclaim the praises of Him who called you out of darkness into His marvelous light; who once *were* not a people but *are* now the people of God, who had not obtained mercy but now have obtained mercy. (1 Peter 2:9-10)

Remember who you are. You are a "chosen" people. You're a "royal priesthood, a holy nation!" You are a people who belong distinctively to God. We are His prized possessions!

Peter pointed out that we are a chosen people in Him. That is another way of saying that God is declaring, once and for all, that He has picked us out of the crowd and has stated categorically: "I voted for you!"

This is also another way of stating that our lives are not accidents, that the courses our lives take are determined by God.

He picked you and me out of the crowd and said that we were distinctly His. He caused us to understand that Jesus invited us to be part of His family. We are His people. We are no one else's people. We have very specific and particular purposes in Him, for nothing can dissuade God's purposes.

While driving home from church one day with his dad, little Johnny asked, "Dad, is God watching me?"

"Why do you ask, Johnny?"

"Oh, I just wondered," he said.

"Tell me, Johnny, because I really want to know why you're asking me if God is watching you. What's going on here?"

"Well, in Sunday school today, our teacher said that I was to remember that God was watching me," Johnny answered.

Now this father reacted as I often do. God gets so much bad press, it seems. We usually perceive God as watching us like those hidden, closed-circuit TV cameras in banks and stores. Have you ever been shopping and suddenly seen one of those cameras moving around, staring at you? Did you then try to remember whether you'd done anything strange or dishonest in the past ten minutes?

Unfortunately, we tend to think of God in those same terms. We figure that He's ready to cuff us one along the side of the head if we step the slightest bit out of line. Note that the father in this story was really sharp in his reply. I wish I could always be as quick as he was.

Johnny's dad answered calmly, "Yes, Johnny, God is watching you, but do you know why?"

"No, Dad. Why?"

"Because He loves you so much, He can't take His eyes off you, that's why."

That's what Peter was saying to his flock. We're chosen by God. God can't take His eyes off us, either. That's why we're able to move beyond mere survival.

You probably remember the story of Esther in the Old Testament. She was the young Jewish girl who went boldly to the throne of her husband, King Ahasuerus of Persia, when the entire Jewish nation had been threatened with genocide by the evil court advisor to her husband.

Esther, called by God to plead their case, declared that the people of Israel must be spared. She risked her life by entering boldly into the throne room of the king. This story tells us that we, likewise, are priests to a king—the King of kings—and we have the right to walk in boldly to intercede for anyone in the world. We are the kind of people you want working for you. We are the type of citizens you want in your nation, because we have access to the throne room of God to intercede on your behalf to make good things happen.

The man or woman sitting next to you at your job this week will ultimately be glad you're praying for him or her. We're special people. We're not just surviving. We aren't being destroyed; we're being constructed.

Here's the clincher: Peter was *not* saying: "You'd better work hard doing this. You'd better be a holy nation. You'd better be a holy priesthood, and you'd better remember you're chosen, or you're blowing it. Everyone is going to hell in a hand basket because of you. It's all your fault."

No, Peter was really saying: "Get your perspective straight. You can't stop this process, because the very nature you have inside you will cause you to be known expressly as 'chosen.' You are a royal priesthood, someone belonging to God. God can't take His eyes off you, so just refocus on what the program is. The world may look dark and bleak, but remember what God told you. You are His. His eyes are upon you. He is constructing your lives, no matter what happens.

REVIEW

Here are some questions and directions for review.

1. What times in your life most challenged your perspective?
2. Have you ever failed to offer praise to God in a church service or your devotional times because you were under pressure?
3. Do you suppose that those may be the times when your praise would be the most acceptable to the Lord?
4. Perhaps your marriage is falling apart or your job isn't going well or your business is going bad or you've been

misunderstood. Pause a moment to realize that the Lord can't take His eyes off you, that He voted for you, and that His heart is filled with love for you.

5. If your perspective has been lost by the pressure of pain, loss, or suffering, let me encourage you to take a step to share your commitment of gaining a new perspective with someone you love or someone who is near you who knows what you're facing. Then ask that person to pray with you to allow this perspective to become part of your daily living.

Chapter 6

The Pain of Misunderstanding: Hearing and Being Heard
(1 Peter 2:11–17)

I can think of nothing that agonizes my heart more than being misunderstood. It is sometimes overlooked, but this kind of pain can be more severe than physical pain. To be judged cruelly or unfairly, or to be shut out of another's life due to misunderstanding can be most agonizing.

Joe and Susan were getting married. Joe had been a member of our church for a long time. They both had completed the five sessions of premarital counseling and had now arrived at the point of planning their wedding ceremony.

Joe said to me one day, "Pastor, we don't know what to do about Susan's family. They won't be attending our wedding."

Quite astonished, I asked, "Well, why not?"

Susan explained, "They're part of a splinter Roman Catholic group and refuse to be part of any wedding that isn't part of the Roman Catholic Church. In fact, they don't believe we're really going to be married."

Joe added, "Her father yelled at me the other night that our refusal to be married in their church was proof that we don't respect or love them. They believe God's judgment will be on our relationship."

Susan asked, "What should we do, Pastor?"

My response was, "The only thing I can think of is to try to understand, in a loving way, your parents' response."

Susan was in her mid-twenties and Joe was in his late twenties, so I didn't feel that they needed to be subject to such an unreasonable demand by her parents.

We outlined a plan to determine whether they were clearly communicating their respect and love for Susan's parents. We also discussed the necessity of being big enough to live in the face of misunderstanding by others. Then we committed the matter to prayer: "Dear Lord Jesus, thank You for Your model of standing strongly in the face of misunderstanding. Thank You for Your model of courage, that when You were loving the world, You were interpreted as hating the world. We ask that You would somehow cause this misunderstanding to be submitted to the loving reality of Your Presence in Joe and Susan's lives."

I wish I could say that Susan's parents changed their minds and attended the ceremony. Sadly, they didn't. It was embarrassing for both families and very agonizing and painful for Susan and Joe. I'm certain that it's a pain that recurs.

I'm proud to say, as their pastor, that both Joe and Susan remain lovingly committed and respectful to her parents. I'm certain they have never brought up this instance again, as they have regularly discussed with me their visits to her parents' home and their conviction that the love of Christ will win them over. It is their life lived before the Lord, they believe, that will bring understanding.

> Beloved, I beg *you* as sojourners and pilgrims, abstain from fleshly lusts which war against the soul, having your conduct honorable among the Gentiles, that when they speak against you as evildoers, they may, by *your* good works which they observe, glorify God in the day of visitation. Therefore submit yourselves to every ordinance of man for the Lord's sake, whether to the king as supreme, or to governors, as to those who are sent by Him for the punishment of evildoers and *for the* praise of those who do good. For this is the will of God, that by doing good, you may put to silence the ignorance of foolish men—as free, yet not using *your* liberty as a cloak for vice, but as servants of God. Honor all *people*. Love the brotherhood. Fear God. Honor the king. (1 Peter 2:11–17)

Pain has a way of shutting our ears off. Peter encouraged his followers to submit, even in the face of being misunderstood. This is a skill to be learned. The Greek word for "submit" in verse 13 in Paul's simple, straightforward instructions, is *hupokuo,* which literally means to "hear under."

It is apparent that Peter was concerned that, in the face of their misunderstanding, the people would close their ears utterly to the reality that God might continue to speak to them through those who were, in fact, persecuting them.

We are to be listeners more than talkers. In fact, a Christian can easily be described as a God-listener. Even in the pain of misunderstanding, God can continue to speak to us.

This past Christmas, I shared a message on the life of Joseph, out of the nativity scene set forth in Matthew. Imagine being Joseph, about to marry a young virgin, discovering that she is carrying a child.

It is clear from other passages in the New Testament that Mary's pregnancy was a scandal in the small community in which Joseph and Mary lived. In fact, the timing surrounding the conception of Jesus was a matter of hot discussion later on by his antagonists.

The Bible says that because Joseph was a just man, he desired to divorce Mary quietly after the baby's birth, but he didn't. Instead, he faced the misunderstanding of his village squarely and, under God's direct command, married Mary.

Usually, when God begins to work in our lives, He brings a kind of misunderstanding to the situation. This is a particular kind of misunderstanding that only Christians know, but all humanity faces the agony of people misunderstanding their motives. What differentiates Christians from others in this kind of suffering is our attitude.

Peter wanted to make certain that Christians exert a great deal of effort in keeping our attitudes straight. We are not to shut off our ears just because we're being misunderstood. At that point, we would cease to be true Christian followers.

This Greek word for "submit," *hupokuo,* and its derivatives appear in verse 13 and again in verse 18, dealing with servants. It will be referred to again in 3:1, where it describes how the marital relationship is to be carried out with wide open ears.

It's important, as Christians, that even in the agony of pain—and particularly in the agony of misunderstanding—we keep our ears wide open to the fact that God may be trying to speak to us through that pain. Outside of Christ, the Bible says, we can't hear God. In fact, Christ said it this way in John 3:1: "Until you are born again, you can't perceive what the kingdom of God is like."

When we are born again, our hearts are in a position to be listeners. We are sensitized, once again, to hear Him and to be infused with courage to obey what we hear.

The Old Testament Hebrew phrase *Shemā Yisroēl,* in Deuteronomy 6:4, translates as: "Hear, O Israel, the Lord our God is one." God's people have always been called to be sensitized listeners. We can never allow our pain and suffering to shut our ears to His voice, even when He would speak to us through those who have treated us wrongfully. I think Peter was worried that his followers would just sit in a heap in a corner, wringing their hands and saying, "They just don't understand," and let it go at that.

Peter was determined to help us to understand that this kind of thinking will only get us off course. He encourages us to live a life that can never be misunderstood. That way, if there is a misunderstanding, it is their problem—not ours.

The misconception the believers of Peter's time were facing was that outsiders believed that Christians and Jews sacrificed Greeks and Gentiles to their God.

By researching the secular culture at the time of the early church, we find that the Romans actually believed that the church was attended by cannibals, because Christians were commanded to "eat the body" and to "drink the blood" of Christ. Evidently, some unconverted people had attended meetings and heard a pastor do an exposition out of John 6, which says, "Unless you eat My body and drink My blood, you can't have any part of Me" (paraphrased).

The Romans maliciously spread the rumor that Christians ate people alive in their "secret" meetings, and this really didn't do a whole lot for evangelism. They also believed that Christians were incestuous, because they called each other "brother" and "sister."

They believed further that the church was antimarriage. The occasion for writing 1 Corinthians 7 was precipitated by the occurrence in certain cities of the Roman Empire of the wives of noted Roman citizens meeting Christ and changing their lives dramatically. As a result, these converted wives would no longer attend nor participate in the orgiastic-type of ceremonies in the cult worship held at the Roman temples.

For the now-Christian wife not to participate in these pagan rituals was a disgrace and usually extremely embarrassing for the social standing of her Roman husband. Hence, the Roman husband would often dissolve the marriage, and his wife would be disowned and thrown out on the street to fend for herself.

These kinds of circumstances obviously precipitated Paul's call to all believers, that if any were married to an unbeliever, not to divorce him or her, but if any were kicked out of their homes, she or he was free in the Lord. That is the only teaching reference in the New Testament about divorce and remarriage. At any rate, the rap the early church received throughout the Roman Empire was: "Watch out, folks! These Christians will divide your home!"

Throughout this entire section, Peter was saying: "Make certain you send the right message. Make sure, even in your sufferings and misunderstandings, that you are rightly perceived. Make sure you're poised to continue to listen. Don't just talk all the time. Be ready to listen."

So often, I think the rejection of our message of Jesus has caused us to shut our ears to a hurting world. It seems that we can no longer hear people's cries for help, nor do we seem to sense their needs. In fact, we've become embarrassingly brash and prideful, believing that we're the only ones who have anything worthwhile to say. This posture leads to further misunderstanding, more pain, and certainly less effective communication about the wonders of Christ.

Admit it. Don't you get bothered by Christians who have all the answers all the time? There are a great many questions for which we just don't have any answers. That's why it's so important for us to listen for and to hear God's voice.

If you happen to be facing a time of misunderstanding, try pausing for a moment to write down some of the thoughts the Lord may be speaking to you.

When our daughter was born prematurely and was subsequently challenged with cerebral palsy, a well-meaning Christian asked my wife if there was anybody she hadn't forgiven who might have inhibited a healing. I have to admit that I was quite angry when I heard about it. That person's tone was accusatory and not at all in the Spirit of Jesus.

Evidently this person had somehow been led to believe that there must be a reason Raissa hadn't been healed. He felt there must be something wrong with either my wife or me. Words can't describe the pain that came to our hearts when we were purported to be the cause of our daughter's lack of healing.

We contend for and believe strongly in divine healing. Yet, we also understand that it is God Who does the healing—that is, it's His prerogative whether He wants to heal us or not. Should He desire to heal someone, it is still in His time frame, not ours. Incantations and rigorous and excessive efforts don't seem to help much.

We've seen positive, encouraging progress in Raissa's life, and we're excited about the spiritual reality that fills her. But that misunderstanding was so hurtful that it only added to the pain we were already experiencing. We decided that we would forgive the tactless inquiry and listen instead to what the Lord might be trying to tell us in the midst of this. Several points came through clearly:

- Don't be so quick to judge when people are suffering.
- In the middle of pain and suffering, the last thing anyone needs is a "Job's helper." I've determined never to be that.
- By prayerfully reassessing the steps taken, we can be reassured more than ever that we have taken the steps the Lord requires of us.

The absurdity of the well-meaning person's suggestion also gave us something to laugh about.

YOU REALLY DID SAY WHAT SOMEONE HEARD

I've always believed that the quality of our communications can be summed up in this one statement: You really did say what someone else heard.

Many times, while counseling couples in my office, I've heard one of them say, "I didn't say that!"

The other usually responds, "Yes, you did!"

"No, I didn't!"

"Yes, you did!"

Finally, as the referee, I break in and say, "Now, you really did say whatever she (he) heard."

So, Peter was stressing also that we make sure our communication is clear.

Even in your pain, make certain that you communicate clearly what you mean. I think we've all fallen prey to our stressful times because we're human and we're frail in our resolves. At times we take out the stress and agony of a hard day or week on those we love most and, before we know it, we've spoken words we didn't mean to say at all.

CONTROLLING OUR IMPULSES

Beloved, I beg *you* as sojourners and pilgrims, abstain from fleshly lusts which war against the soul, having your conduct honorable among the Gentiles, that when they speak against you as evildoers, they may, by *your* good works which they observe, glorify God in the day of visitation. (1 Peter 2:11–12)

I think the "day of visitation" Peter talked of is not necessarily the day of the Lord's return. What he possibly meant is that we can all count on the day when the Lord's visitation will come and He will right all injustices. These verses are also replete with the strong promise that people who hear the gospel receive a higher quality of life.

Peter said quite frankly that the only way we can deal appropriately with misconception is to heighten our standard of living so that people can't deny that we practice what we believe. The primary way the message gets distorted is when Christians give in to their impulses and unchecked desires. By letting our desires control us, rather than Christ's Spirit, our souls are actually hampered and even destroyed. Peter asked Christians, therefore, to abstain from these impulses and unchecked desires.

The original text could easily be freely translated as: Natural impulses, when given in to, become sinful and actually tear our souls apart. The overall text suggests that giving in to these bad impulses could make it impossible for us to hear God. Unchecked anger and unchecked desires gradually cause us to be unable to hear the sweet, gentle guidance of the Lord.

The Bible makes it clear that these impulses are always lurking around to captivate us. But when we seek Christ, we are given a new nature, which helps us to hear His voice from the inside out.

The dilemma is that we have this veneer, this outer shell, that has been habituated to bad attitudes and conduct. It has been given in to; every craving has been answered. We've allowed every habit imaginable to dominate us. In fact, all of us carry around impulses that have no regard for the longtime well-being of our lives. And not one of us is exempt.

These impulses war against our inner person. In fact, they will destroy us if they can. Now, as Christians, we aren't duelists, believing that we will have a knock-down-drag-out battle between Christ's life in us and our flesh, because we believe that we are more than conquerors. As long as we stay in fellowship with Christ, our new nature will dominate our outer person.

Often, what happens in our painful times, especially in times of misunderstanding, is that anger takes over. Soon we are no longer nurturing or feeding our inner person, at which time it gives way to the dead person in us. Impulses we once had under control now take over again.

I once heard a preacher share a story about an Eskimo who owned two husky dogs that he had trained as fighters. As he roamed from village to village, he encouraged people to bet on the dogfights he staged. One of the dogs was darker than the other, so he took turns betting on either the lighter or the darker husky to win each match. Somehow, he was always able to pick the winning dog, and he reaped a big profit each time.

Finally, someone asked him, "How do you always know which dog will win?"

"Whichever dog I'm feeding is the one that will win," he replied.

The same is true of us. Whichever nature we feed is the one that will win. In the face of agonizing loss or a hurtful accusation, the reactions of fear, anger, and mistrust have a way of distracting or diverting us from nurturing our souls. Sometimes, we even give in to an impulse to get back at God or those we love.

Retaliation is a destructive force that worried Peter. He knew so well that in times of persecution, when believers were being falsely accused and attacked, if they failed to continue nurturing the part of their beings that enabled them to hear God, they would be vulnerable to bad impulses, which would further weaken their ability to hear the Lord. Therefore, they were to keep alert in order to survive and to thrive during the times of accusations and persecution.

Exercise

If you are facing a time of suffering and loss or false accusations, let me encourage you to ask yourself the following questions:

- Am I continuing to feed myself in the Word of God and nurturing my spirit?
- Can I be honest and admit that I gave in to the emotion of anger and the desire to retaliate? If so, I must choose to forgive, because forgiveness resensitizes my soul, my heart, and the Spirit of God.
- Have I stopped to think that my negative reaction in the middle of this pain and testing may, in fact, be preaching volumes to me that I had never imagined?

UNCHECKED IMPULSES

Some of us have grown up in more disciplined environments than others. We've been programmed on the whole issue of abstinence.

Sadly, some of us had poor models for parents. We were taught to cultivate our lusts and cravings. We were taught that whatever the whim, fancy, or pleasure of our impulses, we should give in to them—you know that familiar catch phrase of the 1960s: If it feels good, do it. After all, isn't that what it is to be an American—to be free spirits? Well, now we have become adults, and we finally realize that giving in to our impulses will only destroy us, which all too many persons have experienced.

I'm allergic to chocolate, which is really a sad state of affairs because I love it so much. Shortly before Christmas one year, our missionary friends in Germany sent us a large box of German chocolates. Take it from a connoisseur of chocolate, nothing beats German chocolate. American chocolate is waxy tasting, as far as I can tell. German chocolate isn't; it's pure chocolate.

Anyway, they sent us this wonderful stuff in three different shades of chocolate. The outside was a light, crunchy kind of chocolate with really dark chocolate inside. Then there was the gooey kind that was almost fudge-like, while the others had hard or dark centers.

When facing stress, I have a tendency to medicate myself with chocolate. My only problem is that I'm allergic to it and become asthmatic the more I eat. Last year, I found out that when I eat apples or chocolate, or there's pollen or cat hair in the air, I can't breathe. I told myself that I wasn't going to eat this chocolate because of that problem.

One day, when I walked by that chocolate, my mouth practically salivated; I was almost drooling. I have to admit that I was somewhat upset that things weren't going the way I'd hoped for our Christmas season, so I ate a piece of that yummy chocolate to appease myself. After all, I was justified, wasn't I?

My intention was to eat only one piece. But then, I thought, because I'd worked out pretty hard that day, one more wouldn't hurt me. Before I knew it, I'd eaten a dozen pieces!

Then I compounded the matter. I knew Debbie would be upset with me, so I took that box of chocolates and put it at the back of the fridge, under the other boxes. I had it all strategized.

This overindulgence went on for about ten days. By Christmas Eve, I couldn't breathe. At the Christmas Eve service, I blamed my condition on the trees, but the truth was that I was so loaded up with chocolate, if you bumped into me, I would have oozed chocolate out of my pores.

Before I knew it, I was buying chocolate on the way home from services. I was hooked. I was out of control. My wife finally caught me sneaking chocolate from the fridge. Of course, trying to convince her I needed just one more piece didn't fool her at all. By now, my taste buds craved that chocolate so much, it could be likened to needing a "fix." My taste buds didn't care whether I could breathe or not.

That's the way our desires work. I'm "clean" now. I've been freed from the dependence of chocolate. I've lost several pounds since then, and my breathing is much better.

Well, our impulses are also a lot like a horse I had when I was growing up. His name was Lucky, and he was a big quarter horse, a huge horse. Dad loved that horse. In fact, when Dad whistled, Lucky would run right up to him, though he never did that for me. We kept Lucky with several of my cousin's horses on about two acres, so they had running room.

One day, Dad said, "Doug, I tell you what. Treat Lucky like he's yours. You can take care of him and ride him any time you want. You take old Lucky."

Wow! I thought that was great. But the first few times I went out to ride Lucky, he wouldn't come to me. I whistled, and I whistled, but he just stood there, smug. Sometimes he stood in the far corner whinnying, with a snide look on his face. He would look around at the other horses as if to say: "Watch this, guys!"

He would not come to me. I'd chase and chase him. He was having a great time giving me the slip. Finally, he'd run into the corner and let me approach him. This whole ritual usually took forty to forty-five minutes.

When I caught up with Lucky, I'd take hold of him and put the bit in his mouth, which he promptly spit out. At the time, as you may have guessed, I didn't know a whole lot about horses. I finally discovered that if I pinched his nose, he'd be more prone to take the bit.

Then it came time to saddle him. I didn't know he was holding his breath. The saddle seemed tight enough when I cinched it up. But the first time I jumped on, I swiveled around like a cartoon character and fell off the other side. My cousin took pity on me and taught me to "knee" Lucky in his stomach while cinching him up. Gradually, the horse learned that I was up to his tricks, and he didn't try them every time—just two out of three times!

Lucky had one other trick. While I was cinching up the saddle, he would step back, trying to step on my toes. If he felt he had a shot at stepping on me, he'd step back quickly, without warning and before I could react. If you've never had a large horse step on your toes, you've never experienced real pain. Nothing hurts quite like a horse standing on your little toe. Between cries of pain, I would holler and push, but he wouldn't budge.

Still another of his favorite tricks was to try to knock me off his back by running under a low limb. I'd be hanging on, yelling and screaming, "Stay on the trail!" I had the strange feeling he was smirking the whole time.

Finally, I'd had enough. "Dad, this horse stinks! He's not a good horse. I don't like him."

Dad laughed and said, "Well, Doug, do you know what the problem is?"

Still angry, I growled, "No! What?"

"The problem is that he knows he's boss. He's taking you for a ride. You aren't riding him. You just have to show him who's boss, that's all."

I don't think Dad had a clue as to what he had just set in motion. The next time I chased Lucky down, it took thirty minutes. Sure enough, he sucked air into his lungs when I cinched him up, so that I swiveled around again, giving his buddies a good horse laugh. This time, though, I picked up a board and cracked him one across the top of his head. I finally got his attention. At first, he looked kind of stunned, and he whinnied. For a moment, Lucky looked like Mr. Ed from the TV series of years ago. That day Lucky didn't try to step on my toes or to knock me off. It was a number of weeks before Lucky gave me any more problems. I soon learned how to keep him in line.

Our impulses are a lot like Lucky, the horse. They will take you for a ride, though not necessarily a good one. God has given us many impulses that are gifts from Him, but we have to let them know who's boss. Often, these impulses can become our way of surviving through times of suffering.

Exercise

Here are three questions you can ask yourself to give you some insights about yourself when tempted by wrong impulses.

1. Do you have certain impulses you're particularly prone to in times of suffering?

2. Do you ever find yourself feeling gratified when you get back at those you love the most and are the closest to you?

3. Have you ever thought about creating a pattern of discipline to try to control these negative impulses?

DON'T CLOSE YOUR EARS

Therefore submit yourselves to every ordinance of man for the Lord's sake, whether to the king as supreme, or to governors. . . . (1 Peter 2:13–14)

This section of the book of 1 Peter has a very practical message to those of us who are being misunderstood.

God speaks to us constantly through forms and patterns He sets up in society. In Peter's time, it was the governmental authorities through whom God was speaking to His believers, on the one hand, but who were persecuting and falsely accusing them on the other hand. This must have been incredibly confusing to the believers at that time.

I've had the privilege of visiting Eastern Europe and seeing firsthand the darker times of the nations of Poland and the Soviet Union. I've experienced what it's like to be with believers who are daily confronting truly evil governments head-on, who are intent on dispossessing them of their innate rights.

I have a pastor friend in Poland who, prior to the recent sweeping changes, was arrested on a regular basis and taken to the local police station for questioning—for no other reason than because he had Western preachers visiting him! On one occasion, his interrogators actually caused him to have a heart attack by placing his feet in ice-cold water as they questioned him throughout the night. They so traumatized him and his family that not only did he have a heart attack, but his wife subsequently had one too.

It would be difficult to live under that kind of direct persecution and still believe that God could speak through these non-Christian authorities. Amazingly enough, believers under such persecution are able to keep this in perspective. In America, we've been privileged, for the most part, to be able to avoid these kinds of dilemmas.

We can't be good hearers of God, especially in our times of suffering, unless we are willing to realize that He desires to speak to us through the very people who are hurting us the most. It is the Christian conviction that He speaks to us through the laws and authorities as well.

You are probably aware of God's speaking to you on many occasions. For instance, as you drive down the road, you come to a stop light or a stop sign. Who is speaking to you through this traffic light or sign? God is, in a roundabout way, speaking to you through the laws. He has given a person in the transportation department of your city authority to decide to put that sign where it is, and you stop, when you come to it, for your own safety.

Now, some of you will say, "Boy, I never hear from God. God never says anything to me." Well, when you come to a stoplight or sign, say, "Thank You, God, for speaking to me today through this traffic sign"—because He just told you to stop.

Have an ear to hear God. This can be a beginning exercise to help you make certain that your heart is sensitive to hear the Lord.

Peter challenged believers, even in their misunderstandings, not to be egotistic or to think they could live beyond the confines of God-established laws and relationships. He urged us to hear God through those misunderstandings, though we probably don't want to. I don't think any of us really want to hear God speak through our pain, particularly through those who have hurt us the most. But we don't have a choice, for a willingness to stay respectful to those around us will allow us safe passage through times of horrendous pain.

Peter concluded with four sterling attitudes that will allow us to be forever poised as listeners to God. First, he said for us to show respect to everyone by *honoring all people*. Second, we should *love the brotherhood of believers*. Third, we must *fear God;* and fourth, we are to *honor the king*.

1. *Honor All People*

The first attitude, honor all people, is commanded with the realization that we are all potential God-containers. We're to treat everyone with respect as a conduit of God's voice to us.

Not long ago, Debbie and I were en route to attend a football game at the Kingdome. As we traveled through a section of downtown Seattle, near the Alaskan Way Viaduct, we passed by a young couple who were huddled together in a doorway, both quite drunk. That kind of scene just breaks my heart, because I know that, except for the grace of God, my drug habit would have taken me down to that depth.

As I glanced over at them, I'm certain I heard Jesus say, "I'm cold. Don't forget about Me."

Even in our pain, we are not to forget others and their needs. All humans have dignity. By isolating ourselves, however, we often lose touch with opportunities to help others. Psychologists have proven that altruism (the inclination to help others) releases in us a natural chemical that brings with it a sensation of pleasure and happiness.

When I counsel people who have suffered greatly from a loss or because of a misunderstanding, I ask them to make certain that they respect those who are attacking them and to make an effort to help someone else who is suffering and hurting. This will ease their own suffering and help bring them back into the right perspective.

On one occasion, I was visiting a friend in a hospital. I was delighted that so many people from our church had come to see this particular person, and there were cards all over the room.

Across the room lay a small, frail, very emaciated woman in

her eighties or nineties. A respirator was obviously keeping her alive. Her eyes—the only part of her being that were still speaking—seemed to say: "I'm still very much alive."

As I walked by her to my friend's bed, I looked into her fear-filled eyes, and a surprising thing happened to me again, not unlike the experience I had near the Alaskan Way Viaduct. I thought her eyes spoke "I'm lonely" to me. Again, I was sure Jesus said that to me through her.

Empathy, compassion, and respect for her welled up in me. In that millisecond, I realized that here was a woman who had lived a long time, and I was given a sense of the history that had passed during her lifetime. I reached out, took her frail hand, and prayed for her. A silent thank-you appeared in her hollow eyes for a fleeting moment before I moved on to my friend's bed. Even though I was in pain over the serious condition of my own friend, my heart was lightened by extending love and concern to this lonely, dying woman.

2. *Love the Brotherhood of Believers*

Peter said for us to love the brotherhood of believers. In other words, in the face of misunderstanding, don't withdraw from fellowship. It is our position, as believers, to stay in fellowship, for "no man is an island."

Hope has always been part of belief. It says, in a time of misunderstanding, that perhaps even persecution will draw us together with those who are listening. That is, let the words we hear from God resonate between us to encourage us.

3. *Fear God*

Third, Peter told us to fear God. I think this was his way of saying: Live in the awareness of God's Presence. Here, the Greek word Peter used to mean "fear" is *phobeomai,* which is related to our word *phobia.* In an effort to escape its usual meaning of "fear," I looked the word up, but found that it literally does mean "fear."

Living in the awareness of God's Presence in the midst of suffering can greatly encourage us. Realize that God is the Creator, not a creature. His omniscience and omnipresence are always available to help us to stay on a straight course, right through the middle of a suffering situation.

4. *Honor the King*

Peter concluded his attitude checklist by telling us to honor the king. We remain listeners because we respect those who are in positions in which God has placed them so that we might hear Him. In this instance, Peter reminds us that our situations of pain can, in fact, be the very avenues of God's voice to us.

A Christ-listener always understands that God is able to speak to us in the places of our deepest agonies—perhaps even through the very people who are causing this agony. Let's commit our lives to being listeners to Jesus.

REVIEW

We conclude this chapter with a rehearsal of some of the learnings we've been able to grasp, for it may help us to survive our times of suffering. It may also give us some guidance when formula Christianity doesn't appear to be working for us. Perhaps we can discover ways to receive the life we're intended to live in Jesus.

1. In times of stress and pain, we need to be aware of our tendency to revert back to destructive impulses.
2. In the face of misunderstanding, we can never lose respect for people without compounding our own problem.
3. In our situations of deepest pain and agony, God may, in fact, be speaking to us.
4. Christians primarily need to take the posture of listeners.
5. In the middle of our pain and suffering, we may be preaching our greatest message, if we take the effort to make sure that people are hearing what we intend for them to hear.
6. We usually say what other people think they have heard.
7. None of us will ever escape the pain and agony of misunderstandings, which seems to be one of the crucibles of maturing through Christ.

PRAYER

Lord, give me strength and grace to stand in the face of misunderstandings. Give me discipline to control my impulses, as well as the courage and insight to recognize when my anger would destroy me. Thank You for Your grace to stand through the pain and agony of misunderstandings in a growing fashion and in a God-glorifying way. May the true message of Jesus be clearly heard through us in our pain and agony.

Chapter 7

When Your World
Needs Change
(1 Peter 2:18–25)

Do you have someone close to you whom you would like very much to change? Don't we all! Is there someone near you who must change in order for you to survive?

Here's an axiom you don't want to forget: *We can really change no one*. We all, from time to time, end up with "toxic" people around us. Perhaps even our husbands and our wives become toxic to us.

When our world becomes unlivable, how do we change our world in these times? One of our hidden fears is that people and situations will never change, especially when they're painful. On the other hand, it's rather ironic when most people fear change more than anything.

As a pastor, I've been surprised at the number of chemically dependent persons whose families have fallen apart after that person has been healed of his or her addiction. Even though we usually want people to change, when they do, we don't know what to do about it. Our lives are so altered by the change itself that we become shocked.

Yet, God does have a way of making us influencers, all the same. It's the way that Jesus walked. In fact, love expressed in the face of suffering is often the change agent the Lord will use.

Servants, *be* submissive to *your* masters with all fear, not only to the good and gentle, but also to the harsh. For this *is* commendable, if because of conscience toward God one endures grief, suffering wrongfully. For what credit *is it* if, when you are beaten for your faults, you take it patiently? But when you do good and suffer *for it*, if you take it patiently, this *is* commendable before God. For to this you were called, because Christ also suffered for us, leaving us an example, that you should follow His steps:

> *"Who committed no sin,*
> *Nor was guile found in His mouth";*

who, when He was reviled, did not revile in return; when He suffered, He did not threaten, but committed *Himself* to Him who judges righteously; who Himself bore our sins in His own body on the tree, that we, having died to sins, might live for righteousness—by whose stripes you were healed. For you were like sheep going astray, but have now returned to the Shepherd and Overseer of your souls. (1 Peter 2:18–25)

The Scripture here deals with a response that our human spirit can have to injustice that will change the world. Scripture says that the mean spirit of this world can be neutralized and can become part of changing our world around us by responding with the opposite spirit. To confront the mean, abusive spirit that fills this world of ours, we will be supplied by God's grace, through the model and example of Christ.

Before we move on, I would like to insert something here for anyone who may be in a harmful, abusive, or severely dysfunctional environment. Peter was talking specifically about suffering for our Faith, for being physically abused because we are Christians.

However, it is possible that many of you reading this book are in a situation where your life is in physical danger. Cocaine or alcohol abuse by someone in your family or by your spouse may require you to flee. By responding in an opposite spirit to an alcoholic, you may be doing nothing more than enabling that person. The model you ought to follow is the model of "tough love" in this situation. Though you can never change the person, you don't have to accept the danger that person's habit may bring your way.

It is not your fault that the person reacts in this manner. I don't want you to walk away from reading this book, feeling as if you can just suck it in and love that person more perfectly if she or he just wouldn't go off on binges or fly into a rage. That is not the case at all.

In your situation, you must respond in a healthy way by doing what is the most healthy for you and, yet, realize that you can never change that person. You can forgive and love that person, but you cannot enable him or her or, by the same token, allow him or her to carry on in this behavior.

With that out of the way, let's move on to talk about what I would call the "normal" kind of hostility with which the world surrounds us. How do we respond to the normal level of antagonism, the agony and suffering that come in quiet, subtle ways in the closest of relationships?

I recently read an interesting study. The experts postulated that our family life develops only about 10 percent of our personality, while most of it is genetically coded in us before we are born. This is really more biblical than we would think. The Bible says quite clearly that we are all inflicted with Adam's genes, which give us the propensity to act like stray sheep.

The Bible says also that the only hope for us pitiful humans is to be born again. *We can then become forgiven, hopeful, and wonderful people who can anticipate living forever!* But to achieve this, we need an entire new birth—it's that radical. Actually, when you think about it, much of what Jesus said is radical.

Peter began his address about responding with the opposite spirit by addressing the scattered believers as "slaves." The word he used for "slaves" is not the word used earlier in 1 Peter. The word he used earlier meant to be "utterly under the domination of another." In the earlier case, it was under the domination of God.

Christians really are slaves of God. We're called to serve Him and, in serving Him, we serve others. The word used here is a compound term, and literally means: "You are part of this house." It most likely refers to a house servant. The meaning is a little stronger than "employee," but it is closer to "employee" than the word used for "slaves" earlier on.

In the Roman Empire many of the slaves were not people forced into slave labor. Very few of them were, in fact. Most Roman slaves were either born into slave families or persons who voluntarily signed themselves up for economic reasons.

This was so even in Israel. Often when a large debt burdened persons, they would sign themselves over to their debtors for a period of seven years. That was the law in Israel. They essentially became servants or laborers in the house or business of the person to whom they became indebted. For instance, if you were a carpenter then, you would have had servant laborers and/or slaves attached to your carpentry business. Many of the slaves Peter talked about here were these kinds of people. It may even be that they are the ones to whom Peter referred to exclusively.

This slavery was not the same kind of slavery that existed in the early Western, pre-industrialized civilizations. Slavery in Israel and the Roman Empire was not nearly so heinous as the slave trade in parts of the United States prior to Lincoln's Emancipation Proclamation.

Let's look again at what Peter had to say: "Servants, *be* submissive to *your* masters with all fear, not only to the good and gentle, but also to the harsh" (1 Peter 2:18).

The word *harsh* can mean "twisted" or "perverted" as well. Regardless, we're not talking about the best of situations here. Peter wanted to affirm the fact that Christianity does work, even when we're living in harsh situations.

Retaliation is a strong emotion in the face of harsh treatment. In that instant, when we are most tempted to set aside the rules and attack, self-preservation becomes a very strong instinct.

But Peter said, "Keep it in check, kids. In the middle of suffering there is grace, and God may be at work in the situation, more than you ever imagined."

He went on to commend and to advise believers that a blessing is attached to this kind of suffering.

For this is commendable, if because of one's conscience before God, one endures grief or suffering wrongfully. For what credit is it if you are beaten for your faults, that you take it patiently? But when you do good and suffer for it, if you take it patiently, this is commendable before God. (1 Peter 2:19–20, paraphrased)

We're reminded here that, even in the midst of our harsh treatment by others, God is still watching. He is prepared to hand out commendations.

World-changers change their world—not by trying to change others, but rather by concentrating on the kind of people we are becoming in the middle of our suffering.

It isn't what happens to us that makes us weak or strong. *It is who we become in the face of suffering.* The terrible thing about all suffering is that, in every pain, there is the potential for betrayal and for becoming a distorted and dysfunctional person. Also, in the face of every kind of suffering, there is the potential of becoming more Christlike—that is, becoming more powerful.

Peter said that not only is there the likelihood that we will suffer under the hands of harsh people in this world, but also that we are called by Christ to suffer. In fact, He left us an example: We should follow in His footsteps.

I tried to think of the types of suffering that would likely bring us the most agony in the kinds of situations Peter addressed. I can think of several. Perhaps you have some of your own to add:

- Suffering that comes from rejection;
- Suffering that comes from being taken advantage of;
- Suffering that comes from being manipulated;
- Suffering that comes from needless ridicule;
- Suffering that comes from indifference;
- Suffering that comes from being forgotten; and
- Suffering that comes from deliberate attack.

A number of persons have talked to me about their harsh environment at work and in our culture today. One man described the lack of teamwork in his company as being "like a group of vultures working together, waiting for the first one to go down." The better jobs in the firm were so coveted that devious plans were put in motion to obtain them. Sometimes, two or three plans were set in motion to bring down a manager or an upper echelon employee in order to grab that person's slot.

One man lost his job after working for this company for nearly twenty years. Evidence was strong that his Christian beliefs became one of the reasons for his removal. You can imagine the trauma he experienced. He'd given tremendous amounts of energy to this company and was making a very high salary. Boom! One day, without notice, they fired him!

His temptation, at that moment, was to become retaliatory, to appeal his case with the same vengeance he had suffered. However, the Lord subsequently opened up a position for him in another company. To his credit, he never weakened in his Christian commitment, nor did he in any way "talk down" his previous company. Interestingly enough, in his interview process, that was one of the points his new employer brought up, knowing a little more of the details than the applicant realized. The new employer said that he admired this Christian man because he didn't run down his former company when he had applied for the new position.

Now, you may be thinking, "Great! You mean that because I've received Christ, He has saved up for me all these terrible tortures, so that once I say, 'Yes, Lord,' I'm in for a lifetime of misery? Is that what I'm called to?"

To this, you may also be thinking that the Lord would reply: "Oh, goody, goody! Here we go. Now, here's the torment and suffering I've saved up for you for years—just especially for you!"

Let me reassure you. That's not what it means at all. For one thing, it would be rather egotistical for us, as Christians, to say or to think that we're the only people in the world who suffer. It would be even more ridiculous to say that we suffer more than most people. In fact, my observation of American Christians is that we're all as addicted to comfort as anybody.

I personally know of many unbelievers who suffer a great deal! In fact, Jesus put it this way: "The way of a Christian is easier than the person in the world"; and "My yoke is easy and My burden is light" (Matt. 11:30). He was saying that the spirit of this world is a heavy burden; it weighs you down. It is, in fact, easier to walk as a Christian than as a nonbeliever.

Yet, suffering has been a consequence of a fallen world since Adam's time. Conversely, it is a false gospel that if you receive Christ, you won't suffer anymore and everything will be hunky-dory. That isn't true at all. Christ didn't promise that life would be any easier for Christians. He said that He would be with us in our troubling times.

Peter pointed out that Christians are called to face normal human suffering in a fallen world. Perhaps some persecution-type suffering may come upon us as well. It's a rare privilege for us in our culture to experience that kind of suffering, so when we do, we ought to rejoice about it and praise the Lord.

Please understand that we aren't necessarily called to suffer any more than others are, or to a higher plane of suffering. We are simply called to face suffering with a Christlike attitude. This kind of attitude not only brings victory to us, but also glorifies God. This attitude also results in our becoming stronger and better people in the face of suffering.

In this section Peter specifically dealt with a number of kinds of suffering that arise out of being treated unjustly and falsely accused—possibly even abused physically and mentally, and being misunderstood and misperceived. Take heart, though; Jesus Christ faced every one of these kinds of suffering.

Have you ever bought your kids a coloring book with the figures already outlined, needing only for them to fill in the spaces between the lines with their crayons? Well, the Greek word which describes "a life that has been outlined" is *hupogrammos*. The pattern for our lives has been set by Christ. That is what it means to have Jesus as our model. To walk in His pattern means that He has already established the lines. We simply fill in His lines with our own lives.

Now, I'm no artist; I can't draw at all. What's more, I can hardly write, to which my wife and secretary will attest. So, when I'm called upon to do anything artistic, I have to use see-through paper to trace the picture. To be honest, I traced my way through school. I remember one school project that my cousin did for me. It worked great because I got a good grade—he was a good artist, and I was a poor one.

The idea here is that if you lay your life over that of Christ's, trace an outline, and fill it in with your own coloring, the outcome will be pretty exciting! Christ faced the worst mistreatment possible at the hands of sinful, worldly persons; yet, He responded with the right spirit. Consequently, His response, using the opposite spirit to that of the world, has been changing the world ever since!

Hupogrammos can also describe a track that keeps one on course. It's a track-like groove. For example, those bumper cars at carnivals or amusement parks move around in grooves attached to the ceiling. No matter which way you turn the steering wheel, the cars will turn at the right time anyway. The same would aptly describe the point Peter was making. When we place our lives completely in submission to Christ, we simply follow His grooves, using His responses.

Though we can never change other people, we can oversee who it is we become. By responding in the opposite spirit to the mean spirit of this world, we actually become influencers and world-changers.

> *"Who committed no sin,*
> *Nor was guile found in His mouth";*

who, when He was reviled, did not revile in return; when He suffered, He did not threaten, but committed *Himself* to Him who judges righteously. (1 Peter 2:22–23)

Peter recalled Christ's horrible abuse under Pilate, along with the harm and damage heaped on Him by the Jewish authorities. Yet, even during this mistreatment, Christ did not revile nor retaliate. He faced the ordeal and won! He did so by entrusting Himself to His righteous Father.

Christ models this reality for us. Our lives really are in the hands of no other. Ultimately, no one can actually harm us, even in the face of terrible suffering, because of our Father's watchful eye. If we're tempted to say that we've gotten an unfair shake in life, we're wrong. Peter promised his fellow sufferers that God would make certain that all things turn out fair in the end.

Our response to suffering that is probably the most destructive is self-pity. It says: "Why am I suffering more than so-and-so?" It usually comes from comparing our lot with that of another.

In our pursuit of comfort, we often cry out in pain and agony: "This is unfair!"

This kind of thinking erodes our inner person, however. Peter encouraged his followers, in facing their pain, loss, and agony, to lift up their heads and state emphactically that they could trust their Father with their lives!

We all want a world in which there is no injustice, no brutality, and no suffering, in which there is no sin and no disease. This is not the world we presently have, though. We all want a world in which there are multiple blessings and nice, obedient children everywhere. We all definitely want a world in which everybody is really mobile, in which everybody gets enough to eat and has a home to live in. I know I certainly want that kind of world. However, it appears that until Christ returns that kind of world may not be possible.

Though we all work hard and aspire toward these ideal ends, we may possibly be part of creating the kind of world ours is now. We need to face the fact that we are living in an abnormal world. We're living in a world in which people are corrupt. None of us is the Holy Spirit, Who is the only One Who can ultimately change people.

You can continue to live in a fantasy world, point your fingers, scream and yell all you want, and get mad at God, but it won't change anything about the world you live in. The reality is that this is a crazy, mixed-up, troubled world needing the redemptive touch of God. No surface touch by God or our puny efforts will ever change this world.

Believe me, what is happening is a gradual process. It may even happen in our lifetimes with the appearing of Jesus Christ. In the meantime, we are stuck with deciding how to respond in a Christlike manner while the cleanup process is going on around us. Hurray! Peter gave us an explanation of how to do this. He told us what Christ did when His back was against the proverbial wall. Christ chose to respond in the right spirit in two ways: (1) not to retaliate, and (2) to commit Himself to God the Father.

The Greek form of the word *commit* can also be translated as "entrust." As the tense used here is an imperfect participle, it always suggests continual action. The idea is that Christ didn't entrust Himself to His Father for just one moment, but for every moment in every hour! On an ongoing basis, He committed Himself to God's trustworthiness.

In *Christianity Today* a couple of years ago, an article appeared on Dr. Robert Coles, who was an Air Force psychiatrist and a specialist in child development. He now teaches at Harvard University in the Master's Business Administration program. In addition, he teaches on matters of Christian ethics, in which he covers the classics of ancient Christianity and the teachings of Jesus Christ.

In the article, Coles commented, "Even MBAs need this kind of teaching."

The article chronicles Coles's process of committing his life to Christ, and is titled "The Prayers of Ruby Bridges." Ruby Bridges was a grade-school youngster in New Orleans, Louisiana, in the early days of the civil rights campaign. Her family moved into an all-white neighborhood and she enrolled in the local all-white school. Ruby was not only the first black child to live in this particular, all-white suburban area, but also the first black child in this school.

The local white populace was offended by a black child's attending their white school. However, Ruby and her parents bravely and boldly stood up to their verbal attacks, and she continued to attend the school.

By the time Robert Coles met her, she was already big news. He came to the New Orleans suburb in which Ruby lived to observe her daily ritual of attending classes.

A typical morning for Ruby began with federal agents meeting her at her door and escorting her to a car. Neighbors stood on the sidewalk, spitting at her, jeering her, and calling out verbal insults to Ruby.

When Ruby arrived at school, another crowd of forty or so people had gathered. Once she was inside the classroom, however, her classmates were far more sympathetic to her. It wasn't exactly a safe haven, but, as Coles observed, Ruby at least felt safer and more secure inside.

Coles studied Ruby and her family for several months, and he became quite perplexed that Ruby showed no signs of emotional harm from her stressful environment. After all, she was living daily in a life-threatening environment and should be exhibiting some stress reactions.

One day Ruby's teacher called Dr. Coles aside and told him, "I saw the most interesting thing today, Dr. Coles."

"Oh, yeah? What was that?" he asked.

"Ruby was standing by the fence on the playground talking to the people outside as they cursed and yelled at her."

Coles was quite interested in this, because he thought this was abnormal behavior. He couldn't quite fathom what made this little girl so fearless.

When he interviewed Ruby that day, he asked her: "Ruby, why were you talking to the men out at the fence today?"

In childlike simplicity, Ruby responded: "Oh, I wasn't talking to them, Dr. Coles."

"Well, what were you doing? Your teacher said she saw you saying something."

"I was praying for them," she replied.

This took Coles by surprise. This little girl had been praying for her accusers! Amazing! That evening, while interviewing Ruby and her folks, he discovered that they attended a black Baptist church. Every Sunday their pastor had the entire congregation extend their hands in prayer toward the Bridges family, and the pastor would declare: "Lord, help Ruby, and help us to forgive our accusers."

Coles asked Ruby, "Why were you praying for them?"

Ruby responded sternly to his "silly" question: "Because they need praying for!"

Ruby was modeling her pastor's prayers, in which she was forgiving her attackers. In the midst of this harsh suffering, Ruby was, in fact, becoming a stronger and better person.

> Who Himself bore our sins in His own body on the tree, that we, having died to sins, might live for righteousness—by whose stripes you were healed. (1 Peter 2:24)

Christ's response, using an opposite spirit, resulted in the availability of healing. Our hope is that we too will respond with the Spirit of Christ to the mean spirit of this world, and that healing will be the outcome to those around us.

This is really a fantastic promise. Christ responded in the awareness of His mission on Earth. He was commissioned to bring healing to this planet, and it was through His suffering that healing came. First Peter 2:24 suggests three things:

(1) The primary spirit of a believer, when under the influence of the Holy Spirit, is nonretaliatory while experiencing injustice and abuse.

(2) As we live our lives trusting our Heavenly Father, we change our world, even when we are in the hands of unjust people.

(3) Christ's pattern always brings the reality of healing to hurtful situations.

The beautiful attitudes—or the Beatitudes as they are traditionally called—had to have been in the mind of Peter when he wrote this section of Scripture. Recall Christ's words in His Sermon on the Mount: "You have heard it said: 'An eye for an eye and a tooth for a tooth.' But I tell you: Do *not* resist an evil person. If anyone strikes you on the right cheek, turn the other cheek also" (Matt. 5:38–39, paraphrased).

My evangelist friend Ron Rearick has been known for years as the Iceman. Ron used to be a strong-arm man for the Nevada mob some years back. He now speaks to as many as 250,000 students a year, sharing how God dynamically released him from drug addiction and turned his life around after spending nearly twenty years in prison.

One afternoon, after Ron was saved, he was witnessing in a park. An unsavory guy sauntered up to him and asked, "Does the Bible say that if I hit you on the cheek, you're supposed to turn the other one?"

"Yeah," Ron answered.

The man then asked, "What if I hit you? Will you turn the other cheek?"

Ron thought a moment, "Well, I'll have to pray about it."

So the guy hauled off and popped Ron on his right cheek with his fist. Ron then obligingly turned, exposing his left cheek. In a moment of insanity, the guy hit Ron again.

"The Bible gives you only two shots," drawled Ron.

As Ron was still standing after the two blows, his challenger conceded that Ron had proved his point. A moment later, Ron took one shot at the guy and decked him. I don't think that's what Christ had in mind when He said that, but then, Ron's human too.

When Ron tells this story to students today, he's not promoting violence in any way. He's just trying to show us that the point of this verse in Matthew is not quite as simplistic as being on the receiving end of two punches, but that we're to live non-retaliatory lives. Once a vicious strong-arm guy for the Nevada crime syndicate, Ron is now a gentle, effective voice for his Savior.

Christ continued: "If someone wants to sue you to take your tunic, let him have your cloak as well. If someone forces you to go one mile, go two with him" (Matt. 5:40–41, paraphrased).

In Christ's day, several Roman occupational forces were stationed in Israel. These soldiers could ask any Jewish citizen to carry something for them, but for no more than one mile. That was the rule in order to avoid a total social upheaval in this Roman outpost of Jerusalem. So, Jesus was telling the people that if a Roman soldier asked a Jew to carry his goods for a mile, the Jew shouldn't stop at the end of the mile and hand the stuff back to the soldier. Instead, the Jew should say to the soldier: "Oh, goodie gumdrops! May I carry this another mile, sir?"

In other words, our attitude is to be that of an ungrudging servant. That is, when we employ the opposite spirit to that of the mean spirit in this world, we will change the world back to the plus side!

Christ said further: "Give to anyone who asks you, and do not turn away from one who wants to borrow from you" (Matt. 5:42, paraphrased).

Again, the point is that both Christ and Peter taught us that the effective way to change the world around us is to respond with a kind spirit when confronted by a mean spirit. When confronting the vicious spirit of this world, we are to respond with the loving Spirit of Christ. When confronted with greed, *respond with generosity*. When confronted with hate, *respond with love*. When confronted with fear, *respond with faith*. When confronted with abuse, *respond with respect*. The counterspirit will always change any situation from bad to good.

I know a number of couples who have been helped immensely by one spouse's being determined to respond to hateful words with kind words. The person won't react with anger, but will respond with peaceful statements. Then a marriage begins to change and transform, rather than the couple's trying to figure out who is at fault. No-fault marriage allows us to respond in the opposite spirit—to respond in the spirit that will bring the greatest healing to the marriage.

Even in friendships, we should try to work out our conflicts amicably. Someone, somewhere along the line, ought to guarantee you that in any relationship someone will stop and say, "I'm going to respond in a counterspirit to the one that's been going on here."

In 1979, I experienced the apparent symptoms of a stroke, brought on by migraine headaches. It seems that when we are under intense pressure and stress, oxygen can actually be cut off from the vascular system in the brain, resulting in strokelike symptoms.

It was a frightening experience for me in my late twenties! I thought I was actually having a real stroke induced by blood clots. So did my wife.

Deb and I previously had been part of a church staff whose business manager had embezzled hundreds of thousands of dollars from the church. The backlash and fallout from this had been swift and harsh to all of us staff members, who suffered a great deal of personal and material loss as well. Here we were a young couple with two small children, struggling to start a new church.

The large, now-disgraced church we'd been part of was in all the papers and on the evening news every night for several weeks. We saw nine years of labor on that staff go up in smoke. I don't mean to suggest that we were the only ones who suffered. Hundreds of others likewise suffered the agony and embarrassment of watching what they had been committed to in faith and love be destroyed by the greed and mismanagement of a person in the church's leadership.

In addition to all of this, Debbie's father died. I found myself unable to handle the pain she was experiencing, as well as the anger I was feeling, along with the anxiety of leading a young church while still trying to finish graduate school.

I went a number of days without sleep. I was studying for my Master's exam and working on my thesis as well. During the day I worked to establish a new congregation that was less than a year old. Though this church was growing wonderfully, I wasn't growing inside.

My wife returned from taking care of the affairs of her father's estate and her family, and sharing their grief together. That first evening after she was home, as I stood up to leave the dinner table, my right leg and arm suddenly went numb. Then the muscles on the right side of my face went limp and slid down. I couldn't talk properly. I couldn't even remember my own name.

Startled, Debbie asked anxiously, "What's wrong, Doug?"

Being a man of faith and not wanting to admit that anything was wrong, I replied as casually as I could, "Oh, nothing. I just need to go for a walk."

But when I tried to leave the table, I immediately realized that something was seriously wrong. Debbie hurried me off to the hospital emergency room. As I lay in the hospital bed, the doctor checked my blood pressure, which seemed to be moving back to normal. He was certain I didn't have a blood clot.

Looking at me intently, the doctor asked, "Young man, what is it you do?"

I can remember hating to answer that question. After all, who wants to admit he's a pastor when he's in the middle of something that is obviously related to stress and anger in his life?

"I'm a pastor," I replied somewhat sheepishly, while thinking to myself, *Oh, yeah, I'm a pastor, all right. Join our church, and see what it will do for you!*

The doctor asked, "Are you also going to school?"

"Yes, I am."

The doctor said, "This is common for people under great stress. Young man, I would encourage you to stop whatever you're doing."

I'll never forget his words or the intense, concerned look in his eyes. It was as though I was hearing the Lord speak to me directly.

In one of those milliseconds in which the Lord speaks, I suddenly realized that I had been reacting negatively to an unjust situation. My suffering had caused me to thrive on anger, and I was becoming an ugly person because of it. I had been gradually moving into retaliatory thinking, because I wanted to get even. The only one being hurt, however, was myself. I had to admit that I needed a total cleansing from within.

I'd seen plenty of pastors and Christian leaders who had become bitter under the pressures of church leadership. I'd also seen plenty of pastors and their wives constantly spewing forth embittered words about how their congregation wasn't following their lead or respecting them.

Debbie and I had determined, when we first started pastoring, that we would never cultivate a bitter attitude toward our work. Yet, here I was wallowing in that kind of attitude—maybe not articulated, but nevertheless building up steam inside.

In that moment, as the doctor stepped out of the emergency room, I heard the Lord speak to me: "You do need to change. You need to change your attitude. You're becoming someone ugly—someone I haven't ordained you to be. Look at My model, Jesus. Sure, you've suffered, but you can walk away from this situation a stronger, more powerful person if you choose to."

It was a number of months before I recovered fully. If it hadn't been for some close friends, who picked up some of my load, allowing me to get back on my feet, I don't think we would have ever made it as a church.

During the months of recovery, I made a list of lessons I was learning through that situation, such things as:

- the importance of honesty;
- the value of accountability;
- the importance of responsible management in church leadership;
- the importance of delegating authority to good, qualified people, because one person can't carry the whole load alone;

- how sensitive a person's faith is;
- the extreme responsibility, as well as joy, of leading people spiritually; and
- the importance of knowing when I need to check my attitude or be aware of stress in my life, which is manifested by certain biological signs.

Those realities, through the experience of pain, were being etched on my heart in ways they never could have been in a classroom. I gained a great deal through my suffering.

I praise and thank God that He allowed my body to react to my wrong response to suffering, because it has helped me immensely over the years.

The reality of this life is that God has given us the ability to change the world, which is only one of God's strategies. He has other strategies as well. One of them is that, through signs, wonders, and miracles, He draws people to Christ so that they will have listening ears.

He is a constantly healing God. Because Christ faced and conquered suffering, healing is available to us. I've seen many people healed. I don't understand healing at all, and there is often no rhyme or reason as to how God heals. I am convinced, however, that it does come to us through the attitudinal channels of our hearts.

Christ's Presence in our lives will always result in a healing life of one kind or another. He is the great Healer! "Jesus Christ *is* the same yesterday, today, and forever" (Heb. 13:8). He still heals us physically, emotionally, and spiritually. This is a promise we can contend for and hold onto, even in the middle of toxic relationships that have scarred us.

I'm sure some of you reading this have suffered at the hands of an abusive parent or spouse, or both. Let me just encourage you that Christ the Healer is at work in your life, right now. Choose to respond in the same Spirit that Christ has—that is, in the spirit of forgiveness that is combined with wisdom, and with faith that releases the healing promises of His life.

It is His healing life that draws people to Christ. A recent Gallup poll of Americans who attend churches across the country indicated that less than 10 percent of the people attending churches had made decisions for Christ from watching Christian TV or going to an evangelistic crusade. You might also be surprised to learn that the remaining 90 percent said that they had come to the Lord through the influence of a friend or relative who had brought them to church. In other words, people are more likely to attend a congregation because a loved one or a friend had brought them there.

These figures surprised me at first, although they really shouldn't have, as we are all very relational in the way God has made us.

I spoke recently with a young woman after a service. She asked for specific prayer and wanted me to know that she had been attending our church for several months.

I asked her: "How is it that you came to be a part of Eastside Church?"

She replied, "It was through the influence of a young woman."

"And how did that happen?" I asked.

"Well, I was just watching her. She seemed to have all the pain that I did. Her husband had left her with two kids, just as I'd been left by my husband. But, week by week, she seemed to become a better person, while I was still hurting. She seemed to be unflappable. I had seen her, week after week, going to church on Sundays. Finally, I had to ask her how this happened and get her help. It was really through her example in the middle of her suffering that I came to know Christ."

This woman's story calls attention to another interesting observation:

If statisticians probed this matter deeper, they would find that many of those who met the Lord would say they were convinced that Jesus was Lord after they observed and were impressed by the quality of life in some Christian around them!

Exercise

1. Do people around you observe how you respond to suffering?

2. Have you ever taken the time to release, pray for, and believe that the Lord could heal you from the damage brought on by toxic parents or a spouse?

3. Are you committed to the fact that your life preaches louder through what you do rather than through what you say?

I'm reading the book *The Trusting Heart,* by Redford Williams, a cardiologist. Over a period of time, Williams had analyzed heart patients, and he was convinced that diet plays only a very small role in cholesterol levels and helping to prevent heart attacks. Of course, it is still important that we be careful about our diets.

Dr. Williams discovered that our inner heart attitude has the deciding vote about how susceptible we are to heart disease. He found that people who were less cynical and mistrustful had fewer heart attacks. Those who were cynical and didn't trust people were candidates for heart disease.

As we grow older, we do have a tendency to grow more cynical and skeptical about everything in general. For instance, I find that as I age, I try to anticipate what's going to go wrong around me. At times I find a lot of cynicism and skepticism slipping into my heart about people and the work of Christ.

It is usually pain that has caused me to be this way. I don't want to get hurt again, I say to myself, so I'm going to be more careful. The only problem is that this kind of self-preservation does great harm. The healing attitudes of Christ will protect us in times of suffering from being damaged and scarred in our attitudes. That is why Peter reached out to those he loved to make sure they were not scarred in their spiritual attitude . . . scarred so deeply that they would become totally ineffectual for the kingdom.

The second factor Dr. Williams found was that people with a higher frequency of hostile feelings also had a tendency toward heart disease. Last, he discovered that those who were more respectful and considerate of others had fewer heart attacks.

CHRISTIANS ARE NOT VICTIMS

Several months ago, someone I respect a great deal, described to me a terrible situation in her marriage. She and her husband are still together, however, and great things are now happening in their relationship.

She took me aside one day and asked, "Doug, if I'd come to you a few years ago, when this was going on, you would have told me to get a divorce, wouldn't you?"

Pausing for a moment to be sure I answered properly, I said, "You betcha! I would have told you to take him to the cleaners for the way he had treated you . . . and I would have been wrong, wouldn't I? How did you work it out, anyway?"

She replied, "Well, I determined that I would respond the way I thought Christ would. I put my foot down. Now, don't get me wrong. I wasn't nasty about it. I just told him how it was going to be in a matter-of-fact way. Instead of feeling victimized, I began to feel that the Lord was now in control of my life, and I responded in ways that were loving and would remedy the situation. We're both better people for it."

While she was telling her story, I was thinking, *Gee. She's talking about decades of abuse; yet, a wonderful healing has come out of it! This woman appears to be one of the happiest people I've ever met. I think she deserves a medal!*

I believe the real change came in this woman's life when she determined that she would no longer be victimized. The helplessness of feeling victimized causes the most stress and anguish in our lives.

Studies suggest that chief executive officers (CEOs) don't have ulcers or heart problems. They give them to everyone else! They're just carriers. Why is this? Most CEOs are in charge. It is the feeling of victimization that causes the most distress and problems. When you determine that someone can be as abusive to you as she or he wants, but you refuse to be victimized by that person externally and internally, you are back in control with Christ as your Lord. He is in control of your life. Christians are *not* victims.

Likewise, Peter wanted to convince the Christians of his day that they couldn't be victimized by anyone because of the factor of Christ's Lordship in their lives. The Lordship factor and the model of His living assure us that our lives are not out of control or in the hands or the whim of others. The key is walking in His Lordship!

Søren Kierkegaard told a great story. One night a theater filled with people caught fire. When the manager looked around for someone to warn the theatergoers, he found only a clown wearing a red nose, a polka-dotted suit, and a funny-looking wig. Undaunted, he sent the clown out on stage to tell the audience they had to leave immediately because the theater was on fire.

So the clown went out on stage, yelling loudly, "Everybody out! The theater's on fire!"

Instead of heading for the exits, the people stayed in their seats and started laughing. They thought it was a great skit and part of the show. The more agitated the clown became, the more hysterically the crowd laughed.

The clown jumped up and down, waved his arms, and repeatedly yelled, "We're all going to die in the fire if you don't leave immediately. Get out, right now!"

Ultimately, the theater burned down, and everyone perished, because the theater crowd didn't believe the clown. Kierkegaard asked two questions: (1) Why did God leave His message to a bunch of clowns? and (2) Shouldn't we try not to be clowns so people will hear what we're saying?

Peter's message is: One of the ways we get our message about Christ heard and are able to change our world is to respond with respect and the loving grace of Jesus Christ. When asked to go one mile, go two. When someone tries to rob you, figure out how to give. When you're abused, respond with prayer, loving respect, and forgiveness.

In a documentary I recently saw, sociologist Tony Campolo shared with the audience a scene he saw on a bridge in Selma, Alabama. The sheriff told some civil-rights demonstrators to leave the bridge, but they knelt down instead. They would not leave. The sheriff warned them that if they didn't leave, they would be attacked with clubs and by dogs. It even ended up with shots being fired. But the demonstrators began chanting: "We have overcome. We have overcome." At the sheriff's command, his men charged into that group of mostly Afro-American demonstrators and began beating them with clubs and having their dogs attack them.

While watching the replay on the confrontation on TV, Campolo made an interesting statement: "They won! They won! At that point they won!"

How did they win? By responding with the opposite spirit. Nonviolence had overcome violence. Commitment to honesty and human rights have overcome abuse and threats. Whether you agree with that scenario or not doesn't matter. What does matter is that the response of the demonstrators shifted our entire country over to the positive side concerning racial issues. No doubt we have a long way to go, but we have already come far.

As radical and as unfair as it may sound, when God doesn't take us out of an unjust situation, He doesn't give us problem avoidance as well. I wish He would, but He isn't going to.

He said, instead: "I've voted for you. I'm praying for you. And, by the way, there is healing available."

Christ does promise this: If we will determine in our hearts to respond in a Christlike spirit to an abusive and hostile world, He will give us the grace and ability to pull off His masterful plan.

Finally, Peter wanted us to know that we're under the strong, watchful eye of the Father. The response of our hearts to the Shepherd and Overseer of our souls will keep us on track. The person whose knee is bowed to Him will be saved in the midst of suffering.

For you were like sheep going astray, but have now returned to the Shepherd and Overseer of your souls. (1 Peter 2:25)

Chapter 8

Loving *vs.* Controlling
(1 Peter 3:1–7)

The stress of loss attacks our families and marital relationships more than any other part of our lives.

My personal opinion about American culture is that 50 percent of the members of my generation get divorces, not because they devalue marriage, but because they expect so much from it.

A woman was asked whether her husband made her happy. When she responded, "No, not really," the room suddenly grew silent. I noticed that her husband, who had been involved in a conversation with a group of men approximately ten feet away, leaned over with an interested ear to catch what his wife was saying. I was also interested in what she had to say about this.

She continued: "I learned long ago that God didn't intend for my husband to make me happy. God intended me to bring happiness to our relationship."

Not too long ago, a couple came to my office for counseling. They were trying to put their marriage back together, which had failed after they lost their second child through a tragedy.

They had somehow kept their marriage going for a number of months during the tenuous existence of their little child they had both loved. When their child finally died, following a long comatose period, their inability to communicate their pain and grief caused them to drift further and further apart.

The husband would come home inebriated, and alcohol gripped his life in destructive ways. Soon they were divorced. They lost all they had built up together. Financially, they were in a shambles. Though he was only in his late thirties, the husband's career was all but over because of his alcoholism and the bad reputation he had gained.

Now, this couple were sitting in my office a little more than a year later. During our conversation we had an interesting exchange of questions and answers. Since they had both decided that they still loved each other and were willing to work things out, they asked how to find each other again.

At one point, the wife said, "You know, it's in a time of stress that you find out what you've really built your relationship on."

Being the parents of a child with a handicap, Debbie and I were treated with some concern at the hospital when Raissa was born. We learned that it was quite common for parents facing their children's severe health problems not to make their marriage survive. Through a lot of grace and patience and, at times, a lot of work, Debbie and I have hung in there together and have a very fruitful, loving relationship.

Peter addressed his flock on the entire issue of marriage. He knew that they were facing a great deal of stress. I'm sure he anticipated that the health and viability of their relationships would be in danger also. When humans suffer, it seems to be the very strategy of hell itself.

LISTENING TO ONE ANOTHER

Likewise *you* wives, *be* submissive to your own husbands, that even if some do not obey the word, they, without a word, may be won by the conduct of their wives, when they observe your chaste conduct *accompanied* by fear. Do not let your beauty be that outward *adorning* of arranging the hair, of wearing gold, or of putting on *fine* apparel; but *let it be* the hidden person of the heart, with the incorruptible *ornament* of a gentle and quiet spirit, which is very precious in the sight of God. For in this manner, in former times, the holy women who trusted in God also adorned themselves, being submissive to their own husbands, as Sarah obeyed Abraham, calling him lord, whose daughters you are if you do good and are not afraid with any terror. Likewise *you* husbands, dwell with *them* with understanding, giving honor to the wife, as to the weaker vessel, and as *being* heirs together of the grace of life, that your prayers may not be hindered. (1 Peter 3:1–7)

Listening hearts make for strong marriages. Listening hearts, in times of crisis, allow for a quick recovery. I think Peter was suggesting that in times of turmoil our capacity to submit to one another will allow us to grow in strength as Christian people. I think Peter's hopes were that, in a submitted spirit toward one another, we will not only be able to hear the voice of the Lord through relationships, but will also learn to hear the Lord speak to us more clearly as individuals.

This is a very emotional section of Scripture, and this text has raised a great deal of controversy. I think the reason it does so is that it walks right into our living rooms and addresses our lives.

Historically, this text has produced some of the wackiest interpretations imaginable. I hope we can avoid some of the land mines and receive some helpful input from what follows.

A clear understanding of love must be in focus before we can handle this text. Actually, we need to convert our thinking. Christians love without control. *Submission* here is not used in the controlling sense. Submission is a sensitive process of our listening, hearing, and respecting one another.

Our ability to understand this text will depend on our degree of conversion and the level of our thinking. The intention of Scripture is that each time we read it, our conversion process will continue. I've given some thought to the word *convert*. The other day I was rereading Isaiah 55, which has given me some very worthwhile input concerning the issue of conversion.

Isaiah 55 probably gives the clearest illustration of what the Bible means by conversion. It commences with an invitation: "Come, all you who are thirsty. Come and I'll give you drink" (paraphrased). Then Isaiah stated: "Let the wicked change their minds, and let those who would come to the Lord turn from their ways" (paraphrased). Then verse 8 states strongly: " 'For My thoughts are not your thoughts, and My ways are not your ways,' says the Lord" (paraphrased). This entire chapter basically discusses the concept of conversion as being our willingness to exchange our thoughts for God's thoughts.

The word *convert* is very interesting. Here's an example of what that text really means: If you went to a foreign country, say West Germany, and wanted to buy German goods, but had only American currency, you would first need to *convert* your American dollars into deutsche marks. This exchange (or conversion process) then would allow you to turn your U.S. money, which previously couldn't buy anything in West Germany, into German currency so that you could purchase German goods. Likewise, when people come to America from West Germany, they must convert their money from deutsche marks into U.S. dollars.

The Bible suggests that we have a problem far worse than just trying to exchange money. We don't have valid currency of any kind when it comes to living in the heavenly realm. We just have "Monopoly" play money. It's phony money. It doesn't work. It doesn't buy us real life.

So what the Lord invites us to do when we become converted is to begin a process that continues as our lives interact with His Word. We take our phony "Monopoly" money (our worthless ideas, our earthly thoughts) and give it to Him. In other words, to be converted is to give God our phony money, and He will give us back bona fide kingdom of God dollars! As we exchange our thoughts for His thoughts, we receive legitimate thinking for His kingdom.

When He taught His disciples about leadership, Jesus was concerned that they would latch onto the spirit of this world when it came to the issue of leadership. He felt that their overly competitive natures would lead them down the path of the Gentile kings, for believers were not to "lord" it over one another.

Unless one enters into the interpretation of this text with a whole-Bible view, the word *submit* may be easily misinterpreted. Control, domination, and manipulation are always wrong for a believer, whether in or out of marriage. This text is *not* talking about control. In fact, it is really telling us how to love and how to avoid controlling and manipulation.

Suffering has a way of testing the mettle of our relationships. Peter shared with his fellow followers a preparatory input for times when we will all suffer as couples. In this passage, he gave us insight into how we can strengthen our relationships rather than destroy them when we are under stress.

As we look at this chapter, we see that it also contains some perceptive comments that deal with husbands and wives who already have charged emotions. It contains potential gospel guns and bullets, loaded and ready to be fired, if we don't approach it with a converted mind.

THE DILEMMA OF THE FIRST CENTURY

I've rarely heard this text taught with careful, scholarly regard for the specific setting and context in which 1 Peter 3 was written. Invariably, it's lifted right out of context and applied very generically across the board, as though it were a section on the order of the Christian family.

It isn't that at all. The historical context of this passage is that the early church—at least in Rome, where Peter was writing—was being blamed for disillusionment in many marriages. When a Roman citizen's wife became saved, she no longer participated in the pagan rituals of the Roman culture, which was considered defaming and insulting to a Roman businessman. Hence, it followed that there was a great deal of pressure in Roman homes. Often the now-Christian wife would be kicked out of her home and left, literally widowed and needing to fend for herself.

We've seen earlier that this was one of the sociological tension points facing the church. Peter addressed probably the most agonizing kind of suffering. It's the kind of suffering that originates in a home that's divided between two value systems. This is still true today.

Thus, Peter's instructions were for those Roman wives who were attempting to walk according to the values of the kingdom while still living in a home dominated by a man committed to the values of the Roman world. Any person who has ever lived in this kind of situation knows the pain and agony involved, along with the friction that occurs in a divided home.

Peter offered hope and help to those suffering in this situation, as well as insight as to how we ought to interact with our brothers and sisters facing this kind of divided home.

This also accounts for the many instructions in Timothy

about caring for widows. These "widows," for the most part, were those women whose Roman husbands had abandoned them because they had accepted the Lord. Consequently, Peter tried to nip in the bud a special problem before it got out of hand—that when a wife became a Christian, she often became nagging and controlling to persuade her husband to convert to Christ as well. Her rationale was, perhaps, twofold: Her husband would be saved, and they would have peace in their home again. So Peter specifically addressed the wives of unsaved husbands. We should never forget that.

Peter committed six verses to the wives, yet only one to the husbands. I don't really know why he did this. I hesitate to say this, but perhaps the wives needed more help.

It is probably more accurate to say that this wasn't as difficult an issue when a husband was converted first as it was when a wife first became a Christian, given the male-dominated homes in Roman society.

Peter's primary concern, however, was placed in that specific Roman setting and time frame of the first century. Now I wish to emphasize that, as is the case throughout the Bible, many principles can be extrapolated and applied to our lives. There's much being said to us here, whether we're single or married, man or woman.

THE INFLUENCE OF
RESPECTFUL LISTENING

The overriding principle in this section of Scripture is *respect*. We can almost hear Peter saying: "Hey, folks. Don't exacerbate your situation. Through clear thinking and thoughtful living, you can influence your situation for good, though it may be painful."

Peter stressed that the way to influence people is *not* from the outside in. Exterior pressure, nagging, and constant badgering aren't going to help anyone become converted. Peter assured us that we'll get a lot further and have greater success if we influence people by the quality of our lives and character. That's a message to all of us. There is no attitude more contrary to Christianity than that which dictates that we must control, maneuver, and manipulate others to agree with us.

The essential message of this chapter—especially when you look at verse 6 (a difficult verse), wherein Sarah called Abraham lord—is that we can, by building up our inner strength, find a way, even in a less-than-ideal marriage, to define God's lordship at work.

The ideal setting for every marriage is equality and partnership. Unfortunately, not all marriages work out this way. Peter's point here is that if a situation isn't abusive or life-threatening, though the marriage may have a normal degree of suffering, we should not scrap it to seek the "ideal" marriage.

Neither do I think that Peter discouraged wives from wearing jewelry. I think he merely pointed out that influence does not come from the outside in. I believe that jewelry and ornate adornment may have been the basic value system in Roman society, as it is in our own overly materialistic culture here in America. We seem to believe that our true self becomes visible only by what we know, what we own, and what we wear.

But Peter said that our true self is expressed through the cultivation of spiritual values, and that our real self can be recognized by the manifestation of our moral and spiritual values.

OUR TENDENCY THAT DESIRES TO CONTROL

I really think all humans have the tendency and desire to control others. In this passage it is possible to see that the wives of unconverted husbands were so desirous of converting them that Peter felt they might run the risk of entering into a controlling spirit that is the opposite of Christ's.

Peter did not encourage the wives to cower before their husbands as their masters because, in verse 7, he did not afford Christian husbands that right. Christian husbands are to dwell with their wives with understanding, to give them honor as the "weaker vessel," and to treat their wives with astounding respect as partners so that their prayers won't be hindered.

Verse 7 makes it very clear that marriage is an equal partnership for Christians. With great sympathy, Peter, the shepherd of the early church, understood that women living in an atmosphere of male domination have a large task ahead of them.

A controlling spirit can enter into individuals, families, and churches alike. The desire to dominate others to get our own way is common in societies everywhere. So, Peter cautioned believers: "Don't do that; don't fall prey to that wrong spirit of power."

One way to tackle this is to refuse to use any kind of power at all. The spirit of servanthood is always the heart of love. I'm sure we all know of instances where one spouse met the Lord and began stacking Christian books around the house, leaving biblical messages, and inviting Christian friends over for dinner. Eventually the conversation is steered in an "appropriate" direction so as to set the stage for a conversion. Most people, I find, delight in resisting that type of pressure, however. In fact, it can often become a game spouses play.

What Peter referred to is that there's a vocabulary that exceeds the quality of words. It's the vocabulary of a right spirit that listens, hears, and responds respectfully to those we are called to live with.

Here's the gist of what Peter was conveying: "If you can't respectfully trust yourself to powerlessness and influences, you will be gripped by fears—fears that will not rehabilitate you, but will, instead, destroy your precious marital relationship and inhibit the ongoing message of Jesus Christ meant for your unsaved partner."

So whether we are single or married, this passage gives us a clear message: *Don't try to control and manipulate others*. Rather, exhibit the inner character traits of Christ, and you will have plenty of influence.

Peter urged the wives (as he did the men a moment later): *"Listen respectfully to your husband (wife), and you're likely to hear God speaking to you."*

Fear grips all our hearts when we give up control. In doing so, however, we leave the door open for the Lord to work in us, even in the midst of our suffering.

ALLOWING ROOM FOR JESUS' LORDSHIP IN OUR SUFFERING

Peter gave these simple instructions to wives facing suffering in their marriages:

1. Concentrate on developing your inner character traits.
2. Learn that a Christian's basic posture is always that of giving up control. Don't give in to this fear, which fills every heart at the thought of being victimized.
3. Where both the husband and the wife are Christians, that marriage is a partnership.
4. Be convinced that other women have successfully followed this pattern in serenity to Jesus. The word *submission* means "to hear under" or "to approach another with respect." It is entirely possible for Christian wives to gain a sense of superiority over their unsaved husbands, and this will only exasperate an already painful relationship. Refrain from this.

WHAT IS A CHRISTIAN HUSBAND?

I think it is a distinct possibility that Peter also addressed the Christian husbands of unsaved wives. It appears to be part of the total context of this passage—that is, husbands are to have the same ability to hear God in the middle of situations that are less than optimal. Human relationships require a great deal of interpersonal skill.

I'm sure he was also referring to all Christian husbands, but I can't help but feel that he was dealing with husbands who faced a particularly painful situation at home.

When Peter stated: "Husbands, in the same way . . ." I believe he meant: "Okay guys, in the same spirit that the wives have been asked to have, you also must be servants. You are likewise to listen respectfully to your wives."

Loosely defined, the word *considerate* means that when you turn into your driveway at night after work, don't turn into a blob. Don't turn into a gutless, mindless wonder. Actually, you guys should work as diligently at being good, successful husbands as you do at your jobs. That's what *considerate* encompasses.

Now, when Peter told the husbands to give honor to their wives as the "weaker vessel," the term *weaker* is *not* used in the sense of being an inferior partner, having no strength, or being frail and feeble. Here, in the Greek, this term suggests the context of being of finer quality.

At home, I get to wash the Corningware. Now, if Corningware is accidentally dropped on the floor, it rarely chips. And it doesn't really matter how you put it in the dishwasher. In other words, it's your industrial, all-purpose kind of tableware. On the other hand, I never get to wash our china. Debbie usually washes it by hand, because it is more precious and delicate.

I don't think we could say that either the Corningware or the china is better. Though the china is certainly more valuable, in terms of usefulness, the Corningware is better; it is used on an everyday basis. Yet, they both have distinct purposes.

Essentially, Peter is telling us: "Now, guys, I know you're used to hanging around each other (a bunch of tough Corningware). You don't chip or break as easily, and if you're thrown to the floor, you bounce right back up. Husbands, don't be so interested in talking and ruling, but be interested in listening as well."

It is possible that, in the midst of a relationship characterized by pain and suffering, God may be trying to get our attention through our spouse—even when we don't care to listen. This entire text strongly points out that we won't get anywhere unless we are *listeners*. In fact, the only way we get heard is by listening first!

Peter concluded with this valuable insight: We are to conduct ourselves, aided by the grace of God, as *joint heirs*. That means that we are equal partners, a couple who shares equally in God's inheritance.

Then he tacked on this last little gem: ". . . so that nothing will hinder your prayers." Now, just as it is possible for wives to act insensitively toward their husbands, trying to manipulate them, so also it is possible for men to live guilt-ridden with their wives. To clarify this, when husbands mistreat their wives, they are trapped by guilt, and their relationship with God then suffers and is impeded as well.

So, if you husbands will live in submission with and respect for your wives, your spirituality won't go down the tube. If you think about it, it really is hard to seek and to hear God when you feel guilty.

I'll wrap it up with this comment: I believe what Peter was trying to impress on us is that the way to be heard is to give a truly listening ear that is sensitively tuned to what God may be telling us through those around us. By doing that, we will gain far more influence for Christ's sake.

Could it be possible that marriage is an exercise in listening, an exercise that allows us to hear the Lord more clearly? I believe so.

I think marriage will assume various shapes and forms in our culture in the 1990s. The younger generation, sometimes referred to as "baby busters," aren't marrying in the numbers that their parents (the "baby boom" generation) did.

Did you know that baby boomers average 50 percent of all the marriages and divorces in America? From my observation, it seems as though the baby-buster generation is not too inclined to marry legally (or at all) because of the pain and agony they suffered at the hands of their divorced baby-boomer parents. Most human pain, from my experience, seems to arise out of relationships between the genders.

When wives attempt to manipulate their husbands, it usually blows up in their faces. Then, too, overly dominant men who are abusive and destructive end up destroying not only their wives and their families, but themselves as well.

About four times a year, our church offers a course called "Marriage Enrichment Seminar," in which we discuss such subjects as family budget, communication, romance, and other pertinent topics. One of the concepts we endeavor to put across to the couples attending the seminars is the idea that we actually experience multiple marriages within the life span of one marriage. In fact, the couple who help direct the seminars say that they have already experienced as many as five marriages to each other. Deb and I have been married nearly twenty years, and I really feel that it is true that we have had multiple marriages. It seems as though we repeatedly pass through vital junctures of our relationship.

Let's admit it. Who stays the same his or her entire life? I know my wife, Debbie, is entirely different now than she was at sixteen, when I first met her. I probably appear quite different to her as well.

Could it be that some of the pain and suffering we experience within the context of marriage is of the healthy variety, put there to make us better people? It would seem so.

In this section, Peter brought back to my heart again the conviction that God is in my marriage relationship with Debbie, though it is painful at times to grow together. But it is this pain that makes me a better listener.

Let me cite an instance from my own marriage. Early on in our pastorate I became very busy, working almost around the clock at times. I often went away to conferences and speaking engagements. Quite frankly, for several years, I didn't pay enough attention to my wife and kids.

One day, Deb sat me down and gave it to me straight: "Doug, this isn't the way it was going to be! Things have to change around here."

I remember being quite mystified by her attack. In fact, at first, I felt that she was totally out of line. After all, I was serving God, wasn't I? It was a painful, but necessary, conversation we had that day. In fact, at the time, it was a painful phase in our marriage relationship, but the problems had to be addressed and adjusted nevertheless.

Upon reflection, I'm very glad my wife decided she would no longer tolerate the imbalances in my life. Because she put her foot down, it helped me to listen to God concerning my priorities. I would hate to imagine what might have happened if I hadn't had a listening ear to what she had to say.

The other day, when I reached out to take her hand and squeeze it as we walked across a parking lot together, Debbie looked at me with a quizzical smile on her face.

"What's gotten into you, Doug?" she asked.

"Gee, I don't know. Maybe 'cuz it's a nice day. Why do you ask?"

"Oh, I was just curious. You just seem so much warmer lately than you've ever been before, that's all."

I realized then that the Lord had been changing me . . . again. No doubt about it, change is painful. Perhaps it is this kind of pain that Peter wanted the believers to be braced for. If so, wives would be living with husbands who had different values. Husbands, on the other hand, would be living with wives who were learning to be more sensitive and were sharing the fruits, as well as the responsibility, of their relationship. As a result, one thing, for sure, would happen: We would all learn to hear God better!

Exercise

1. Have you ever considered that some of the pain you suffer in your relationships is because God is training you to hear His voice?
2. Do you ever find yourself desiring to control or manipulate others so they will agree with you or do as you ask?
3. As you've grown in your relationship, have you allowed for change in your spouse's life?
4. Are you practicing the skill of being a good listener?
5. Have you been tempted in the last ninety days to take out your own personal pain and suffering on your marriage partner, or those who are closest to you?

HOW TO BE A GOOD LISTENER

This chapter has presented several good insights on how to be a good listener. I believe these insights will also lead us to become better listeners to God, especially in less-than-optimal situations such as those faced by the husbands and wives discussed in this chapter.

1. Be painfully honest about your temptation to manipulate others. Tell yourself: "I will state the facts just as they are, and will not embellish them."

2. Don't be fearful about giving up control in your relationships while trusting God to work matters out. Be willing to accept the fact that your opinion may not be accepted.

3. Always maintain a tone of respect, as well as a real commitment to respect the other person in your conversations.

4. Refuse to be treated with disrespect. Remember: You're both heirs together.

5. Appreciate the differences between yourself and another person. Respect where she or he is coming from. Don't communicate from a superior position. The Greek word for "submission" is *hupokuo,* which literally means "to hear under."

6. Seek to understand the other person. Don't just state your own position and ignore the other's. The old Indian adage "You'll never understand a man until you walk a mile in his moccasins" is very appropriate here.

7. Be very sensitive to the fact that your inability to communicate with others can definitely inhibit your ability to communicate with God. Your prayers may well be hindered also. After all, if we can't hear others, how will we ever hear God?

8. Realize that hearing can be the most difficult when you're suffering. Put your life in the proper perspective.

9. Know that the loudest way you speak is the way you live. A loving heart will create a loving environment. A respectful speaker creates a respectful listener.

10. Realize that communication is sometimes a painful process. Misunderstandings are common and normal for all relationships. This kind of pain is a good kind of pain, though, for it creates growth. Listening with ears that are willing to accept the reality of pain as the pathway to growth will help. This will avoid disappointment and disillusionment, which create anger and hostility that would need to be released somehow.

Note that there is an inheritance or great reward to be gained by putting forth the effort to listen respectfully and to share your lives lovingly with each other.

PRAYER

Lord Jesus, we pray that You would release us from our desire to control others. Lord, we embrace the pain that comes with growth, and we trust that, by concentrating on inner qualities, You will begin to influence and change the world around us from the inside out.

Chapter 9

Traits of a Successful Heart
(1 Peter 3:8–13)

Success is discussed a great deal in our time. In fact, I think one of the principal ways we suffer in this age of such ferocious competition is because of perceived failure.

One of the first emotions that strikes our hearts in a time of loss is the feeling of doing something wrong or that we have failed or God wouldn't be treating us this way.

Peter had a reassuring slogan for those of us who would be tempted to feel we have led unsuccessful lives: *Success cannot be measured from the outside in. The successful heart is always measured from the inside out.*

Even in times of suffering, there is an opportunity to grasp and apprehend true success. It may be that in these times we are closest to true success—the success of a unique heart. A successful heart, according to Peter, possesses special character traits. If we master these traits, we will all prosper and be blessed in the best of ways!

The basic impact of successful living, as we all know, does not stem from the accumulation of worldly possessions, nor does it come from the acquisition of fame or an excellent reputation. We can all have fantastic vocational success; yet, we all know people who are utter failures as people.

I think that Peter's great fear was that we would lose touch with those traits of a truly successful heart. If we master these traits, we will have spiritual IQs that will soar off the charts!

Finally, all of *you be* of one mind, having compassion for one another; love as brothers, *be* tenderhearted, *be* courteous; not returning evil for evil or reviling for reviling, but on the contrary blessing, knowing that you were called to this, that you may inherit a blessing. For

> *"He who would love life*
> *And see good days,*
> *Let him refrain his tongue from evil,*
> *And his lips from speaking guile;*
> *Let him turn away from evil*
> *   and do good;*
> *Let him seek peace and pursue it.*
> *For the eyes of the* LORD
> *   are on the righteous,*
> *And his ears are open to their prayers;*
> *But the face of the* LORD *is against*
> *   those who do evil."*

And who *is* he who will harm you if you become followers of
what is good? (1 Peter 3:8–13)

TRULY DEFINING SUCCESS

In a broken world, one of the greatest gifts a person can have
is a proper definition of what success is.

I hope you have realized by now that suffering will be inevitable for all of us. We will all face troubles of one kind or another.
People used to call these troubles "acts of God." For some
reason, God gets the rap for all that goes wrong in the world.

I've found that one of the methods for surviving suffering
used by people I've loved and pastored is that they already have
a predetermined definition of success. It's clear in their minds
what they're truly about.

The loss of such things as material possessions, a vocation,
or even the loss of a near and dear loved one, when put in the
proper perspective, are much more easily handled with satis-
factory wholeness when you know what you're about.

I recently reread *Leaders* by Warren Bennis. It is a presentation of data collected from ninety leaders in our society who
were deemed to be successful. This book's purpose was to analyze the traits of these leaders to determine any consistencies
that would possibly yield an explanation for their success. Pro-
fessors, college presidents, inventors, educators, chief execu-

tive officers of both small and large companies, and persons from all parts of the country were interviewed.

Five common personality traits were discovered among these persons. Now, these traits may be different from the ones Peter offered the church, but they are, nonetheless, interesting. I think you'll find them surprising, as I did. Knowing them might even put us in the frame of mind to consider the attributes of a truly successful heart, like Peter's.

First, these ninety leaders had the ability, far above the average person, to accept people as they were without feeling compelled to change them.

Second, these leaders had the capacity not to recall and rehash the past failures of themselves or anyone else. That is, they rarely made a decision based on a person's past successes or failures. They lived in the present and based their decision-making on the veracity of the facts currently available. In other words, if someone failed at something today, they did not rub that person's nose in it years later.

Third, these leaders treated their family members and closest working peers with the same courtesy and politeness they would extend to a stranger. That is, they were extraordinarily kind, considerate people.

Fourth, all ninety leaders had the ability to trust other people, even though doing so presented high personal risks. They were the kind of people who would invest in someone else's dream. They would invest time, effort, and money in the good character of another person. They would take risks that depended on the performance of others, not on themselves, and they were comfortable with that.

Fifth, these ninety leaders had the ability to live without the constant approval and recognition from others because they were extremely secure within themselves. This trait was expressed in self-assurance, self-confidence, and a strong feeling of self-worth. They didn't have to prove themselves to anyone. They did what they did for the sheer joy of sharing the skills, talents, and resources with which they had been endowed. They didn't seek out pats on the back, but simply wanted *to do something* rather than *be someone.*

It was interesting to learn about the common traits of these successful leaders. Peter, the great leader of Christ's church, had his own list of traits to describe a successful heart. Let's find out together what they are.

PETER'S LIST OF TRAITS

Trait One: Be of One Mind

The first trait of a successful heart, as a believer, is *to be of one mind, to live harmoniously with others*.

What does it mean to live harmoniously? It does *not* mean that we will live with only those who are like us, but that we are to harmonize with all those around us. I think it means our ability to have, in the context of Christianity, relationships based on what we agree on, rather than being caught up in what we disagree on.

A harmonious heart is a successful heart. This kind of heart is always discovering how to work together with others. We should have minds open to other ideas or perspectives to avoid the common pitfalls that seem to betray and to beleaguer Christianity.

Hasn't the church been noted for rejecting the Isaac Newtons and Galileos of the world and the new ideas they presented? The church seems to be the last bastion to accept and to receive changes warmly and enthusiastically—not that we should accept *carte blanche* every new idea that comes along without first examining it in the light of the Scriptures. However, we are known to be rigid, disharmonious people.

From my own experience, one of the problems that made it difficult for me to accept Christ as Lord of my life was the squabbling I saw among the different church beliefs. The Baptists hurl grenades at the Pentecostals, and the Pentecostals project their own venom at the Baptists, the United Methodists, and so on. Roman Catholics won't have anything to do with the Protestants, and vice versa. Not to be outdone, the Eastern religions throw their darts at the rest of us, and we hear constantly that this doctrine is better than that one. Every group in the kingdom of God is divided and separated from the others by its distinctive doctrines and different positions—so on and so forth, *ad infinitum* and *ad nauseum*.

None of this lends itself to the biblical definition of a successful heart. I think Peter sensed that in times of personal suffering we would need each other more than ever. That's why a character trait that allows us to live in harmony with one another is vital.

This kind of heart finds out what we do agree on and then concentrates on that. I'm certain that we have phenomenal differences on a variety of issues in our own congregation.

Someone asked me recently, "Doug, what's your attitude toward SDI?"

I replied, "What's that?"

Now, don't get me wrong. I really do know that SDI means Strategic Defense Initiative, though I don't know all the ins and outs about it. A number of my friends are involved in secret aspects of it, but they can't tell me anything about it. I've tried to read up on it so I'd be a little more knowledgeable about it. It's interesting, and I know it's important, but what does it really matter what I think about it?

Not long ago, I started to put together a message about the "delayed stress syndrome" of Vietnam vets, but postponed it when I found that delayed stress syndrome is, in fact, symptomatic of many of today's abused wives and children. It has become a very broad problem in our society. It's more complicated than just categorizing them into one unit, such as the Vietnam vets. So I felt I would need to do a great deal more work on the subject in order to share the message.

Another reason I backed off was that when I began interviewing people to obtain different opinions, I realized that I might not live through that evening's service. I discovered that very strong, unresolved feelings existed about the Vietnam War. People of the same age, with the same backgrounds, had dramatically different interpretations of what the Vietnam War meant, ranging from: "We shoulda nuked 'em" to "Let's exhume LBJ"—incredible emotions!

We all disagree on a lot of stuff, but what does that matter? Not a whole lot, does it, in the long haul? The church ought to be a place of harmony where people concentrate on important issues of the day to fight for and about, and don't have time for unimportant issues.

Now, don't misunderstand me. I think there are some issues worth fighting for and about, issues like the necessity of the Lordship of Jesus Christ in our lives. I will argue vociferously with you about the Scripture's infallibility. I will fight about the necessity of having a born-again experience and the infilling of the Holy Spirit in order to live a Christlike life. I'll argue with you that the gathering together of the church of Jesus Christ is necessary and creates a place of growth in Him, for "no man is an island" and cannot survive alone.

There are a number of issues we are to contend for. However, if my essential heart's trait is disharmonious or argumentative, I know I won't be able to survive times of suffering. Conversely, a person with a harmonious heart is one that is able to reach out and involve others in his or her life.

I've been a believer now for nineteen years, and I've met all kinds of different Christians. I've met people whom many of us would claim aren't filled with the Holy Spirit because they don't speak in tongues (*glossolalia*). I'm sorry to disagree with you, but I'm quite convinced that they are! I've met Roman Catholic priests who are more sound doctrinally than some of the "evangelists" we hear on radio and TV. Surprising? Not really.

I've had fellowship with a Seventh Day Adventist pastor, who comes to our pastors' meetings every year. He believes that Jesus Christ is Lord. He also contends strongly for the experience of grace. I don't understand all of my friend's theology, and I may think he has strange ideas about God's laws, but guess what? We don't talk about them. I eat my Big Mac, and he eats what he wants to, and we don't mess with our differences in beliefs.

What I'm getting at is that harmonious hearts don't divide Christ's body. Big hearts find the points of agreement and dwell on them instead. Incidentally, this attitude helps to make a marriage happy too.

I contend that we are far better off finding the points that we *can* agree on and talk about. Let's face it: We aren't going to change one another's opinions very much. We may pretend to agree, but usually what happens is that the more eloquent person or the more dominant personality wins.

One psychologist proposes that every relationship—be it a church, a marriage, or a business partnership—experiences four phases.

He calls phase one the *forming phase,* where you discover all the reasons for joining together. Then he says you enter the *storming phase,* that phase wherein you discover all the reasons why you can't possibly establish an alliance. The third phase, the *norming phase,* consists of learning how to live with all the ideas and attitudes of the other person, which you previously claimed you couldn't possibly tolerate. The fourth, final phase is the *fruitful phase,* where you have finally worked through the first three phases and are now producing good results.

Unfortunately, many churches never reach the fruitful phase, and many marriages never reach that point either, because those first three phases are very agonizing. To reach the fourth phase, it takes a heart that is inclined to compromise, to tolerate, to be accepting, and to be harmonious. That's the analysis of a good heart—a quality heart that senses when to fight and when not to.

Trait Two: Be Compassionate

The second trait of a successful heart is that it is *compassionate.* It is moved to act on another's behalf on the basis of feeling for that person. But you don't just feel; you do something to right the situation.

Prior to the Christian "Operation Rescue" sit-in at Seattle area abortion clinics in the summer of 1989, our Foursquare Gospel Headquarters advised us pastors that we were free to follow our individual convictions. Further, if we wanted to spend a night in jail to defend this cause, they wouldn't fire us. This posture reflected wisdom on the part of our leaders.

A fellow pastor made an apt comment on this issue: "It's refreshing, in an age of such apathy, to see a group of people actually doing something about what they believe?"

That's a perfect definition of what compassion is all about:

actually doing something about what you feel and believe. In case you wonder where I'm coming from, I don't expect to be arrested on the abortion issue. For anyone who is arrested, I'll be glad to visit you.

Trait Three: Be Sympathetic

The third trait of a successful heart is being *sympathetic, tenderhearted*. That's a pretty simple trait. It just means being able to feel what another person feels. It's the ability to feel and to view life from another's perspective—to get into another person's skin, as it were. In fact, the Greek word *pathos* means "to feel together." Kind of neat, huh?

The Native Americans have an excellent proverb: "Don't judge a man until you have walked a mile in his moccasins." That's what the word *sympathetic* literally means: to view a problem or situation from another person's angle. It's the marvelous ability to enter another's mind and emotions and to feel that person's problem or situation right along with him or her.

Being truly sympathetic and empathetic make a congregation really great. Here's why: Christianity often creates myopic people. In fact, this is what a submissiologist (one who studies submissive behavior) calls a "cultural lift." Allow me to explain the process of myopic Christians.

Christian myopia occurs when individuals receive Christ, but come to Him with extreme needs. As the Lord meets their needs, they become better people, better employees who work harder and save more money. They tithe and don't waste their money on unnecessary items.

Before they realize it, they have a "cultural lift," because they are now beyond the needs they once had. At that juncture they often become hardhearted and desensitized to people who are still hurting and still have needs.

I would bet money that some of you reading this are possibly alcoholic or drug dependent. Now, imagine that you're visiting a church today where you're sure the people are—we're not that way in our church, but let's use the term anyway—"religious." So you figure you better not tell anyone at the service that you're an alcoholic or that you snorted cocaine last night. The cocaine made you feel like Superman, but you're kind of edgy now because you're on the down side, and a buddy talked you into coming to church with him today. Just imagine how you feel being there and thinking you're, perhaps, the only person present who isn't "clean" today. It's not a lot of fun, for you might be discovered and, worse yet, you figure you'll be rejected.

Here's another sad situation: After the last service one morning, a young woman approached me and asked whether I would pray with her about her missing mother. She's an adult child of alcoholic parents, and her mom is on skid row somewhere in Los Angeles and can't be found. I couldn't begin to feel what she must feel, because I don't know what it's like to have an alcoholic mother you still love, yet have no idea where she is. Sad!

Try this one on for size. Last Christmas Eve, I was really tired after several candlelight services, when a man whom our church had helped that spring walked up to me. I had three more Christmas services in the morning, and I just wanted to go home.

At first, I thought he was spaced out on alcohol or drugs and that the expression on his face meant he needed at least an hour's counseling. Boy, was I wrong! Upon looking into his eyes, however, I stopped thinking that.

He had been determined to work his way through the Christmas Eve crowd up to the front of the church to search me out. With tears in his eyes, he grasped my hand fervently and said with much feeling: "Thank you, Pastor Doug, for all your help this year!"

Now, that's a great heart! I don't hear that a lot, even from my own kids. While driving home, I swallowed the lump in my throat several times.

This fellow had an incredible story. The spring before, the economy had crashed down in the Oregon community where he, his wife, and their three kids had lived. They lost everything and didn't know where to turn. When someone told him there was work in Washington, they packed what they could in their old trailer and headed for the Seattle/Kirkland area. But when they arrived, they found no positions open in his teaching field, starting a downhill spiral for this unfortunate family, who were now out of food and money.

Someone had directed him to Eastside Church for help. When he told us his sad story, we could sympathize with his desperate plight. I thought to myself: *Dear Jesus, help them!*

We found a place for them to stay and helped them to get established. But as I drove home that day, I tried to imagine what it must feel like to have a wife and three kids, with no money for food and no place to live. That must be an awful feeling.

Or imagine a young child who was brought by a friend to one of our Sunday school classes. He didn't know where his daddy was, and hadn't heard from him for a long time because his dad didn't care about him. It has to be pretty hurtful for that little kid.

I guess my point is that a successful heart is one that has been trained to have the capacity to feel what others are feeling, to see life through their hurting eyes.

One of the assignments I enjoy challenging male pastors to do is to pretend that they are a woman when they come to church. Seriously, though, just imagine what it would feel like, as a woman, to know that your level of contribution to the church has already been capped because of your gender. This slight doesn't even occur to men and to pastors, because this area has always been a man's world. The guy goes to seminary and becomes a pastor and the head honcho.

I believe this is an arbitrary barrier that is not godly nor of Christ, and I have discussed this problem at length with my wife, Debbie. I feel this way because I've imagined what it would be like to be a woman a number of times. I've concluded that it would feel terrible to be limited just because of your gender. And it is morally wrong besides!

I believe that bigotry and most of the idiocy perpetrated on others would be taken care of if people would learn to look at life from another person's viewpoint. This attitude makes for great people and a great church!

Therefore, *be sympathetic. Love one another as brothers and sisters*. Before leaving this subject, let me just say that we don't get to choose our brothers and sisters. In other words, if we wanted to vote for a different brother or sister, we wouldn't get a vote. My point is that we are to love one another as brothers and sisters, knowing that we have no other recourse.

When suffering hits your life, it's very easy for you to feel as though you're the only one in pain at that moment. A sympathetic heart, however, will look around for someone else to help, which will possibly help disperse some of the pain in your own heart.

The ability to extend sympathy and empathy, I believe, brings with it a correlative capacity to accept kindness and sympathy in return. If your definition of success does not include extending empathy and sympathy to others with ease, you're using the wrong pattern. In a time of suffering, hardheartedness will make it difficult to receive the kind of help you need. This kind of independence and distancing of yourself from others will serve only to impede your grief process, as well as to exacerbate the pain and scarring that occur.

Trait Four: Be Humble

The fourth trait of a successful heart is *humility*. Being humble simply means having a realistic appraisal of yourself, not having to win all the time. Know what your place in life is and be happy with it. Don't wish that you were someone else. Don't be afraid of being fourth, tenth, seventeenth, or thirtieth down the line instead of first. Be sensitive to other persons.

One of the questions I ask prospective pastors who say they want to take on a church is "If you were not a pastor, what would you do?" If the person answers: "Well, if I weren't going to be a pastor, then I'd be rich," I crumple up the application and toss it out.

This kind of mentality astounds me. If they can't be the head honcho and boss people around, then they're going to be rich. I don't know where they get the idea that people actually listen to and act upon what their pastors say, anyway. That outlook is contrary to the gospel, because I truly believe that the Lord may call some pastors to be poor. I'm not volunteering, you understand, but He may call some of us to be poor. He may also call some of us to be only servants, who are never heard of—not in a million years.

I do believe that the Lord wants to meet our needs and that He does plan to provide for us. And I believe that the Lord rejoices when we are fruitful on His account. But I also think that people who truly want to become pastors should act on the basis of simply desiring to serve the Lord and other persons.

Trait Five: Nonretaliatory Living

The fifth trait of a successful heart is *not repaying evil with evil or an insult with an insult*. In other words, we are called to give a blessing to others so that we may inherit a blessing.

Have you noticed, throughout the book of Peter, how often he used the phrase "to this you are called"? He mentioned three or four distinctive tasks to which we have been called. Here is one of them: We are called, as believers empowered by the Holy Spirit, to bless others and not to curse them.

Let me explain, by citing a story from the Old Testament, what a blessing means. Probably the blessing you might remember most is in the story about Isaac and his twin sons, Jacob and Esau, the firstborn.

When it came time for Isaac to bestow his blessing, Jacob and his mother contrived to steal Esau's blessing (inheritance). Because Isaac was nearly blind, they figured they could fool him by dressing Jacob in a goatskin to simulate Esau's hairy body. Though Jacob's voice was higher pitched than Esau's, Isaac's initial suspicions were allayed because Jacob's arm felt hairy like Esau's, and Isaac's wife reassured him that it was Esau standing before him. So Isaac laid hands on Jacob and mistakenly conferred on him the prospering touch of God that was intended for Esau, the firstborn.

The concept of blessing originated here and its meaning has carried over to the New Testament's understanding of this word. It literally embraced all of the following meanings and attributes:

• That Jacob would succeed at all he set out to accomplish;

- That he would be affirmed and have the confidence of his destiny ending in God; and
- That Jacob's path was, in fact, acknowledged and blessed by God and lighted by His light.

Esau, on the other hand, had squandered his inheritance, his birthright, for just a bowl of stew. With great chagrin and anger, Esau fought with his brother until their later years. Even though Isaac and Esau had discovered Jacob's deceit, it couldn't be reversed because once you are blessed, you are blessed forever.

We live in a culture that thrives on curses. We get cursed on the freeway. We get cursed on the basketball court and on the football field. We hear curses on the TV and in movies.

A letter came the other day advising me to enter into deep intercessory prayer, because covens of witches were cursing pastors in our area. But what the witches don't know is that one small phrase—"the blood of Jesus"—has just taken care of that problem.

Once, when I was working on a Sunday message, it occurred to me that our society really believes in curses. Why don't we believe in blessings, which are truer and far more beneficial? Why not bless others instead of cursing them? If witches can curse people and ruin their lives, why don't we bless people and give them wonderful lives instead? For example, when you go through a store's checkout counter, you could say, "Bless you" or "God bless you" or "God be with you" or "In Jesus' name be blessed."

Debbie and I have been blessing our kids for years, and we encourage you to do it. We lay hands on the heads of each of our kids and say, very simply, "I bless you in the name of Jesus. I bless all that is in your heart to dream about and do." Our kids just soak it up. It doesn't have to be an elegant, masterful bit of rhetoric at all.

There are people all around you right now who need to be affirmed, to be blessed. We can be world-changers by using this power, this mysterious ability that God gives us to bless others. In fact, it would do both of you a world of good to hug your wife or husband and say, "I bless you in the name of Jesus."

This is one of the reasons we celebrate in the name of Jesus when we come together in church. Wouldn't it be a great attestation to God's glory if people said that they left a service feeling better than when they came? Wouldn't that be a great statement about our homes and gathering places?

When people say that, they are saying that the presence of God's blessing was there. Blessing means "to speak well of, to confer prospering intentions." By inference, it means also that we have the right to live and to dream our dreams, and our God in all His power will accomplish them through us! To that end we gather together.

And that's what Peter urged us to do. Don't be victimized. Don't retaliate, but bless and change the world.

Try it sometime. It really works. I have a friend who blesses the airplane seat he is assigned to, and he prays for the person who will occupy it after him. Wherever we are, we are to bless others.

Did you know that waitresses dislike waiting on Christians? Why? Because they don't tip worth beans; they leave a tract on salvation instead. They don't seem to know how to say "thank you." Pity.

Why are we that way? I think we, perhaps, shift our Christianity to superhuman levels and forget to keep it working in our everyday lives. If we wish to touch people's lives, we have to be kind to them. We have to be aware of people and their needs. Be sympathetic. Be compassionate. Help others when you can. Bless them.

While a friend and I were riding in a taxi the other day, he said suddenly: "God just spoke to me, Doug. He said: 'Give this cab driver $20. He's really hurting, right now, and I want you to tell him it's from Me.'"

When we reached our destination and got out, my friend paid the fare and then handed the cabbie another $20, saying: "I don't know what's going on, but God told me to give this to you. It's His way of letting you know that He knows what your needs are and that it's going to be okay."

The cabbie just broke down and cried, right there in his car, for God had taken time to speak to him through my friend.

Christianity and the gospel work best at that level. It works the worst at the radio and TV levels.

As Christians, we are called to be blessers. Some people have made a pattern of being blessers in their lives rather than cursers. That is, these people have desired to touch the dreams of others and to encourage them to see these dreams happen. People who extend blessings in prayer and by their attitude are reaching out and saying: "In the Name of Jesus receive a blessing." These are the kinds of hearts that, in their own times of need, are open to receive a blessing as well.

I think an appropriate text to cite here would be Paul's admonition in the last chapter of his letter to the Galatians: "God is not mocked. We reap what we sow" (paraphrased).

If we're committed to sowing blessings, the blessings will be returned to us in our own times of need and suffering.

Exercise

1. Have you ever evaluated and written down your definition of success?
2. Is there a tendency in your own life to define success from the outside in? If so, suffering is likely to take its toll on your life.
3. Have you made it a regular practice to extend blessings to people around you? For example, you can direct your hand toward your neighbor's house and say: "I extend the blessing of Jesus to you."
4. Have you ever thought about how the preparation of your own heart can help you to thrive in a world that, by its very nature, is filled with pain, suffering, and abnormality?

I recently picked up a book by Rabbi Harold S. Kushner titled *When Children Ask About God*. Kushner is best known for writing *When Bad Things Happen to Good People*. This is a great book for Christians. It deals with preparedness to face the true issue of pain and suffering in this world.

In chapter 4 of *When Children Ask About God*, Kushner exhorted us to watch how we use the phrase "act of God." Why is it that when things go wrong or fall apart, it is erroneously considered an act of God? I cringe when I hear this phrase used on the evening news. I was quite happy to see that Rabbi Kushner also picked up on this, giving us some valuable insights to share with kids.

Our distorted thinking in times of trouble can effectively block our hearts from being properly prepared for suffering. For example, to ask why God allowed some tragedy to happen is to miss the point of the true condition of this world.

Rabbi Kushner told the story of a young Jewish congregant who told the fifteen-year-old son of a woman who had just died of cancer that God took his mother because God needed her in heaven more than He did down here. This put God in a bad light by presenting Him as the divine kidnapper.

Kushner has given us some helpful points so that we may discover the true acts of God, which he outlines as follows.

1. *God places order and stability in the world.* That is why, when instability or suffering happen, we feel abnormal. It is obvious to us all that that is not an act of God.

2. *God has helped us to discover ways to minimize tragedies.* This is reality. For instance, a drive resides within all of us to minimize the risk of plane crashes or to enhance safety through building codes, and so on. Something in us tells us that we must make the world safer. This is a true act of God.

3. *God gives us the resolve to rebuild our lives after experiencing a disaster.* This is another true act of God in the midst of tragedy. I think we observed this after the last great earthquake in San Francisco on October 17, 1989. The news was filled with stories about people who willingly thrust their lives into rebuilding their community.

In the face of suffering, these are the true acts of God. But understanding and recognizing these acts is most available to us when our hearts have been prepared for times of suffering.

Thus, the truly successful heart daily practices and prepares for the kind of success that dust and rust can't corrupt. These are the traits that are deposited in heavenly realms!

Chapter 10

Getting Along with Yourself
(1 Peter 3:13–22)

. . . Having a good conscience, that when they defame you as evildoers, those who revile your good conduct in Christ may be ashamed. For it is better, if it is the will of God, to suffer for doing good than for doing evil. (1 Peter 3:16–17)

Facing suffering with joy, Peter contended, comes down to one issue: Am I suffering for doing good, or am I suffering because I deserve it?

I suppose this is the acid test of our endurance of the pain we confront. Praise God that there is forgiveness for those times when we suffer because of our own wrong actions. This passage suggests there are certainly times when we suffer, as well, for doing righteous things. Let's face it, though, this kind of suffering is an incredible gift—one that we rarely get to experience in America.

As I was riding with a group of men from our church to a prison for outreach ministry one night, I was surprised at how much subtle persecution those men faced on their jobs. One engineer commented about my sweatshirt as we headed into the penitentiary. On it was inscribed: "Born to Choose" and "Jesus Is My Lord" in bright, red letters.

He said, "Boy, I'd never wear that where I work."

"Why not?" I asked.

"Well, they'd eat me alive. They already know I'm a Christian, and they're just waiting for some reason to ride me. I really have to be on my toes around those guys. I can't afford to go in there with anything bothering me. One of the things I appreciate about that environment is that I'm always in tune with Jesus Christ. They're just waiting for me to fall so they can eat me up."

Another friend chimed in, "Pastor, you just don't know what the real world is like."

I thought I did, and I have to admit that I was mildly insulted by that comment. However, I did have my eyes opened to the fact that there is far more persecution on a subtle, one-to-one basis than you could ever imagine.

Peter said that this kind of suffering would make us strong. It is also the kind of suffering that every Christian ought to aspire to, if it is the will of God, for it's a better way to live.

I think Peter highlighted some of the worst kinds of pain and suffering in this chapter. I've become convinced that the worst kind of pain we suffer is the pain that is natural to a bad conscience.

Clear-hearted suffering is a Christian's aim. But often when pressure comes from without, and we know from within that we have failed, the agony is almost unbearable.

Guilt is not a legitimate emotion that God wants to send to any of us, but I don't believe a pained conscience is the same as guilt. Guilt is a feeling of being condemned. In the Gospel of John, chapter 3, we're told emphatically that God did not send His Son into the world to condemn the world. Essentially, John boiled sin down to one issue in his teaching: Have we accepted Christ? That is the only guilt point God will legitimatize. Of course, we know that multitudes of sins exemplify and declare our rejection of Him; hence, they carry His continuing wrath and our continuing bad conscience and guilt.

Nonetheless, I cringe at how often the church uses a negative emotion like guilt to motivate people. The Bible is very clear that Christ never used guilt to motivate. He used love!

Yet, I think most of us would agree that the most painful kind of suffering we can experience is a conscience that has been injured, leaving us with the inability to live with ourselves, especially when things are falling apart.

I recently received a lengthy call from a young woman in our church. In anguish, she described the terrible guilt feelings she had agonized over for years, stemming from an abortion she'd had when she was nineteen. She had never come to terms with this guilt. Sobbing, she shared with me how she tried to bury her guilt feelings about ending that little life growing in her.

"Pastor, I have nightmares still and often see myself going into that clinic. I know I silenced the voice of God, because He told me not to do that, and I did it anyway. I've worried ever since whether I could still hear Him."

I don't think it was mere coincidence that the Holy Spirit was having me prepare a message on this subject at the time. I described to her how her conscience worked and how to bring it into proper repair so that it would function properly again.

At the time, she was having extreme difficulty at her job as well. At her job she was apparently the target of much sexual harassment, combined with physical abuse from her husband. For years, she'd been telling herself that she deserved this kind of treatment. After all, she thought, she couldn't make good decisions.

The guilt of her past wrong actions caused her more suffering inside, however. On her own, she managed to come to grips with some of her pain without resorting to lengthy, expensive therapy. But because she had judged herself unworthy of love from the time of her abortion, she was willing to assume any kind of abuse on the outside to somehow diminish or drown out her agony within.

After we prayed together, she discovered a new joy, a new sense of forgiveness. Forgiveness is always the beginning point for recovery in these matters. The receiving and giving of forgiveness is what resensitizes and fine-tunes our conscience so it will function properly again.

My parting words to her were, "You deserve all that Jesus died for. He died for your forgiveness. He died for your healing, and He's giving back to you your real life. You can now hear His voice again."

I'm glad to report that this young woman's internal suffering ended when her conscience became healed. She was also able to return to her marriage relationship and demand that their problems be straightened out. She realized that she wasn't the cause of the sexual harassment directed toward her at work, so she put her foot down and demanded that her supervisors clean up the situation. They did.

Some weeks later I heard from her, "Pastor, there is such a new boldness in my life, now that I've dealt with the matter I had submerged and carried around improperly all those years. Thanks so much for your help!"

We both rejoiced in her newfound freedom and that the extra baggage of guilt had been lifted. Do you also see that the healing of her conscience brought with it self-worth, self-confidence, and self-assuredness as well?

HOW OUR CONSCIENCE WORKS

The Hebrew equivalent of "conscience" conjures up a humorous picture in their phrase "the little man inside." This brings to mind the cartoon depicting a character with a little angel on one shoulder and a little devil on the other, each attempting to persuade the guy to behave in a particular way.

Paul referred to this part of us as the "inner man," so the word picture of "the little man inside" is a good description. By reading the Scriptures, you will see that the word *conscience* is used to describe the part of us that is most sensitive to God's pleasure or displeasure with us. It is, of course, the base and center of our moral and ethical gyroscope. It's that inner voice we listen to—or don't listen to. God's marvelous, divine provision gave every person on earth a conscience. It can be healthy. It can be in disrepair. It can be overactive, or it can be untuned (insensitive). Let's go through a brief outline of the different conditions in which we can find our conscience.

Biblically Tuned Conscience

The Bible suggests four kinds of conscience that may abide in us at different seasons of our lives. We shall call the first one a "biblically tuned conscience." This kind has been schooled by Scripture to feel good about what God feels good about, and to feel bad about what God feels bad about. That's a pretty simple concept to grasp.

You have all probably, at one time, listened to a radio that was not set squarely on a station's radio frequency. When the needle is slightly off the station, what do you get? Distortion. It's fuzzy-sounding and full of static. Though you hear some sort of radio signal, you don't get clear reception. Then, when you adjust the tuner, the signal comes in clearly.

Okay, a biblically tuned conscience is one that has the Bible set squarely on the signal. So when you read the Bible consistently, you are, in fact, keeping your conscience in tune. Paul said for us to live richly—that is, to enrich our minds and hearts by listening to and reading Scripture.

Your inner gyroscope will automatically be fine-tuned. I would encourage you not to emphasize any single section of Scripture, however. Spending a great deal of time in the Old Testament, for instance, can tilt your inner dial off course. Likewise, spending too much time in the book of James can tilt your inner dial as well. I like to spread out my reading in the Word by reading some proverbs, the Gospels, the writings of Paul, the psalms and, occasionally, some of the Pentateuch. These all help to keep me squarely on my dial.

Violated or Injured Conscience

The second kind of conscience is a "violated or injured conscience." What often happens if we don't deal biblically with sin (inane things that we do, anything counter to what we should do), we realize that we're wrong and our conscience becomes pricked or injured. A low-grade presence of guilt then fills the entirety of our being and we deface or disfigure our self-esteem. That's one of the horrors of sin. We don't escape the effects of having committed even a single sin. Each one extracts its toll. We actually deface and damage our dignity as well by each sin.

Soap companies are great at taking advantage of guilt. For instance, the TV ad about the man with a ring around his shirt collar registers consternation on his wife's face. Clamping her hand to her face in shocked disbelief, she says, "Oh, my gosh! What do they think of me?"

Each time that ad runs, Debbie says, "Why doesn't he wash his own shirt, then, if it makes him feel so bad?"

That would be one solution to the problem. Merchandisers are really shrewd at taking advantage of our feeling of not quite measuring up in the eyes of others.

A wonderful thing happened recently. A young woman, realizing she would be too late for our 8:30 A.M. service, decided to have coffee at McDonald's and catch the next service. At first, she hesitated about taking her Bible in with her, but then she decided to.

Shortly after she started openly reading it at the table, another young woman walked over and said very wretchedly: "I've lost my soul. Would you help me?"

This young Bible-reading woman then gladly shared the message of Jesus with this "lost" woman and brought her to our 11:00 service, where she accepted the Lord. Evidently, through serious personal failings, she had lost both her husband and her kids. Because of this, she felt she had lost her soul as well, and her conscience tortured her constantly. That morning, Jesus freed her from her heavy burden and is now allowing her to live with herself again. Hallelujah!

Seared Conscience

The third kind of conscience is a "seared conscience." This is the worst kind to have. A good example of this conscience would be Ted Bundy, the serial murderer. Eventually, what happens is that a person sins so much that he or she totally silences the "inner man." It's like having calluses on one's conscience. In the Old Testament, it was called a "hardened" heart.

I have calluses on the tips of my fingers from playing guitar. If a callus becomes thick enough, it won't even feel a lighted match touching it. Likewise, if we silence the voice and anguished cry of God the Father, we actually don't feel bad any more about doing sinful things. In *The Problem of Pain* (chap. 4), C. S. Lewis stated:

> In trying to extirpate shame, we have broken down one of the ramparts of the human spirit, madly exulting in the work, as the Trojans exulted, when they broke down their walls and pulled the horse into Troy. I do not know that there is anything to be done but to set about rebuilding as soon as we can. It is mad work to remove hypocrisy by removing the temptation to hypocrisy: The "frankness" of people who have sunk below shame is a very cheap frankness.

That's what is so idiotic about someone's saying: "Well, I went ahead and did it anyway, because I didn't feel bad about it."

Ordinarily, our conscience is our ultimate guide about right and wrong. However, when we sear our conscience, we don't feel bad anymore about matters we should feel bad about.

Weak Conscience

The fourth kind of conscience is a "weak conscience," an overactive one. We feel guilty about small, unimportant matters, like an opinion or a cultural preference.

For example, when we were in a church service in Poland recently, all the men sat on one side of the sanctuary and all the women sat on the other side (very much like a Jewish synagogue in the days of Jesus). We thought that was stupid, so we had the people intermingle. At first, many of the Polish women had difficulty with that, because they felt guilty sitting with their husbands and sons, when they had no reason to. Of course, this was not justified, and eventually they got over it.

We can also feel bad about things that are totally stupid. In fact, much of our compulsive behavior stems from a conscience that is overstimulated. For instance, the adult children of alcoholics often assume responsibility for attitudes and happenings that are not their own; their consciences are overstimulated.

This constitutes a weak conscience. It needs to be retrained and schooled according to biblical principles. Because certain things and events are not our responsibility, we have no business feeling bad about them. They are someone else's problem.

While speaking with the woman who had the abortion problem, I described the four kinds of conscience to her. I told her: "Let's take a moment now and bring your conscience in contact with the Bible. Let it be biblically tuned, in other words. Have you asked Jesus to free you from guilt?"

"Yes," she replied.

"Do you believe He did that?" I asked.

"Yes, I do," she answered.

"But now you're telling me you still feel bad."

"Yes."

"Okay, let me explain to you what receiving forgiveness is. It's having the penalty of sin removed from you. Receiving forgiveness now allows a reinterpretation of your past. Believe me, God is not against you; He is for you. He has forgiven you, and He will not look for ways to punish you. Now, we can interpret your past as being free from the threat of punishment. Second, your new status, because of God's forgiveness, is as though you'd never committed that sin. That means that God does not define you by your sin. So if you still feel bad, that's a feeling of remorse and regret."

Wouldn't it be great if Jesus erased our memory every time we came to Him for forgiveness? But let's forget before-and-after-Christ distinctions, because we've all sinned plenty since Christ brought new birth to us. But wouldn't it be wonderful if every time we knelt down and asked for forgiveness, our recollection of that trespass was wiped out also?

There's just one little problem with that process, however. Jesus would also have to wipe the recollection slates clean of all the persons we had sinned against, which would create quite a different situation. We would all be mindless people, wandering around like zombies, perhaps, so that wouldn't really work out. Actually, if you think about it a moment, you may see that it's very practical and logical for us to be forgiven and to experience guiltlessness, yet still feel regret—even remorse—over our mistakes.

There is a wide gulf between emotional pain and true guilt. When we are faithful to confess our sins to God and ask for His forgiveness, we become guiltless, because God is for us. When we are forgiven and walk in that forgiveness, we are experiencing and practicing what is known as "strategic forgetfulness."

In other words, there are some things we shouldn't even try to remember, or even try to get over. We should just forget them, because the Bible says that's what Jesus has done with our sins. As far as the east is from the west is the distance that He's removed our sins from us!

The apostle Peter suggested that when times get rough (and they will), when we're experiencing less-than-optimal circumstances, we don't have much to fear from those circumstances or from those opposed to us or from an injurious reaction of life. What we must be concerned about is the condition of our hearts. Is our conscience clear? Peter suggested that a clear conscience will give us empowerment in the face of a fallen and less-than-perfect world so that we can courageously face less-than-optimal circumstances.

Your conscience is clear when your heart is right before the Lord. That is, the "little man" inside you is walking in stride with God's will and the warning light on your "dashboard" isn't bleeping on and off. When that oil light flashes, you have to stop at a service station and get oil, or at some point your car will quit. It's the same thing with your conscience. Its warning light signifies a problem here . . . a problem there. Listen to it before your whole system blows.

Having the boldness to face suffering defiantly is an important issue to the believer, and it was an important issue to Peter. While addressing the people he loved, he came up with several key steps to help them stand securely and boldly in a world that was falling apart around them.

Peter listed several steps to keep a conscience that is strong and feeding the boldness that would allow them to defy those elements of suffering that could have possibly weakened their declaration of faith while struggling in a fallen world.

1. Make sure you practice daily forgiveness to free your conscience.
2. Know that you have access to and have been received by God.
3. Remember your baptism.

And who *is* he who will harm you if you become followers of what is good? But even if you should suffer for righteousness' sake, *you are* blessed. *"And do not be afraid of their threats, nor be troubled."* But sanctify the Lord God in your hearts, and always *be* ready to *give* a defense to everyone who asks you a reason for the hope that is in you, with meekness and fear; having a good conscience, that when they defame you as evildoers, those who revile your good conduct in Christ may be ashamed. For *it is* better, if it is the will of God, to suffer for doing good than for doing evil. For Christ also suffered once for sins, the just for the unjust, that He might bring us to God, being put to death in the flesh but made alive by the Spirit, by whom also He went and preached to the spirits in prison, who formerly were disobedient when once the longsuffering of God waited in the days of Noah, while *the* ark was being prepared, in which a few, that is, eight souls, were saved through water. There is also an antitype which now saves us, *namely* baptism (not the removal of the filth of flesh, but the answer of a good conscience toward God), through the resurrection of Jesus Christ, who has gone into heaven and is at the right hand of God, angels and authorities and powers having been made subject to Him. (1 Peter 3:13–22)

Key Number One

Perhaps your conscience is dirty. If you aren't feeling good about yourself because you've violated God's will, and the "little man" inside you is reminding you about it, or you've confronted a situation in which you're suffering, but your life is falling apart anyway, you probably lack confidence before God at that point, which could be your only hope in facing and surviving the suffering that you're experiencing.

There is a remedy. God hasn't left you hopeless, even when you find yourself in inner despair. However, I believe that it's absolutely inane to think that God is somehow dealing with you or judging you when things go wrong. I don't understand how this erroneous concept was included in church theology, for it is *not* New Testament doctrine. The real reason we get ourselves into tough straits is because we make stupid decisions—nothing more, nothing less.

The other day my car collided with the car of someone from my church. It was a frightening experience and an unpleasant situation, but I'm certain that God wasn't trying to teach either of us anything. What I did learn from it was to concentrate on my driving. I learned not to let my mind wander and to keep my eyes on the road and traffic, or I may injure someone.

Let's face it. Life is made up of many situations that are less than ideal. Things do go wrong from time to time, regardless of what you do or don't do. Children do have problems. Money does become scarce. People do make stupid, unwise decisions. The stock market does go bad. That's the nature of life.

Consequently, if you're not clear about whether you're solid before the Lord, the first thought you grab onto is that God's mad at you and that's why this happened. This erroneous line of reasoning, however, won't bring you confident solutions. It's not God. It's you!

That's why Peter stressed: "Be prepared! Have your heart in such a clean condition that you can explain to anyone your hope of salvation at any given moment."

On Mondays, after three Sunday services, I'm shot. When the adrenalin drains out of my system, I collapse in a heap and don't crawl out until about Tuesday night. Well, one Monday Debbie and I went shopping at a nearby mall. I was getting tired and figured we'd seen enough. My idea of shopping is that I decide what I want to buy and buy it. Just looking at stuff and not buying it is for the birds.

Well, Debbie likes to look. She never buys anything; she just looks. Though the money in her purse is screaming to be let out, she won't spend it.

Debbie wanted to look at "just one more thing." You're familiar with this scenario, I'm sure. Most of the time I enjoy shopping with her, because it's usually interesting, and I'm normally a nice, kind person. However, this particular Monday evening I decided I'd had enough of shopping for one evening.

Brusquely, I said, "We're not looking at anything else, Deb."

"Oh, yes! Let's go over there, Doug."

"Now look! I'm tired! Okay, I'm going home, and you can get home any way you want!"

"No, Doug, just one more thing, please."

"Look. You're being really selfish!" I could tell by the expression on her face that she disagreed with that opinion.

"I'm selfish?"

We were in the midst of getting the "selfish" matter settled when someone from our church spoke up behind us: "Well, hello, Pastor Doug and Debbie!"

Instantly, I was chagrined, embarrassed, and felt guilty. I sure didn't want to talk to anyone right then, because I was being less than a man of God at the time. In fact, there's a word for what I was being that we won't discuss here.

Of course, Debbie and I immediately slipped into our roles of the "happy couple." At the same time, we gave each other the I'm-going-to-kill-you-when-we-get-home look that couples engage in. We exchanged small talk with the person for a few minutes, and then went on our way.

I share this episode to demonstrate how a bad conscience doesn't allow us to interact properly with others. If our conscience is off center, we won't make it through suffering times. The issue is not what can happen to us without our conscience. The issue is, rather: What's the condition of our heart? That's the acid test of being able to make it through life's rough situations.

Key Number Two

"Christ died for sins, once, for all." Peter's language here asserts that Christ did not die as an Old Testament sacrifice of many times over. No, Christ was required to die only once, and because He was the perfect sacrifice, He didn't have to repeat the procedure.

In the courts of the Gentile kings, one of the staff persons was a fellow called "the giver of access." This person brought new guests in and introduced them to the king. It was a very prestigious position. He usually had to be bribed, or you had to be a pal of his or in his good graces to be presented to the king. Jesus is our Giver of Access into the throne room of God.

This steward was the appointment secretary for the king. If you wanted to see the king, you had to apply to this giver of access. If he liked you, you were granted an audience. If he didn't, you were escorted to the proverbial door.

This phrase for "that he might bring us to God" was used in this passage to point out that Jesus became our Giver of Access. This means that when we turn to Him with an impaired conscience and say, "Lord, by Your precious blood, please come and free me and forgive me," we are not only forgiven, but also are now authorized to enter the very Presence of God Almighty Himself, with both joy and a clear conscience.

Let me explain the logic presented here. If you have had dinner with the president of the United States, it doesn't matter if the mayor of Seattle canceled out on breakfast with you. Likewise, if you have access to God's presence through Christ, it doesn't matter what anyone else says to you or about you. It doesn't matter that you've failed in your job, your marriage, or in your behavior, for the supreme fact is that because of Christ's intercession on your behalf, Father God accepts you into His Presence. Because of that unalterable fact, you can have the confidence to know that God the Father accepts you. The Bible states categorically: "If God *is* for us, who *can* be against us?" (Rom. 8:31). No one! That's why we have a strong conscience—because God has accepted us.

Key Number Three

Peter drew a parallel here between Noah's ark and the church. In his mind, the outpouring of the flood rains and baptism were related. He said, first, that a good conscience comes from being prepared by having your conscience freed. It follows, then, that if you don't practice to clear your conscience on a daily basis, you won't be prepared to face suffering.

Second, he said we would be ready to face suffering by knowing that we have access to God. Christ died but once for everybody's sins, and He lives now as our Giver of Access. By our friendship with Him, we have confidence and courage to approach our Father King to address any situation and pain we may be facing. Third, he says that water baptism is the basis of confidence that leads to boldness.

For our conscience, water baptism is vital to confidence building. Yeah, I know. As soon as I mention baptism, I can sense what you're thinking: *Oh, gads! Not that old song again!*

Now, I admit that baptism is a rather strange practice. In fact, when I received the Lord, water baptism seemed like the dopiest practice I'd ever heard of. But when I got baptized, I suddenly realized that it was the flip side of dopey. It's a *powerful phenomenon!* In this passage, baptism is presented as the seal of a good conscience.

The Greek word Peter used here is *eprotema,* "to seal." It is a legal term and was the "oath unto death" that Roman soldiers pledged when they entered the emperor's service. In business dealings in that era, the *eprotema* was included at the end of every contract, not unlike exchanging the marriage vow of "until death do us part." Verbal assent to any Roman contractual agreement was as binding as anything written—quite unlike today's business dealings.

Baptism becomes the seal of our conscience, because both our entire being and the entire world now know where we stand. No ambivalence is present. We are *for* Jesus Christ!

Quite often, I'm asked about baptizing infants. I've reached the conclusion that both sides of that issue have an equal basis for argument. Our church's tradition is to dunk people in a tank, so if you get baptized around here, you can bet on getting wet.

One woman who had never seen a baptism asked, "What will I look like when I come out of the tank, Pastor?"

I replied, "You'll look utterly ridiculous. Your hair will be sopping wet and hanging in strings, and your clothes will cling to your body like static electricity, but it will be the most marvelous experience of your life, because you'll be making a stand for Jesus!"

When you are baptized, you commit your life to Christ. At that moment, Christ signs a contract with you, and He frees you on the basis of your confession in the Name of Jesus.

If you've never been baptized, allow me to encourage you to do so soon. It will be not only one of the great highlights of your life, but also one of the greatest strengtheners your conscience can acquire. When rough times hit, you will need a strong, biblically based conscience. At those rough times, you may need to look back over time and restate what you said the day you were baptized: "On this day I gave my life to Jesus."

I know of countless numbers of believers, struggling with issues in their lives, who, when they were baptized in water, came to tell me: "Man, my life has taken a whole, new turn!" or "Man, my life has turned completely around!"

Peter told us that it isn't the water. It isn't washing dirt off. It's what has been stated in the spiritual realm—that is, you've made a statement that says: "This is where I stand!" Your conscience then latches onto that as an anchor in times of trouble.

CONCLUSION

For the Christian the issue of suffering isn't *whether* we will suffer. The issue is what *kind* of suffering will we face—the kind we deserve or the kind that comes from doing what is right? Even if we deserve the suffering that comes our way, we still have access through our Giver of Access to forgiveness and boldness to approach God the Father.

For the Christian facing suffering, the issue is not how one will maneuver one's exterior world. The issue is what's happening inside. Christians do, and will, face suffering as all humans do. Yet, Christians are offered a boldness, a forthrightness, and a courage with it—and they are strengthened from the inner person out. Now, let's review how to access this inner strength:

1. Understand that our lives are committed to the will of God, and remember that the will of God itself may, at times, be painful.
2. Take great care in nurturing and feeding the "little man" inside us—our conscience. It is a vital source of strength when everything in the world seems to be crumbling around us.
3. Remember that Christ died once, for all sins, for all peoples. We are made alive by the Holy Spirit because of Christ's sacrifice.
4. Our loud and bold proclamation of Christ, through our public declaration of water baptism, fortifies us and gives us boldness.
5. We have access to and acceptance by our Father God through Jesus Christ, the Giver of Access. He has made a way for us to go to Him in the middle of any crisis, because we have been freed and forgiven.

We are people who live in the reality that everything is subjected to the Name of our Lord Jesus Christ—the Name that is above every name.

In *The Lion, the Witch, and the Wardrobe,* C. S. Lewis wrote some prose that gives us pause to realize the power and strength of that Name. It is important that Christians understand that this Name, Jesus, to which we come, does cause the world around us to stand in submission to it!

> "They say Aslan is on the move—perhaps he has already landed."
> And now a very curious thing happened. None of the children knew who Aslan was any more than you do; but the moment the Beaver had spoken these words everyone felt quite different. Perhaps it has sometimes happened to you in a dream that someone says something which you don't understand but in the dream it feels as if it had some enormous meaning—either a terrifying one which turns the whole dream into a nightmare or else a lovely meaning too lovely to put into words, which makes the dream so beautiful that you remember it all your life and are always wishing you could get into that dream again. It was like that now. At the name of Aslan each one of the children felt something jump in his inside. Edmund felt a sensation of mysterious horror. Peter felt suddenly brave and adventurous. Susan felt as if some delicious smell or delightful strain of music had just floated by her. And Lucy got the feeling you have when you wake up in the morning and you realise that it is the beginning of the holidays or the beginning of summer.

Aslan is, of course, the figure of Christ. It is the name of Jesus, to which we go in times of suffering, that causes our own hearts and every realm around us to stand alert and at attention. His name on the lips of His people definitely affects the way we live. This is the boldness that causes us to thrive in the midst of suffering.

The most important person to be able to live with in a time of suffering is yourself. God has provided ample means to make certain that is possible.

Chapter 11

Have You Checked the Clock?
(1 Peter 4:1–11)

The Christian perspective of suffering is an eternal perspective. It is from the vantage point of God's will.

Every once in a while, I fly in and out of Sea-Tac Airport. If it's a clear day when I'm returning home, it's fun for me to anticipate which area the plane will fly over. On many occasions, I'm able to look down and see our church site or my home.

Several years ago, when we were investigating the possibility of purchasing twenty acres for our new church site, I was returning home from a trip, and the landing flight pattern we followed flew right over both our old, existing site and the twenty acres we were attempting to buy.

At the time we were planning to purchase this land, it seemed like such a large step for us. I was really quite apprehensive about it and, in fact, was one of the less aggressive members in the decision-making process.

As I looked down from the plane, I had a heavenly vantage point. At first, that twenty acres looked quite insignificant. But then, I noticed the number of large housing developments and apartment buildings surrounding our potential site. It dawned on me that there were many broken, hurting families with intense spiritual needs in that community circling our property-to-be. From my perch, several large, nearby shopping malls caught my eye, which seemed to dwarf our little project.

That day, the Lord allowed me to have one of those serendipitous gifts of faith that He extends to us. My heavenly viewpoint helped me to realize that, with God, all things are possible. Viewed from His standpoint, what seems to be so large and painful for us is really no big deal at all for God.

Suffering for the Christian is understood to be bound by time and space, which is a very important perspective. Paul's loud proclamation in 1 Corinthians 15 sounds the battle cry of the eternal, when he asks: "Death where is thy sting?" Death is likewise limited to time and space.

Christians are prepared to understand pain and suffering, because we understand that time is running out on suffering, which is not eternal. It will have its end. The book of Revelation predicts that the day will come when all tears will dry and all fear will be assuaged.

Pain and suffering have been incarcerated in time and space. Christians understand this. Christians also understand that we have been freed from the limitations of time and space to live from an eternal viewpoint.

Several years ago, Barry McGuire, the famous Christian folk singer, performed for our congregation. On this occasion, he shared not only his testimony, but a fascinating story as well.

One afternoon Barry told us, when he was reflecting about sin, death, and eternity, he asked Jesus: "Lord, why did You make time?"

Though the Lord didn't reply in a booming voice from heaven, Barry did hear a quiet voice inside him answer: "I made time so sin wouldn't fill eternity."

Time is a limiting factor to all that is outside of God's will. Yet, eternal life has invaded the realm of time and space with the living reality of Jesus Christ.

I thought that was a fascinating revelation the Lord shared with Barry. Sin and suffering are imprisoned within the framework of time. Christians can have a new perspective, because our time and space have been intruded upon by eternal qualities.

This is the perspective that Peter encouraged Christ's followers and friends to grasp. We may experience suffering, but time is running out on suffering, yet time will never run out on believers.

I really don't know what pain or suffering you may be facing at this time. I would guess, since we're all human, that there is at least some level of discomfort or less-than-optimal circumstances in your life.

I find a great deal of joy in reminding myself in tight spots that time is running out on that problem, but it isn't running out on me. The fact is that I'm going to outlive every problem I've ever had. I'm going to last longer than any suffering. I will outlive every disease, because I've received the gift of eternal life!

> Therefore, since Christ suffered for us in the flesh, arm yourselves also with the same mind, for he who has suffered in the flesh has ceased from sin, that he no longer should live the rest of *his* time in the flesh for the lusts of men, but for the will of God. For we *have spent* enough of our past lifetime in doing the will of the Gentiles—when we walked in licentiousness, lusts, drunkenness, revelries, drinking parties, and abominable idolatries. In regard to these, they think it strange that you do not run with *them* in the same flood of dissipation, speaking evil of *you*. They will give an account to Him who is ready to judge the living and the dead. For this reason the gospel was preached also to those who are dead, that they might be judged according to men in the flesh, but live according to God in the spirit. (1 Peter 4:1–6)

The Bible is not only the book that we study; it is the book that the Holy Spirit uses to study us. In our interaction with Scripture and with the public preaching of the Word, our heart condition is studied continually. Peter suggested that believers pause for a moment to allow the Word to study their use of time.

As Hebrews 4:12 states: "It is the Word of God that divides us into soul and spirit and into bone and marrow, and separates the flesh and the soul from the spiritual life that the Lord wants to release in us" (paraphrased).

You probably remember as well the cry of the prophet Jeremiah that God's Word is like a fire and like a hammer. No one can stand in the face of it.

I have found that there are epochs in all of our lives. Certain issues are vital and urgent to our spiritual growth as we pass from one stage of life to another.

For example, between the ages of eighteen and twenty-three, there are specific topics that are not only interesting but vital to our spiritual growth. Then, from the age of twenty-three to thirty, we enter into our vocations and establish our lives with some degree of permanence. Other issues also come to bear upon us at that time. As we move through this phase, we ask questions about still other issues, and the Word of God is able to address these.

We hear a great deal about mid-life crises. Both men and women are subject to them. When we hit the ages of thirty-eight to forty-five, we wake up one morning with the stark realization that about half of the time allocated to us is gone. Time is a vital resource that has been extended to us. Peter told his friends and fellow followers of Christ not to forget this.

Not long ago, a businessman visited our church. He'd been a close friend of a pastor who had been very successful and had led several hundred people. This man had been touched by our morning worship time, and he caught me afterwards. He was quite broken as he related this sad story: "Hi, pastor. I'm visiting here today. My pastor, who is a very close friend, has done a terrible thing. Last week he stood up before our congregation and said that he was married to the wrong woman! They had been married thirteen years. He just wanted to be released from his pastorate to go find God's will."

I think we can all agree that this would be a painful experience for any congregation to face. Reeling under this blow, that congregation felt betrayed (and so they were). It doesn't make a whole lot of sense.

Having just heard this story secondhand, I couldn't give the visitor a thorough diagnosis, but I suggested that his pastor may have been facing a mid-life crisis. I've seen it many times in the helping professions as well as in businessmen. Women are no less susceptible to the rigors of seeing time run out of the hourglass of life that God has given them.

Emotions turn upside down. Questions fill our minds: What could I have been doing if I wasn't doing this? Did I miss God way back then? Is it possible to start all over? Doing what?

It's a harsh discovery to realize that life's mobility has been stripped from us by the sheer responsibilities with which God has gifted us. The fear of insignificance is probably one of the greater emotions that fills the hearts of intelligent, thinking Christians.

Peter has an antidote for this particular time disease: a heavenly perspective. Our lives aren't over just because the sand drips its final grains from our hourglass. Our lives are eternal. What we are at that time will only begin to be revealed in wondrous ways.

Peter's concern was that when a Christian sees his or her hourglass running out of sand, the Christian would not turn to immediate gratification or to rapid attempts to recover an adolescent dream or evade the responsibilities that become part and parcel of one's life in Christ.

I've found that when we are led spiritually, we ask a number of questions. For example, younger Christians ask important questions, such as: How do I know what God's will is for my education? How do I know where God wants me to live? Should I stay single or get married? What is my gift in Christ? What kinds of entertainment should I bring into my life?

Then, for those of us who are establishing our vocations, there are questions like these: Am I choosing the right vocation? Do I want this promotion? Do I want to move to another city in this career? Should I buy a house or keep on renting? Should I invest my money? If so, where? In what? Is there an opportunity for advancement, or am I in a dead-end job? Do I enjoy working in this field, or am I already bored and unhappy?

Some of you reading this may be moving into your "twilight" years. As you look retrospectively at your past life and at the lesser span ahead, you may ask questions like: What is God's will for my life now in response to the amount of time I've already lived and have left? Should I retire? When? Where? Should I start a second career? If so, in what field? Should I just relax, travel, and vegetate? Do I have enough money to live on and to handle any health problems that may arise? Do I have enough health insurance? What kind of extra health coverage should I buy? Should I buy long-term care insurance? Medicare gap insurance? Have I made wise investments? Should I invest any future surplus funds? If so, in what?

Researchers say that there is one topic that remains a primary concern for believers throughout their lives: the impact of their lives on others. I suggest that, though it's defined differently for the Christian, every human being is concerned about this. Our entire lives can be summed up with this one, basic, underlying concern: Are our lives affecting others for good or bad?

This need fills every stage of our lives. This question can be answered adequately only in a living, vital relationship with Christ. The answer to this question will determine whether we will thrive or be submerged under the sufferings and disappointments in this time capsule in which we live. This question can be summed up by asking the following: Am I doing what will count the most with the years I have been allotted? Is my life having a beneficial impact and meaning? Frankly, is my life even worth living?

I believe that your time perspective plus living in the awareness of God's Presence and the proximity of His will determine how successfully you survive in a deranged world.

LIVING ACCOUNTABLY

Life's major resource is time. Anything is easier to obtain than time. Material objects are easier to acquire than time, because they can always be rustled up somehow. But once time flees, it cannot be retrieved again.

Peter sent a note of alarm to his followers in 4:2 when he said: "He no longer should live the rest of his time in the flesh for the lusts of men, but for the will of God."

The Scriptures invite us to analyze our own hearts. Have we allowed the sheer pressure of the prevailing mentality around us to determine how we shall use our time? Or have we assumed the perspective of that prevailing mentality?

A good friend of mine retired when he was fifty-five years old after having successfully operated four businesses at once.

One day I asked him, "How on earth can you run four businesses at once with any degree of competence?"

Ollie answered: "You don't. You attempt to, but you usually do two jobs well and two very poorly. But you discover, after you've lived for a while, that the price is too high." With a sparkle in his eyes, he added, "The Lord did teach me one thing, though: I'll never get time back. These businesses were chewing up a resource that will never come back. The prevailing mentality of the world today is to use credit to get more faster. The one who gets the most the quickest wins the race."

Reality is that true life is never gained that quickly. The time-pressure disease of this world has destroyed many believers, and their emotional and spiritual equilibria have been lost forever.

My friend continued, with a hint of admonition in his tone: "Doug, remember that your life is a gift that God has given you. You have only so many years. Even in serving Him, make certain that you take time to enjoy Him—to see life from His perspective. I thank God that I caught myself when I still had some years left to spend on what He wanted me to do."

I was fascinated by what he said and the wisdom he shared with me, and I took particular note of his concluding comment.

REVIEW

1. What is your time awareness as a Christian?
2. Have you evaluated your time from the perspective of what is God's will? Or has the peer pressure of this world and its prevailing mentality shaped your view of time?
3. Have you ever taken an assessment of what you're investing your time in? This could give you a key regarding your time perspective.

Suffering can be viewed as a gift to remind us that we are living in a time capsule. Between the ages of eighteen and twenty-five, most of us believe we're invincible. Perhaps mid-life crisis is a gift from God, and we don't recognize it as such.

That's when we face our disappointments, when we face the reality that we have limited options. It is at this point that we come to terms with our true living priorities. Sometimes it can come through the loss of a loved one or a business collapse. Or a dead-end road in our career can bring a kind of agony, though not quite tangible, that is painful all the same. Yes, perhaps suffering is a tool to bring perspective back into our lives. Suffering can be considered a gift to bring us to face the age-old question: How are we using the resource of time?

I think Peter may have been suggesting that the suffering his fellow Christian followers and friends were facing was a great opportunity (and should be viewed as such) to assess the degree to which they had experienced the time disease of the Gentiles—the hurry-up-and-gain-quickly-all-the-pleasure-you-can syndrome (the hedonist's credo).

Accountability is not a popular word today. However, we will all give an accounting. Whether Christian or non-Christian, we will all stand before the Lord Jesus to give an account for that which He has entrusted to us.

One of our favorite parables is the one about the talents. If you remember, Jesus taught that a rich man gave one servant one talent, another five talents, and another ten talents. Those who received the larger amounts aggressively invested theirs at some risk and reaped good returns. The servant who had been given one talent literally buried it in the ground for safekeeping, gaining no return whatsoever. When the rich man returned to collect on his investments, he was delighted to learn that the guys with the larger sums had invested theirs with great returns, but he was very upset with the guy who played it safe by doing nothing with his.

Jesus summed up the parable with this lesson: "To him who has, more will be given; but to him who has not, what he has will be taken away" (Matt. 25:29, paraphrased). Another lesson this parable brings home is the same point Peter tried to endorse here: We will all give an accounting to the Lord.

Jesus' message here is that life is to be lived to the fullest. Paul Tournier says it well: "Many people spend their entire life indefinitely preparing to live." Let me ask you several questions bearing on this point:

- What would you try right now if you knew you couldn't fail?
- Is there anything you have left unattempted in your life?
- Why don't you attempt it? What is stopping you?

The other day we received two notices from our bank regarding overdrawn checks. We were terribly embarrassed. One problem with banking where we do is that several employees at our bank attend our church, and I've also come to know the Christian manager fairly well.

As I studied the statement, I could see that the bank had made an error by confusing a two with a seven. Of course, I don't accept any blame for my sloppy writing! In addition, a $300 deposit was not listed on the statement.

I rushed to the bank, and the bank clerk and I went over each item and each deposit. To my chagrin, we found I'd deposited the $300 into savings instead of into checking. Our bank balance had come up short because I put our investment in the wrong place. Thankfully, the teller had also made an error in the way she had posted the deposit, so we saved $24. Had the bank not made this error, we would have paid the price.

The term Peter used here for "accounting" is not unlike the accounting I went through at our bank that day. We will all, ultimately, at the end of time, give an accounting for how we've invested and how we've deposited the time God has allotted to each of us. Peter said for us to be certain we're investing our time from an eternal perspective. It is this perspective that will cause us to thrive in times of suffering and disappointment.

BUILDING BLOCKS

But the end of all things is at hand; therefore be serious and watchful in your prayers. And above all things have fervent love for one another, for *"love will cover a multitude of sins."* Be hospitable to one another without grumbling. As each one has received a gift, minister it to one another, as good stewards of the manifold grace of God. If anyone speaks, *let him speak* as the oracles of God. If anyone ministers, *let him do it* as with the ability which God supplies, that in all things God may be glorified through Jesus Christ, to whom belong the glory and the dominion forever and ever. Amen. (1 Peter 4:7–11)

Christianity is a life-style that is built out of basic building blocks. I've concluded that the *worst* time to consider seeking guidance is when you vitally need it. Guidance comes not through a last-minute scramble to find the will of God, but through the consistent building of a biblical life-style.

The best time to think about being led by the Lord is *today*. By erecting scriptural building blocks in our daily lives, we are constantly prepared to know His will. Learning and applying these basic building blocks will ensure our ability to know His voice and to know His will.

The end of all things is at hand. One of the better explanations I've heard regarding where we will stand as Christians at the end of time was offered by Oscar Cullman: "For believers to live in the end of time is like running up to the edge of the Grand Canyon." Time, as we know it, has essentially come to an end. From the time of Christ on, our lives can be described as running up to the rim of the Grand Canyon and running parallel with it. We keep living life as a parallel; we are *not* progressing onward.

At the appearing of our Lord, we will all be pushed off the edge of time. As we stand looking down at the edge of that precipice, we realize that all the signs of His return have already been fulfilled. This is Christian time awareness. Christ can come at any time because time has come to an end. We are living at the end of time. The biblical clock is slowly ticking to an end of pain and suffering.

This is cause for great rejoicing and triumph for believers. The last disease may have been suffered today. The Christian lives with this total awareness that his or her last appointment may have already come.

There is a limit to the suffering we're facing now. Trust me; we will outlive it. We won't be pressing on endlessly into time. We are living at its very edge right now. Our hope is that every morning when we arise, this may be the day the Lord puts an end to all our pain and suffering.

God took decisive action when He sent His Son. He has also decreed a limitation to this time capsule. He has set in motion a plan to rescue and to recover those who are incarcerated. He has imparted the reality of eternal life into the heart of every believer. This is our great hope!

Living at the edge of time doesn't require dramatic or traumatic reactions. It does require sensible, consistent building blocks—each day, intelligently building into the fiber of our lives those blocks that will assure our living in the center of His will!

Catch-up Christianity just doesn't work—especially when we confront times of intense pain and disappointment.

My wife is a rigorous exerciser. She walks. She runs. She rides a bike. Last summer I decided to start jogging to keep up with her. We don't run together; however, I decided I would run the same track she used. I soon realized that I was running about two blocks, then stopping and walking, running three blocks and walking a while, then running one block, and so on.

I started running by a group of contractors working on a new housing development in our neighborhood, and I wished in the worst way that I could run the full distance of several blocks past them. As the workers, realtors, and would-be buyers drove by, I wanted so much to keep on running, but I just couldn't—another instance of willing spirit, but weak flesh. I returned home exhausted. My feet hurt. My lungs hurt. My heart pounded. My pride hurt. The next day when I went out, I made it a little farther, however. And the day after that, I made it still farther before dropping.

One of our staff members is a long-distance cyclist. When preparing for a race, he trains regularly and vigorously, gradually building up his endurance. In the races in which he competes he cycles for eight to nine days! I can't imagine doing that.

The lesson in this is that our physical endurance is built up by using consistent building blocks. By building our strength day by day, we increase our ability to endure.

I've had the challenge as a pastor to observe all kinds of persons who have experienced suffering and disappointment. I've noted that those who live consistent, disciplined lives in the Lord don't have less suffering, but when suffering does come to them, they seem to have far more rewarding results.

On the other hand, those who live marginally committed to Christ, those who don't build consistent building blocks that lead to living in His will with assurance, seem to be far more hurt by issues of pain and suffering.

It isn't so much that suffering hurts any more or less for those who have built themselves up properly, but that their perspective allows them to gain much more positive energy from what they suffer and experience.

When the clock starts running out, it is a sign for us to check and double-check whether we are building consistent building blocks in our lives that will lead us into His will.

STAYING IN HIS WILL

One of the greatest sources of strength for Christians who face suffering is the certainty of living in God's will. From 1 Peter 4:7 on, Peter outlined how we can be positive we're living in His will.

Guidance requires a specific life-style—a life-style that brings a surety that our guidance system is sound.

Time was viewed by Peter as a valuable resource, the most vital resource Christians have, in fact. It is this resource that must be managed carefully to maintain the assurance of His guidance in our lives.

Time is running out on suffering. This perspective is often overlooked. Knowing what to do while time runs out in the midst of suffering is vital. The practical life-style that thrives in a less-than-optimal world is the kind that is in the middle of God's will for us.

Peter listed seven steps that lead to a life-style that ends where God is. We're not only to stand constantly and unwavering in God's will, but also to thrive in the face of suffering while time is marching on.

1. *Pray*

Praying is the exercise of speaking and listening to God, asking and receiving, looking within and looking up. How we are to pray is very specific in this verse as well.

Clear-minded. We are to put our thinking caps on as we pray. We are to pray with precise thinking. Our minds are not to be caught up in emotions or distractions. We are to pray with pin-point accuracy.

Watchfully. We are to be alert. Not only are we to have a clear mind, but also we are to be free from the distractions of this world. "Watchfully" praying means keeping our eyes on the landscape before us. We're to pay attention.

2. Life-style of Love

A life-style of love leads us into God's will. The kind of love Peter mentioned is *forgiveness*. This is not the kind that covers just one or two sins, but multitudes of sins. The life-style of love and the motivation of love will always lead us straight into the center of God's will.

3. Hospitality

Hospitality means "to love strangers, to be gracious to guests." We are to share hospitality without grumbling. In other words, in facing this world, which is characterized by suffering, we are not to lose touch with the necessity of a generous heart and an open home.

4. Gifts

Peter continued: "As each one has received a gift, *minister it to one another, as good stewards of the manifold grace of God"* (1 Peter 4:10, emphasis added). We live in a time when the world is falling apart. The gifts of the Spirit are essential in these last days. If we are faithful to steward properly the graces and abilities God has passed on to us by His Holy Spirit, His will shall manifest itself. It is His gifts that bring strength and certainty in a confused and weakened world.

5. Oracles of God

We are to speak as the oracles of God. By our sensitivity to God's voice and our sharing of His insights and Word in our lives, we are to encourage one another that we aren't alone in this world. God is not silent. He is there. As oracles, we can speak with assurance, in the middle of our suffering, that God is not silent.

6. God's Abilities and Strengths

Peter went on to encourage us that if we minister to anyone, we must do it with the ability that God supplies, that in all things God may be glorified through Jesus Christ. It is God's abilities that allow us to thrive in the face of suffering. His strengths and abilities bring suffering into perspective. We are more up to the task.

If we attempt to stand only in our own strength during a time of suffering, we are likely to be out of God's will. Peter's assurance here is passed on to us that if we are standing in God's strength and ability, we'll be in the absolute center of His will, no matter how intense the suffering may become.

7. *Glorification of Jesus Christ*

Even in the middle of suffering, we are to be Christ-focused people. If we do this, we will surely be in God's will.

To sum it up, Peter offered us a life-style that will thrive and outlast pain and suffering. I think what this sage old leader of the church was attempting to get across is that when the pain gets intense, get busy!

A LIFE-STYLE THAT GUIDES

The starting point of knowing God's will is in our attitude. Peter was really concerned about the attitude of his flock. This was a group of people who were facing some very troubling times, just as you and I do. Things weren't working out the way they had imagined. Frankly, I get the feeling from Peter's writing that he was positive that Christianity really wasn't working for his flock. They were looking toward a rough road ahead. From reading the book of 1 Peter I don't think it was going to improve.

The theme of Peter's book is how to survive and thrive in a suffering world. What do you do when something isn't working out for you? Do you tend to curl up in the fetal position and hope life will improve? Or do you fight, scream, and kick in all the systems of pain avoidance available to you?

If so, we can almost guarantee ourselves that our suffering will only become more intense, more confusing, and more painful. Keeping busy and continuing to do what we know to do as believers are sure ways to move beyond surviving to thriving in suffering.

As a pastor, I've shared this counsel many times. Though we can't deny our guilt, and definitely shouldn't or it will return to haunt us, we can continue to do what we know to do. Continuing to do the same things in times of suffering that Christ has taught us to do when things are going well can be the anchor that stabilizes our lives.

I don't know about you, but when things start going wrong for me, that's when I start wondering whether I'm in God's will or not. How about you? Peter says that times of suffering are *not* the times to ask yourself that question. Establishing a life pattern and life-style as outlined above will be certain to keep you in the center of His will in the face of suffering.

TIME FOR A LIFE QUIZ

Let's take a short quiz on how we view our lives. Just for fun, note the statement that most aptly describes your view of your life at this moment.

1. My life is primarily like a jail sentence. I've got fifty more years to serve until parole.
2. My life is a harried rush against the clock.
3. My life is like paying for yesterday's Caribbean cruise. In other words, I live only to make my credit card payments.
4. My life is like a ship at sea without a sail or a captain—it just drifts with the current.
5. My life is an artistic work of God.

Which of these attitudes would best align you with even recognizing God's will in your life every day? When I shared these five possible attitudes about our lives, a man in the congregation suggested that a sixth category be included: all of the above!

Sometimes it's easy to acquire an attitude that says: "My life is just a jail sentence." Of course, it's pretty tough to recognize God's will when that's your basic approach to life.

When you awaken in the morning and say, "I've got ten more years until my parole," it takes the pizzazz out of living. You may wake up and say, "You know, I like that commercial where you drive up to a speaker and say, 'Give me two more weeks' or 'I need four hours more.'" But you're just buying time.

The drudgery of purposeless living will get to each one of us. Now, add purposeless living to intense times of loss or pain, and you're set up for some real problems.

The second attitude that might imprison us is the harried lifestyle. However, if we would cultivate the attitude that Peter encouraged us to have—the one where we rise every morning and say, "Lord, thank You that today is another step in Your artistic process in my life"—I honestly believe that we will experience an exciting, adventurous life! I think we will have the kind of life that grows better in the face of the unravelings we all experience.

Just imagine with me for a moment what that would be like. At this point, let's rehearse our lives hereafter, so that when we wake in the morning, we will say, "Lord, whomever I encounter or whatever decisions are made or whatever goes wrong today are part of Your artistic process in my life, and for that I praise You!"

Wouldn't life then take on a different perspective for all of us? If you answered yes to number five above, I can guess that you're going to survive any pain this world will hurl your way with above-average success.

Once again, heart preparation based on a life-style that leads us into God's will is what Peter was trying to teach us. It seems as though we won't escape it through this book. It seems as though preparation of the heart is vital. We will suffer; that is a given. Yet, how we prepare our life-style and shape our heart could determine whether we are overcome by the suffering or whether we overcome it.

Start building your life around the anticipation that God has already said that you are His workmanship of grace! You are His sculpture! He is molding you into someone very beautiful! Suffering is one of the chisels He uses to shape you from the inside out.

Recently, I spoke with a young woman after one of our services. When she had visited here for the first time, she had just lost all of her assets from being involved in a couple of lawsuits. Then she decided to surrender her life to Christ.

She came to me and said: "Pastor, it's a remarkable thing. This morning, when I committed my life to Christ, I felt encouraged to face life again."

I told her, "I'm always excited to hear this kind of report. Do go on with your story."

She continued, "Well, soon after I'd given my life to Christ, I decided to start another business. At the time I had only $140 a month coming in and just a small amount of food, but I started the business anyway. I knew, no matter what I'd suffered in past business experiences, that the Lord had a purpose for me now."

Well, as you can guess, God prospered her business until she became very successful in just a matter of months. When she realized that the Lord was at work in her life, she gathered courage to face life again, and she launched out to do the thing she had only previously dreamed of doing.

She used a phrase that caught my ear, and I'd like to share it with you. She said, "I have no doubt now that God is making a thing of beauty out of my life."

LIVING IN CHRISTIAN TIME AWARENESS

"Christian time awareness" is looking at our lives every day from God's standpoint. This is the awareness that time is running out. As Christians, we have a tendency to lose our sense of time awareness and move into what I call "delayed obedience" or "postponed living." It is a kind of perspective that says: "Well, in six months from now, kids, we're really going to have fun, because I'm going to be through with this project." Or "In three years from now, I'm going to have such-and-such done, and then the Lord and I are really going to get it on together."

This type of thinking is a postponed approach to life. It certainly isn't living in Christian time awareness. The Christian viewpoint of time says that the vital increment handed to us is each single day—and each single day must be lived to the fullest.

After a recent Sunday service in which we had sung the chorus "Maranatha," a young woman approached me and asked, "Pastor, what does *maranatha* mean?"

I think she was worried that we were singing some Eastern mantra or something similar. I answered: "*Maranatha* was a greeting that the early church members shared with one another. When they finished honoring the Lord and having fellowship, they didn't say 'See you later' or 'Have a great day,' as we do today. Instead, they said "Maranatha," which means "O Lord, come."

She was delighted to learn this new Christian declaration, and I think she was relieved that we weren't chanting mantras.

The word *maranatha* was intended to instill in the early believers a sense of anticipation and a sensitivity to the time in which they lived, that the Lord might very well come before they met again. They knew there wasn't enough time to play catch-up Christianity. We are allotted just so much time, Peter said, and that's all we get.

I recently watched an NFL game. The quarterback leading one of the teams was originally from our Seattle area. My son, Matt, and I used to watch him play at a nearby high school. He also played for the University of Washington the year they won the championship from the University of Oklahoma in Miami. Every Husky fan in Seattle remembers those days.

At any rate, the game was moving into the fourth quarter. It was the fourth down, and his team had to go about 1½ yards to get in a scoring position for a first down. Once they had a first down, there was no doubt they could move into a scoring position.

At the snap of the ball, this quarterback rolled out. You could tell just by the way he ran that the pressure was on. In his hesitation he forgot that it was the fourth down. I don't know how I knew it, but I realized, as soon as he swung out to his right, that he thought it was the third down.

Because he hadn't paid attention to the little stick on the sideline, he threw the ball away as an onrushing defender moved toward him. He could easily have made the 1½ yards necessary if he'd just remembered that it was the fourth down. I know he thought he had one more down, because of his reaction when the whistle blew.

The fans were ruthless. They booed him off the field. They probably figured that a guy who gets a million dollars a year sure ought to remember a fourth down from a third down. Well, the bottom line was that there wasn't enough time left to retrieve the ball and score.

He had played fabulously up to that point and had made very few errors. He had done a good job of commanding his team. But in a momentary lapse of awareness, he'd committed an unforgivable error. Forgetting a fourth down won't keep a quarterback in the ranks of pro ball for long.

So I think what Peter was getting at in this passage is this: "Hey, gang, it's the fourth down. You don't have any more time to play catch-up Christianity. If you want to be in God's will, you have to have Christian awareness of what time it is. Be attentive! Don't mess up! It's too late in the game. The Lord may come at any moment. It's the fourth down."

THRIVING IN HIS WILL

I've discovered that sometimes when we seek God's will on a particular issue, we experience silence on His part. For example, I got away a few weeks ago for a short retreat to pray and to write. I also wanted to get my spirit in tune for the many matters we were facing in our church. I was praying over a number of issues in our church life and for a number of persons. It was one of those refreshing, remarkable times. It was really a great time for reflecting and for getting in touch with myself and some of the real issues I was facing.

I really needed some answers from the Lord, but I didn't seem to get any responses to some issues for which I was seeking answers. I just couldn't come up with any solutions, or even additional steps. The Lord just wasn't answering. Finally, it dawned on me, as I was preparing my notes for that Sunday's message, that the Lord was giving me a firsthand illustration. He was saying: "Doug, don't ask Me for any new guidance when you haven't done what I've already told you to do."

Part of the reason we get confused at times and don't know what to do is that it is God's way of telling us that we haven't yet fulfilled what He has already told us to do.

God may, in fact, be saying: "Step back about three paces. Do what I've already asked you to do, then let's talk about the new issue because time is so short. Don't think that you've got two more downs to go, guy. You've got *no* downs left. Do what I've already asked you, and you'll then be in a position to be in My will for the next chapter of your life."

We usually do, if sincerely seeking the Lord, have sufficient insight for the moment. Confusion comes when we don't fulfill what we know we're supposed to do today, but instead pursue too aggressively what we know we need to do in three or four months from now.

CHASING DONKEYS TO YOUR THRONE

One of the greatest illustrations from Scripture on how guidance has worked for me is found in 1 Samuel 9, where God chose Saul to be king of Israel. The prophet Samuel objected to the whole concept of having a king. In fact, at this point in the story, Samuel was still grumbling in his heart that Israel had not honored him as a prophet. He was also concerned that they would choose a mortal, human king over choosing God as their King.

At the opening of 1 Samuel, we find Saul, the son of Kish, and a servant pursuing several donkeys that had broken away from his father's ranch. The text says that they looked for days, climbing hither and yon through the sagebrush and the sand and, probably, the rolling hills of pasture.

The prophet Samuel started off for a nearby town, under the instructions of the Holy Spirit. Saul and his servant heard that Samuel was in a nearby town. The servant offered this insight: "Perhaps the prophet Samuel will know the whereabouts of the donkeys."

Both the young men scurried into town and found the sage old prophet. Upon setting his eyes on Saul, Samuel immediately knew that this was the young man he was to anoint as king. Now, catch the contrast. Saul thought he was chasing donkeys, but Samuel had been told by the Lord to anoint him king.

I really believe this is how most guidance works. I also believe it is how our lives stay the most stable. If we simply chase the donkeys that we have been assigned to pursue, God always has a way of making us kings. The point is that Saul was obedient to the instructions of his father (and employer), and he fulfilled those instructions as the will of God. Saul's simple lifestyle of obedience led him right smack into the center of God's will—and the donkey chaser became king!

I have observed that people who simply do what has been assigned to them, no matter how horrendous the circumstances or painful the unraveling of their lives may have become, have a way of always coming out as kings.

Our steadfast commitment as Christians to simple, everyday

obedience is what will cause us not only to survive, but also to thrive through suffering. Through our searching we will always be led into the courts of the prophets, who will establish us as kings. God's dreams cannot be thwarted in our lives, no matter how painful this world becomes.

Now, if you search for God's will and aren't getting any answers, let me gently encourage you to review your actions and ask: "Lord, is there anything You have spoken clearly to me that I haven't done as yet, that I need to do before I can expect You to lead me any further?"

If so, let me encourage you to take care of that aspect first. I returned from my retreat realizing that I was supposed to do a couple of things before God would reveal the next step. It was refreshing and releasing. In fact, the steps were quite easy. One or two of them to which I had clearly committed myself were quite simple, but had just been forgotten.

REVIEW

I hope you can leave this chapter with the following convictions about facing suffering:

1. As a successful believer you may suffer, yet still be in God's will.
2. God's will may lead you purposefully and directly into suffering in order for His will to be accomplished in your life.
3. Time is running out on suffering. Pain and suffering will not last forever. At the Lord's appearing, all tears will be dried up, and suffering will end. This is the perspective that a believer lives with.
4. God is artistically shaping our lives, even through suffering, though it may not feel like it.
5. Keep busy with what you know to do in times of suffering. This will increase your chances of thriving through pain.
6. Crave God's will more than a problem-free life. In this way God will surely be glorified in your life.

Chapter 12

When Everything Goes Wrong
(1 Peter 4:12–19)

We've seen already, through Peter, that the big issue for believers during times of suffering is not why it comes. The big issue is how do we stay on track when everything is going wrong around us?

There's a distinct possibility of being derailed in times of suffering. Sometimes we may not be derailed outwardly, but inwardly. Peter once again dealt with heart preparation, not only to survive suffering, but also to thrive during suffering in an abnormal world.

Have you experienced times when it seemed as though everything was going wrong? I know there have been a few times in my life when I looked around and wondered what else could possibly go wrong. To my surprise, a couple of more things did go wrong!

I've discovered at those moments that I needed a theological correction, lest I became susceptible to a folk theology. Now, you're wondering: What's a folk theology? It's a Ben Franklin kind of theology, a homespun philosophy. A folk theology is something like: "God helps those who help themselves"—I hope everyone realizes that is *not* in the Bible. Or that God is 100 percent opposed to divorces and divorcées. Or if you're sick, you think you've obviously angered God. If you read your Bible closely, you'll see that it isn't quite that simplistic.

In this case, the folk theology I've been susceptible to is that if one lives a perfect life (impossible, of course) in God, nothing goes wrong. In fact, this theology claims that one of the ways you know you're right in the center of God's will is that absolutely everything is going perfectly.

Conversely, this theology suggests that when things are going wrong, you've somehow displeased God or have missed

Him entirely. This folk theology of the "good life" and "perfect circumstances" is absolutely wrong!

Peter dealt with this fallacy straight on to make certain this erroneous theology didn't derail those he loved and knew were not only facing suffering then, but were going to face much, much more in the future.

> Beloved, do not think it strange concerning the fiery trial which is to try you, as though some strange thing happened to you; but rejoice to the extent that you partake of Christ's sufferings, that when His glory is revealed, you may also be glad with exceeding joy. If you are reproached for the name of Christ, blessed *are you,* for the Spirit of glory and of God rests upon you. On their part He is blasphemed, but on your part He is glorified. But let none of you suffer as a murderer, a thief, an evildoer, or as a busybody in other people's matters. Yet if *anyone suffers* as a Christian, let him not be ashamed, but let him glorify God in this matter. For the time *has come* for judgment to begin at the house of God; and if *it begins* with us first, what will be the end of those who do not obey the gospel of God? Now
>
> > *"If the righteous one is scarcely
> > saved,
> > Where will the ungodly and the
> > sinner appear?"*
>
> Therefore let those who suffer according to the will of God commit their souls to *Him* in doing good, as to a faithful Creator. (1 Peter 4:12–19)

One of suffering's great negative forces in your life is the element of surprise. Peter warned us to have our hearts poised to remove it. Don't think that you've been separated out or chosen for a particular suffering. It's something that belongs to this worldly realm. Don't think it's strange when pain and agony happen to you. But rejoice in knowing that you are identifying with Christ's suffering in the midst of a world that is out of whack, out of sync.

This section of Scripture suggests that, as Christians, we are not involved in some sort of "life-avoidance program." Actually, coming to Jesus Christ is not a wonderful way to avoid problems. But, then, you've probably discovered that by now. Those who buy into the idea that everything will be just perfect when they come to the Lord are in for a rude awakening. In fact, the Bible suggests in this section (as well as in many others) that Christians may very well have more troubles than other people.

Peter was emphatic about there being no "free lunch." According to the Bible, the rain falls on both the just and the unjust; that's just the nature of life on earth. No one escapes life's adversities—and especially not Christians.

Someone once said: "Life is hard, and then you die." I'd like to add to that the theology of the 1980s: "Don't worry. Be happy." If you think about it, that's a great theology! It may even be what Peter was trying to communicate to us here: "Don't worry. Be happy. You are experiencing an abnormal life. If you're suffering, you're experiencing the realities of a fallen world."

Now, in these moments of suffering, there are three tendencies into which we can fall:

Belief Tendencies	Peter's Answers
• To believe that we've been singled out.	• Don't be surprised if you are suffering; you have not been singled out.
• To believe that we're experiencing an abnormal kind of living.	• This world is abnormal; suffering is consistent with the state of creation.
• To believe that there is no good to be gained from our suffering.	• There is a great deal to be gained from what we suffer.

COMMIT AND CONTINUE

"Therefore let those who suffer according to the will of God commit their souls to *Him* in doing good, as to a faithful Creator" (1 Peter 4:19).

Here is Peter's key statement, which can actually be translated this way: "commit their souls to Him in doing good." The tense of these verbs can be read and understood this way: Those who suffer according to God's will should *commit themselves* to their faithful Creator and *continue to do good.*

These two verbs, *commit* and *continue*, hold the key to what Christians should do at the time of suffering. The fact that suffering will come is a settled issue. But what do we do to stay on track when we're suffering? Peter's simple advice is *to commit* and *to continue.*

The attribute that makes Christians stand out from non-Christians is our approach to problem-solving and how we think about our problems. Christianity isn't something that works *for* us. It is Christ Who works *within* us! Our relationship with Christ is what makes the vital difference. It is this relationship that assaults the pragmatic theology of the problem-free life—a false theology, we all agree.

If you want a how-to program, Christianity is not the way to go. If you want a how-to program on problem avoidance, you'll have to go to a bookstore. They carry many books on this topic. When you come to Christ, you're facing life square-on with the indomitable attitude of the infilling of the Holy Spirit.

What makes us distinctly Christian is the attitude we maintain when we face suffering. We experience pain, trouble, and suffering in life from a Christian orientation.

As I shared earlier, our daughter is physically handicapped. However, she's not mentally impaired at all. Quite the contrary, she's really quite brilliant. Raissa has a sterling character, and her social skills are captivating. She's a great little gal with a powerful personality and an equal amount of determination to live her life to the fullest.

My wife and I determined early on that, even if we couldn't change Raissa's physical condition, we could certainly give her an attitude that would allow her to be a conqueror in life. We've taught her to live her life without limitation while, at the same time, meeting her problems squarely. We feel that this is our call as Christian parents to instill a Christlike attitude in our kids in spite of the real problems they may suffer.

For the most part, Christians haven't prepared themselves well enough to deal with life's real problems; neither have they addressed the issue of suffering that their children will encounter. In fact, we seemingly spend more time trying to find a pathway to a trouble-free life, using Christ as a vehicle to accomplish that, than we do grappling with problems head-on.

It's been a joy to observe the growth of Christ in our daughter's life. I think a vital part of that growth has been our ability to be honest about the reality of suffering in our lives.

We may not all be physically handicapped, but we can be handicapped in other ways. This world has a way of marring us, inhibiting us, and, at times, even scarring us. Peter suggested that we're not to be surprised by that, but to equip ourselves with a Christian mentality; in this case, to commit our lives to a faithful God and to continue in Him.

The other day I brought home a book containing 120 questions devised by a scholar. These questions were designed to help the reader to discover what really motivates and spurs him or her on to seek a higher quality of life. A couple of the questions read like this: If somebody gave you one million dollars to give away, would you give it to Mother Teresa, an orphanage in Haiti, or Oral Roberts? If you could go on a vacation, would you go to the Himalaya Mountains, the Amazon River, or the beaches of Hawaii?

Here's the key question Raissa picked out as she read through the list: What in your life limits you most from fulfilling your dreams? This little girl who, for the first time in her life, had to ride to school in a wheelchair (hating every minute of it), thought and thought . . . and thought. She read and reread the question, and thought some more. Her mother waited for Raissa's answer, holding her breath.

Finally, Raissa brightened and announced cheerfully: "Mom, I can't think of anything. There's nothing limiting me from meeting my dreams!"

What a fantastic outlook! Now, that's real joy! Debbie hurried upstairs and excitedly told me the whole story. We rejoiced. I think Jesus rejoiced too.

Our daughter has no limits because she doesn't perceive

herself to have any. It's life without limitations or reservations for Raissa, even though she still needs healing of her gross motor skills. She's not oblivious to her plight, nor will she ever resign herself to it. Although she is very aware of her physical condition, Raissa moves on with Christ in her life, and she feels that she will become everything He wants her to be, whatever that might be. That's the Christian perspective!

WHY DO CHRISTIANS SUFFER?

There are several reasons why Christians suffer. Let's go over a few of them. After all, Peter's encouragement is that we are to be prepared to suffer—not to know why it happens.

We Are Human

We all suffer because we're human. We are not involved in a Christian fallout shelter. I have had the joy as a pastor to see many people be healed. Sadly, not everyone gets healed, though. I've actually seen people be healed who didn't believe Christ would heal.

Now, I have to admit that it's hard for Deb and me to reconcile the marvelous healings of others in the reality of what we confront daily in our own family. But from this side of the Lord's return, there will probably be many things we won't understand totally.

In trying to reconcile this tension somehow, I have read and reread *The Problem of Pain* by C. S. Lewis. As I read, I realized that, whether healed or unhealed, whether the receiver or giver of the "laying on of hands," we will still die one day. It's the way of humanity. In this fallen world, at least one death is inevitable for us. If we're outside of Christ, we face two deaths: the one we face here on earth and the one at the Judgment Seat.

Any person who has ever been healed on earth, Lewis said, will still die eventually. Because we are mere mortals, we are unable to overcome the forceful blow of death, except spiritually and in Christ! When we cry "maranatha," it is our battle cry of victory that this element of death will ultimately be destroyed. And the sting of death will disappear with the cry: "He is risen! He is risen!"

Nonetheless, suffering is part and parcel of this life, simply because we are human in a world that is being gradually redeemed, in a world that is groaning and awaiting its full recovery at the second coming of our Lord Jesus Christ!

We Often Deserve It

Sometimes we bring suffering upon ourselves. To illustrate, let me tell a story. About a year ago, a friend came to me. He had charged $11,000 on his American Express card!

He groaned, "Doug, please help me out on this bill. I really need your help. I don't know what to do or how I'm going to get this bill paid."

Praying under my breath, I knew immediately how the Lord wanted me to respond: "Not only will I not help you, but I won't even pray for you!"

My friend looked so hurt and bewildered that I almost felt sorry for him. Don't ever come to me for counseling. I've never been very good at it, because I'm too blunt, too candid.

"But, Doug, what'll I do?" he wailed. "How am I going to get out of this mess?"

"Well, I advise you to call the American Express Company and arrange some sort of payment plan. By the way, how did you do such a dumb thing, anyway?"

"Well, I had a chance to get into a franchise. My partner and I were flying all over the country, never thinking that we'd have these enormous bills if we didn't get it. I guess we didn't think far enough ahead."

"Okay, just to show you I'm a compassionate guy, I'll pray for one thing. I'll pray that your wife doesn't kill you when you get home. I know her. She's tough, and I know that's a possibility."

I know the Lord on this sort of thing. Money problems get solved slowly, with much prayer and fasting. At any rate, when the conversation ended, we were both laughing. As he was leaving, he looked more hopeful when I told him I really did love him and would be praying for him.

Often the answer to the suffering we confront is a changed life-style. My friend did change his life-style and did work his way out of debt. He also gained a great deal of business prowess in the process. I solved my propensity toward migraine headaches by changing my life-style from anger and resentment to forgiveness.

God Disciplines Through Suffering

I once read some sage wisdom of C. S. Lewis (*The Problem of Pain*): "God whispers to us in our pleasures; He speaks to us in our conscience; and He shouts to us in our pain." Hebrews 12:6 says: "The son that God loves, He chastens" (paraphrased). This is one of my least favorite messages to preach, because I don't like to be chastened any more than anyone else does.

By the way, you can't determine for someone else whether she or he is being chastened by the Lord. That person knows that in her or his own heart; you will know when you are being dealt with. I think this verse is intended to be read very personally. It was never intended to be a basis for our allies in other situations.

Someone once came to Deb and me and said: "The reason your daughter has cerebral palsy is because God is dealing with sin in your life."

Needless to say, we didn't receive that as a legitimate word from God, and I don't think anyone can make that determination except my family and me. Besides, what an idiotic picture that is of God! It is not only wrong, but it is also terribly mean and inaccurate.

I grew up as a redhead (still am). I was the kid you could always spot in a crowd. On a nice Saturday afternoon, about six of us kids, including one who owned a BB gun, were shooting the smithereens out of the stained-glass window of a Seventh Day Adventist Church behind my parents' house. It was not only great fun, but also great target practice. One section had just about been knocked out when the custodian came charging out of the church.

We all ran like the dickens. We jumped over the fence, ran home, and acted as though everything were cool and normal.

The only problem was that when the police asked the custodian who had broken the window, he remembered seeing a red-headed kid. Of course, when the police questioned the neighbors about a redheaded kid who lived close to the church, their trail led right to our doorstep.

Thankfully, I didn't own a gun and hadn't shot out any of the windows myself. I had simply been an enthusiastic spectator. The culprit who did own the gun ended up paying for the window.

In a very real sense, when you become a Christian, God turns you into a redhead too. You stick out in a crowd. You won't get away with anything after that. You may think you will, but you won't.

The fact that we often have to cope with the full extent of pain when we make wrong decisions is actually a statement of God's love. The writer of Hebrews says that if we get away with anything, we might be considered fatherless children and perhaps ought to question whether we're His.

God uses painful circumstances to chasten and to shape our lives into His image. He also uses pain and suffering as a way of chastising us before our wrong life-styles destroy us totally.

Suffering Helps Keep Perspective

For a long time, Paul endured a "thorn in his side," which the Lord allowed to remain. This great apostle, we believe, suffered from malaria or something related to it. Through prayer, Paul's interpretation of 2 Corinthians 12 was that the Lord allowed a satanic emissary to buffet him so that he would keep the proper perspective.

According to that chapter, Paul was caught up into the third heaven, where he saw wonders that he not only didn't know how to write about, but also was not permitted to write about. As best as we can tell from studying all his writings and trying to read between the lines, Paul may have been losing his sight due to his malady. We can't really tell for certain because not enough information is given, but he prayed to God three times to remove the problem, to which God finally answered: "My grace is sufficient for you" (2 Cor. 12:9).

I think God was telling Paul that He would stand by and comfort him, but He wouldn't relieve the symptoms. Paul felt that he was to experience this discomfort so that his ego wouldn't become inflated or that he wouldn't feel overly important because of the revelations God had showed him. It helped Paul to keep his viewpoint more realistic.

Until you've suffered yourself, you can be an extremely insensitive person. When you've been "tenderized" by the rigors of pain, something inside you softens up. You then tend to be more compassionate for the hurts, plights, and health problems of others. I know this firsthand.

Here are four considerations to keep in mind when you suffer or when you're in the middle of a painful problem. First, God is violently opposed to all pain and suffering, and He looks to the day when the end of this age will come and there will be no more suffering.

Second, God has taken aggressive action, by sending the Lord Jesus Christ to earth, to destroy pain, disease, and suffering. According to Luke, Jesus came to proclaim liberty to those in bondage, and to proclaim and to declare God's nearness to those in trouble!

Each time someone is healed by Jesus, it's like another bonfire has been ignited to remind us that the kingdom of God has come to earth and that Satan's kingdom, typified by disease and suffering, is being destroyed and is on its way out of existence! The kingdom is partially here already, but not totally. God has unequivocally declared Himself opposed to the fallen state of this world.

We are experiencing the redemptive process of Christ's power in our lives. It is how we stand in the midst of pain and suffering that determines the extent of that power we presently experience.

Third, if God completely removed suffering from earth, He would have to use one of two methods: (a) He would have to annihilate earth totally, wipe it out, blow it up. God's providential plan doesn't allow this to happen, for the Bible suggests that there are many persons yet to come to Him. (b) Or God would have to dispose of our free will. Because of free will, we have the potential to worship God freely and spontaneously. For instance, when we sing in church, there are no angels prodding us to sing, and there are no buttons on the backs of our heads that God can push to make us worship Him. We sing and worship because we desire to show God our love and respect.

Free will can also be misused. Throughout 1989, the news media bombarded us about the dishonest bank officers who embezzled many billions of dollars from various savings and loan banks, causing them to fail. It appears that several of these persons embezzled at least a billion dollars, which they shamefully misappropriated for their own selfish purposes so they could purchase beautiful mansions in Brazil, expensive yachts in Australia, fleets of expensive cars, and private planes.

Because they deliberately mismanaged these banks, which were entrusted to their care, thousands of people have lost their life savings, and a number of banks have closed their doors. Instead of using their free will for good, these persons chose to use it to steal. Who will pay? It looks as though Mr. and Mrs. Middle America will.

Here's another illustration of the misuse of free will. The AIDS epidemic is causing great agony and suffering to come upon many innocent people, as well as those directly involved in the sexual and drug-related activities that spread this evil, insidious disease. If people wouldn't engage in illicit sex or use drugs, AIDS could possibly be wiped out in a relatively short span of time.

It's really that simple. It involves the specific law of physics that for every action, there is a corresponding reaction (that is, cause and effect). Put negatively in "computerese": garbage in, garbage out. So it follows that if you feed false, wrong information into your freewill computer, guess what prints out: bad, evil results, leaving a trail of broken, shattered lives!

In January 1989, the medical insurance for our church staff jumped 30 percent and was expected to increase again by the end of the year. In fact, it appears to be a distinct possibility that medical insurance costs will continue to rise due to the far-reaching effects of AIDS.

It isn't just one person who suffers from the misuse of our God-given free will. We all suffer because people tend to do what they want to at any given moment.

The point is that our free will can either be used to worship

God freely and gloriously or it can be used to impose further pain and suffering on this planet when we violate God-given rules.

We've all been given a free will, and we all actually do what we want. Evidently, though, the rewards of our being free will worshipers are so great that God was willing to risk the kind of experience we face each day on a fallen planet in order to reap the fruits that would come upon those who would worship God freely.

Free will carries with it an element of danger, but we have to assume that there is also the reality of glorious rewards for those who will freely worship Christ and respond to His grace.

Fourth, we don't see the whole picture. In 1972, while attending youth meetings in Munich, Germany, Debbie and I were privileged to meet Corrie Ten Boom (nicknamed Conta Corrie, author of *The Hiding Place*). She was a fantastic Christian warrior from Holland. At the time we met her, she was in her eighties, fragile and hardly able to stand.

During World War II, this brave Dutch woman and her family were a Christ-directed force to be reckoned with. They hid, fed, and spirited away hundreds of Dutch Jews, right under Nazi noses, before they were arrested and imprisoned in Nazi death camps, where she also left her mark for Jesus Christ. Corrie was the only death camp survivor in her family.

After the war, God had Corrie tell her spellbinding story to millions of people in Europe and America, and He used her story to draw thousands to Christ. At the youth meetings she taught us by using the illustration technique.

She would say, "Now, kids, today I'm going to give you an illustration." Then she reached into her bag and pulled out a piece of embroidery and showed it around the room.

"What is this picture, kids?" she would ask.

"It's a duck, an embroidered duck," we all answered.

"Good!" Then she flipped it over to show us the back.

"What is this, kids?"

"Threads," we chorused.

"Very good. Very good!" She'd flip it back to the picture side and say, "Now, this is your life as God sees it." Turning it to the back side again, she continued, "This is your life as you see it. Many loose ends. But God sees the whole picture. Now, if you want to see life perfectly, you must see it from His vantage point."

The point Corrie was making, as you can guess, was that when we're in the middle of trouble and suffering, we're to remember that we're not seeing the whole picture.

The Christian response to suffering is to commit ourselves to Him and to continue to do what we know to do. When everything goes wrong, Peter told us, the way to stay on track is to commit ourselves to God, Who is our faithful Creator Who has never ever violated any of His promises!

Promises We Can Hold On To

God has given us the following eleven promises to claim in the midst of sorrow and suffering. I thought these promises might help us to commit ourselves to Jesus and to continue on in Him:

1. God is our *shield* (Ps. 28:7). He has promised us that He would protect us from injury-causing troubles (Gen. 15:1).
2. God is our *refuge*, "a very present help in times of trouble" (Ps. 46:1, paraphrased). "He shall call upon Me,/ and I will answer him,/I will be with him in trouble" (Ps. 91:15).
3. God has promised to be our *strength* (Ps. 28:7).
4. God is always our *Shepherd*. As His sheep, we're under His watchful eye (Ps. 23).
5. God has promised *superabundant provision* (Eph. 3:16–21).
6. God has promised us His *Presence*. "Draw near to God, and He will draw near to you in trouble" (James 4:8, paraphrased).
7. God shall supply *all* your needs through Christ Jesus (Phil. 4:19, paraphrased).
8. If we endure [suffer] with Him, we shall also *reign* with Him (2 Tim. 2:12, paraphrased).

9. He has promised His *overshadowing glory* in the middle of trouble (1 Peter 4:14).
10. He has promised a *special kind of fellowship,* the kind that can be known only in His sufferings. Paul said: "I want to know Christ and the power of His resurrection, and the fellowship of sharing in His sufferings, being conformed to His death; and so, somehow, to attain to the resurrection from the death" (Phil. 3:11, paraphrased).
11. God has promised that, as bad as circumstances may look, *He will make the outcome be according to His purposes if we stick close to Him* (Rom. 8:28, paraphrased).

Committing and Continuing

As Christians, we set the course of our lives according to a specific focus. To have Christ as your Lord is to set the course of your life on the path of several life commitments. They could be summarized in the following way:

1. I will trust God with the outcome of my life.
2. I will not get fearful about loose ends.
3. I realize I am entrusting my life to the faithful Creator, Who can be trusted totally.
4. I will, by His grace, stick to the commitments I have made to Him.

I get concerned for those whom I serve when they encounter really tough times. I know that a lot of pain, agony, and disappointment can really test the mettle of our convictions. At times, it's a great temptation to get off track and turn the reins of our lives onto courses that seem to be the right way at the time to solve our pain. These pathways, however, usually give only temporary relief at best and often have long-term tragedies attached to them.

When we allow this mistaken response to happen, we forget what it is to commit our ways to the Lord, and we withdraw our commitment from Him to look for unsatisfactory God replacers, or some other way to anesthetize our own pain. It fails every time. We end up causing more trouble than we ever imagined. Solutions to agony that are outside of God's will always cause further damage—sometimes irreparable.

Worse yet, when we veer off course and no longer continue to do what we know to do, confusion can often set in.

We have a friend we care about very much whose husband disappeared a few months ago. She was left to fend for herself, along with their several children. He's gone, seemingly vanished from the earth. Frantically, she called me asking for help.

"Doug, I don't know what to do. I can't think; I just sit here paralyzed. I can't even get up to go to work. I can't get to church. I don't know where to turn."

I replied, "Just keep doing what you've always done as a believer. Stay on track. Do what you know to do as a Christian. Commit and continue. Get up every morning, regardless of how you feel. Get dressed, eat, feed the kids, look in the mirror, smile at yourself, and go to work as usual. And continue to worship as usual. If I don't see you worshiping with us, Deb and I will come to your home, tie you up, bring you to church, and lift your hands up in praise, if need be. But continue to do what you know to do, because it's the only way you'll get through this mess."

There is only one way to solve any problem: head-on. Go through it. You can't go around it; you can't sidestep it. *You must go through it*. That's what Prime Minister Winston Churchill told the British Parliament during World War II, that there was no other hope, no solution, that the only way through was through! That is, commit and continue. Whatever is happening, *stay on track*. Committing and continuing are what the prepared heart of the believer does in the face of suffering and tribulation.

Say to yourself: "I will commit myself to the Lord. I will continue to do what I know to do in Him."

This stance must hold, regardless of how agonizing the pain may be, or how severely the problems mount up, because:

(1) We know, according to Peter's words, that we serve a God Who is faithful and can be counted on;
(2) We are constantly under His watchful eye; and
(3) Nothing can separate us from the love of God.

213

PRAYER

Lord Jesus, we praise You that Your presence is not imagined, but is very real. I pray for any of us who are in the middle of trouble. You said that You would be a "very present help in times of trouble." If our pain or agony is coming from seeds that we have sown, Lord, we turn to You and ask for forgiveness. Free us from our own sinfulness. We want to establish a new life pattern, in that we determine to commit and continue and to stay on track with You. We pray for those who are seriously ill and those facing the compounding of the ill effects and suffering resulting from the stupidity of others. We choose to forgive and to open our hearts to the provision of Your grace for the awareness that we will be more than conquerors in this life. Thank You, Lord, for this provision of grace, in the name of Jesus we pray. Lord, I ask You to bless, as we freely give praise to You from our hearts, determining to commit to You and to continue in You.

Chapter 13

What to Expect
from Church Leaders
(1 Peter 5:1–4)

Is Christianity real when leaders fail? Many would say it isn't. Peter was no less concerned about the vulnerability of the church in his time with regard to leaders.

The events of 1988 and 1989 have afforded us the opportunity to see just how aggressively the Lord exposes and deals with leaders who either live inconsistently or take advantage of His people. The mistreatment of God's people at the hands of leaders isn't anything new. This doesn't, however, make it any less painful.

In our city, a very large congregation, through the use of heresy and error by its leadership, fell prey to a devilish practice called "connection." It has been clearly documented that this church has been solely responsible for the breakup of several hundred marriages.

In the practice of "connection," couples were encouraged to be "spiritual" partners with persons other than their spouses. By and large, this usually led to infidelity. The pastor, it was discovered, had had multiple affairs and was also extremely abusive and tyrannical. Our church has been inundated with couples fleeing that church, seeking help.

One of the greatest dilemmas in attempting to help someone who has been seriously injured by errant church leaders, is rebuilding their trust. We've found the recovery process for people involved in errant belief systems to be frightfully slow. One's unquestioning, blind trust always gets one into trouble.

As bad as church life gets at times, the reality of the Scriptures is that none of us can grow alone. Our link with the body of Christ is essential for our health in Him to continue. At the same time, God's people are so very, very vulnerable to leaders.

A young man, whose wife left him as a result of the false connection doctrine perpetrated by this cult, asked me, "How can I ever trust the church again?"

I replied, "I don't know, but we both know that it has to be accomplished somehow. Maybe the way you trust needs to be worked over, but you will have to learn to trust the church again."

"What gets me the most, Pastor Doug, is that lately I've been thinking that maybe God isn't real after all. If He would allow my leaders to treat me so abusively, how could He be?"

In answer, I opened the Scriptures to Acts 20 and showed him where the apostle Peter prophesied that there would be leaders who would fall away and seek to use the church abusively for their own advantage. The Bible is a very realistic book.

Sometimes the leap from simply reading the Scriptures to applying them to our situations is large. However, the Bible squarely addresses in many places the definite possibility that leaders can injure and take advantage of God's people. Perhaps, as you're reading this book, you've been abused yourself by faulty leadership within the church.

I would encourage any of you who lead a congregation not to get smug too quickly. I'm certain that any of us who lead with well-meaning hearts and a commitment to orthodoxy will, from time to time, unintentionally hurt people. Wisdom and forgiveness are always a dual necessity to walk in a healthy way with God's people. Wisdom should not be overly vulnerable, but forgiving enough to allow leaders the opportunity to repent and to grow as well.

Researchers have been able to establish the fact that adolescents were the most negatively affected by the fall of very visible leaders in American religions in the 1980s. The cynicism and skepticism of adolescents about God and the church have been severely affected by the recently publicized failings of church leaders.

It was interesting to learn that the older a person was when researched, the less skeptical that person was and the less impact a leader's failure had upon that person. Perhaps this could suggest that the longer we live, the more accurately we are able to assess the true nature of humanity.

People do suffer at the hands of leaders, sometimes innocently, sometimes not. Peter was intensely concerned that the church would have a pattern to measure God's view of church leadership versus what could be abhorrent forms of leadership.

This pattern, outlined in 1 Peter 5, will help us to recognize the kind of leadership God desires for His church. His desire is that the church would be the one place where suffering would not be perpetuated, but would be set aside. He desired that the church be a place of fellowship, a place of refuge, a place of peace, and a place where one's hurts are bound up and healed.

> The elders who are among you I exhort, I who am a fellow elder and a witness of the sufferings of Christ, and also a partaker of the glory that will be revealed: Shepherd the flock of God which is among you, serving as overseers, not by constraint but willingly, not for dishonest gain but eagerly; nor as being lords over those entrusted to you, but being examples to the flock; and when the Chief Shepherd appears, you will receive the crown of glory that does not fade away. (1 Peter 5:1–4)

Most leaders I've met in the body of Christ are sincere, hardworking men and women. For instance, I know a wonderful man who pastors a group of sixty people in a small town in Eastern Washington. Five days a week he drives sixty miles one way to work (that's six hundred miles a week!), because he can't get a job in the little community he's been called to pastor. I asked him why he did this.

He replied, "Well, Doug, I need to support my family, and I'm definitely called to this town. This little town is so small, it will never support a pastor. So, I see it as a small sacrifice, and so does my family. The privilege of serving God's people is well worth this effort."

I was humbled by his response. I think he is indicative of the vast majority of leaders in the body of Christ. He does this week after week to earn an income so he can lead Christ's people, but I doubt we'll ever see an exposé of him on "60 Minutes."

I can tell you about another guy, upstate in Mount Vernon, who owns a wrecking yard. God has touched his life powerfully. Hundreds of people have come to know the Lord through this man. He simply began reading the Scriptures and caring for a group of people. As a result of his efforts, the congregation has grown to three or four hundred souls. At his own expense, he's turned over a building on his property for the people to meet in. You'll never see his face on the cover of *Time* magazine, but he's there caring for Christ's church.

These are just two examples of hundreds of great church leaders I could tell you about. In fact, if you're being served by a good leader, I encourage you to take a moment to sit down and jot him or her a note of appreciation. In the environment in which we find ourselves today, I believe most church leaders are cringing.

Without strong, healthy, appreciated leaders, Christ's church is greatly weakened. My first experience with church came when I was eighteen, when a pretty girl named Debbie (who later became my wife) invited me to her folks' church on a Sunday night. About twenty people were there, and it was really boring to me. I felt like a fish out of water. I was sure everyone was looking at me because I was new and because I wasn't wearing the "right" clothes; I didn't wear a tie. I really felt awkward and ill-at-ease.

During that service, several people were baptized, which I thought was the weirdest activity I'd ever seen in my life. Every time they dunked someone under the water, everyone spouted Christian phrases like "Praise the Lord" and "Hallelujah!" I thought they were drowning those poor folks. The whole experience was pretty unnerving and frightening to me.

Then I met the Lord. Debbie and I went to a number of churches (each one a little different from the others), looking for one where we thought we could fit in. In one we attended, people actually moved away from us. But then, that was understandable. You see, Debbie dressed a little strangely in those days. She looked a little bit like Grace Slick from the rock group Jefferson Airplane. I had my own problems as well, not knowing how to dress or behave in church. I still haven't figured that one out.

Finally, we ended up in a church, knowing nothing about anything. I'd never sung a hymn in my entire life. Some of the people lifted their hands, and we had no idea what that was all about. But we did know and feel in our hearts that God was at work in His people in this place, and we badly wanted to be part of it. Our desire to be a part of a group of believers was a gift from the Holy Spirit. In belonging we became very vulnerable as well.

I received a report from Princeton University recently that analyzed the pervading spiritual mentality and attitudes that occur in our society. For the first time in seven years (the last quarter of 1988), our culture's perception of the viability and credibility of what is happening in the church has dropped. In terms of church leadership and churches' being esteemed in our culture, the 1950s were a high point. In fact, such esteem for the church had probably never been higher in our country's history.

Then from about 1960 to 1980, the church took a deep plunge by several percentage points. People perceived that the church was not viable or credible and had no importance in their lives. I really think the greatest fear in America stems from the dichotomy that it is not *whether* God exists, but rather, is He really *important* to me?

Suddenly, in 1980, popular opinion began to reverse itself. People's perception of what Christianity is all about climbed steadily upward until the end of 1988.

What happened in the last quarter of 1988 caused the church's standing to dip again by several percentage points. Frankly, I think we have a number of church leaders in the body of Christ to thank for that. When the press covered the credibility (or incredibility) of those lackluster leaders, bringing disturbing spotlights and general disgrace on the church, people began to question our integrity. How could we expect anything else?

Actually, there are plenty of opportunities for a loss of credibility in many churches. I'll never forget, as young marrieds and new believers, when Deb and I watched an usher have a terrible argument with his wife in the parking lot before a church service. We really hadn't been married long enough to have a fight and, if we had had one, I think we would have treated it as no big deal. But I was really quite stunned that this couple would be yelling at each other before the church service, yet smiling as they handed out bulletins.

I was briefly wounded by this episode. It was one of my first doses of reality, though it wasn't the last time I was hurt at church. There are always plenty of opportunities for us to separate ourselves from church.

Peter's point is that the church's approach to leadership should be such that the possibility of suffering at the hands of ill-motivated leaders should be guarded against. There are several things we need to know as we relate to the church: the Holy Spirit places in us a desire to belong; being a member of Christ's body is a very vulnerable state; and God does have an idea or a plumb line by which to measure our behavior toward one another.

PETER'S DREAM FOR LEADERS

We can all point fingers at the highly visible church leaders who have fallen in the last few years. But the other three fingers point back at us. Because we're all frail humans, we also have clay feet. The reality of all this brouhaha is that people are people. However, people are wondering everywhere whether their leader is putting the squeeze on them, or if he is manipulating and maneuvering them to his own advantage.

On the other hand, God hasn't slowed down His work at all, for He will continue to use leaders. Leaders are extremely important to God's work. None of us really grows in the body of Christ without a degree of vulnerability to leadership. In 1 Peter 5:14, Peter discussed what the church should be able to expect from its leaders. His expectations are the pattern for us to discern the kind of leadership we expect and are entitled to.

The kind of leadership he outlined will heal suffering rather than cause it. His outline of their character is as follows:

- Their aims,
- Their dreams, and
- Their mentality.

The church's drop in credibility happened, I believe, because the world has judged us properly. At times, our motivations haven't been square; our focus and visions have veered off-center. People aren't stupid.

The church is blessed with many different kinds of leaders. In our own congregation we have hundreds of volunteer leaders and pastors who help share the ministry load. They are involved in every aspect of the church, from leading meetings to holding women's studies, men's studies, Sunday school, and so on. Still others care for people during the week, counseling and making prayer calls and hospital visitations. We have a fantastic staff, composed of both paid and volunteer workers. They give generously of themselves for the caring and equipping of a large congregation.

The body of Christ is multilayered in its leadership. Peter offered us an opportunity to examine our motives, our dreams, and our mentality about leadership at all levels.

Perhaps I'm strange, but I refuse to be called a "reverend." My wife won't let me be called a reverend anyway, because I'm not reverent enough to be a reverend. In her mind you have to be really reverent to be a reverend. I believe that all the people in our congregation are ministers, so, in that sense, I'll refer to myself as a "minister." My job is primarily that of an equipper, for more and more of our staff are becoming the actual ministers.

I can only hope that all leaders in the body of Christ (especially myself) would exhibit the right attitudes, pure motives, and Christ-centered ambitions Peter outlined. I believe we live in the greatest time ever in the church of Jesus Christ. Sociological and spiritual factors and the intense anticipation that's building in the body of Christ confirm this. I've been a pastor for more than seventeen years, and there has never been an easier time than the one we're living in to share the realities of Jesus Christ. You almost have to work hard at trying not to have someone encounter Christ.

Everywhere I go the conversation soon turns to Jesus. People are interested in Jesus Christ today. When people ask me what I do, I tell them I'm a pastor, and I love telling people that. There's no better place for this opportunity than on a golf course, which generally happens at about the sixth hole.

One day, my son, Matt, and I were playing golf with a guy who was cussing a blue streak. I guess he thought he could guide his ball through the air better with his bleepity-bleeps. Matt, who was sixteen, kept looking at me with a shy grin on his face. Someone behind us who recognized Matt and me had heard the guy cussing.

While we walked from one tee to the next, he strolled over and asked the cussing guy in a low voice: "Hey, Mac, do you know whom you're playing with?"

"No. Who am I playing with?"

"You're playing with Pastor Doug Murren from the church down the street!"

At the next tee the cussing golfer told us about his two kids in YWAM (Youth With A Mission) over in Hawaii, as if God would forgive him his blaspheming because his kids were serving the Lord. At least, he had some good offspring. I suppose he hoped this would encourage me. I must admit I took some delight in the whole matter. Yes, it was quite easy to talk about the Lord Jesus with him the rest of our game.

François Voltaire, an "enlightened" French philosopher of the eighteenth century, declared one day that in his lifetime the church would become obsolete, unknown, and nonexistent. Not only was that not the case, but also the very house in which he penned that ridiculous statement is the headquarters of an international Bible society! Yes, I believe we're going to be around a while—in spite of toxic leadership. And we aren't just going to limp into the end of this age. We're going to be here and experience awesome power! It could be that the events of the past two years have sharpened our focus and brought about legitimate leadership in the church of Jesus Christ!

ATTITUDES, DREAMS AND AMBITIONS

Let's discuss the attitudes and ambitions we ought to expect and be entitled to from our leaders in the body of Christ.

1. *Among You*

The first thing we ought to expect from a leader is that he or she is to be from among us. *Among* is an important word. The notion that an expert from outside a congregation should be brought in is nonsensical. It doesn't work. Sooner or later it doesn't fly.

I personally feel that God never intended for outside experts to come in and lead churches. Now, being an expert is no problem because at times pastors will be brought in from outside a congregation. We're talking about mentalities and attitudes. Any effective leader in a church ought to be, first of all, from among the believers—a leader among equals.

When we started this congregation, we decided to have a church that we would always want to attend, a church where I'd want my family to attend all their lives. Why was that important to us? Because I've talked to enough pastor friends who, after some years, woke up one morning realizing that they and their families didn't want to attend the church they were pastoring anymore. That's a rough situation to be in.

I can say honestly that even if I weren't the leader of the church we're a part of, I would still want to be a part of this church. Regularly, I ask myself: "Doug, if you weren't the pastor of Eastside Foursquare Church, would you still attend?" The day that answer is no is the day I ought to pull up stakes and move on.

Leaders of a church are to be from among you. They are to be an integral part of the church at the human level. They're not to speak as experts from a lofty perch, nor from outside the congregation. Their lives are to be within reach and touch of the congregation.

We're all to live together as equals with different assignments. This is no easy process. Peter wanted to make certain that the church would not be following experts. Real leaders understand that they, too, are fellow members of the body of Christ.

I see myself at about age eighty-nine, listening to and evaluating some young person trying to preach to the congregation we've all grown up in. I plan to spend the rest of my days in this congregation, while, at the same time, understanding and accepting that my life is in the hands of the Lord and the church.

Leadership becomes toxic and can injure churches when leaders do not consider themselves to be part of the people with whom they share the Word.

2. *Remember Whose Flock It Is*

A congregation has the right to expect its leaders to remember whose church they're leading. When Peter told the leaders of his day that they were to *shepherd,* to take care of someone else's flock, whose flock was he talking about? *God's flock,* not their own.

It isn't just pastors who need to be reminded of this. I was recently asked to intervene in a squabble in another denomination. It seems there was quite a rift in that church.

The essence of the battle came down to two prominent families on the church board. Because they disagreed with the senior pastor's choice of youth pastor, they were exerting their votes, muscle, and politics. My ears turned red as I heard the story. The issue was power. Who would control and who would run this church?

When asked for my input, I said: "Actually, the church ought to follow the leadership of its pastor and trust his insight and wisdom as being from the Holy Spirit."

One board member answered angrily: "He [meaning me] hasn't been here all these years! Three or four of us on this board paid for 90 percent of what we have here!"

That was the crux of their problem: It was *their* church, not the church of the pastor, the board, and the congregation. Leadership that has that narrow view of the church will only hurt God's church. Until those board members realize whose church it is, I really feel that the situation in that church is hopeless. Many wonderful believers in that church are languishing in a conflict that is totally unnecessary.

I won't allow my family to be subjected to any leadership that forgets this basic premise. My wife, my kids, and I were bought by Jesus' blood. Don't try to own us!

Every so often, someone refers to our congregation as "Doug's church" or "your church." This noun and pronoun, though very subtle, are very powerful. Ownership is great; the kind of ownership that is submitted to the overall ownership of Jesus Christ is wonderful. I tell our congregation that they will know they're truly members when they shift their pronouns. For example, if they still refer to our congregation as "they," "yours" or "theirs," then they aren't members yet. The Holy Spirit still has a work to do in their hearts. But when they begin to say it's "my church" and "our church," then membership has truly happened to them from the inside out.

With Jesus there is no seniority system, either. All too often, the people who have been around the longest feel they are the largest stockholders. Jesus told a parable similar to this. Let me contemporize it a little.

Jesus reminded us of a construction foreman who hired workers at 8:00 in the morning at $48 for the day. At noon, he needed more guys for the job, so he hired more workers at the same wage of $48. Along about 4:00 in the afternoon, he needed still more guys to finish the job, so he called the union hall and hired several more, also at $48 for the rest of the working day.

Well, when the guys hired first heard that the guys hired last were getting the same pay, they got a little steamed, thinking they should get more. After all, they'd worked through the day's heat and had worked up more sweat. The foreman, however, pointed out that he hadn't welched on the deal and that they had agreed to work for $48, and that's what he would pay them.

Jesus' point was that there is *no* seniority system in the body of Christ. When it comes down to ownership and payoffs, He alone is Lord.

We deserve leaders in all areas of church life who will never forget that the church is Jesus Christ's church. The home meeting or Sunday school class you lead is not *your* meeting or class. It is Jesus' meeting or class.

Give yourself a test sometime. Ask yourself: "Would I stay in this church if they asked me not to teach this class or lead this group anymore?" If your answer is no, you've got a problem. Those are His people you're teaching or leading. Don't mess with them. It's a frightening thing to abuse God's people.

I think Peter was gravely concerned that there would always be leaders who would always be mindful of the Lord's watchful eye. Believe me, as a pastor, I think of the time when I will stand trembling before the Lord Jesus while looking into His eyes, and I will have to give an accounting of the care I've given the flock I have been assigned to tend. What a privilege—yet what a fearsome challenge!

3. Caring Leaders

The church deserves leaders who are primarily motivated by concern and care for others. I care about people, and I know our leaders and other pastors do as well.

When someone says to me, "I can't help it. I've got to express my gift or I'll never be happy," I get a little scared. If my primary motivation for caring for a flock is my own personal fulfillment, I'm actually using God's people to gain my own self-esteem. I'd hate to be guilty of using God's people to make myself look good or feel better. That would be a terrible travesty. The church deserves leaders who really care about what's going on around them.

I phoned a young man in our congregation recently. I'd heard that he was having a rough time. I don't get many opportunities to counsel these days, so I felt I should call him.

I said, "Hi. How's it going? How are you doing?"

"Pastor, you don't have time to call me," he replied, sounding embarrassed.

"Are you kidding? I don't have time not to call you," I retorted.

People caring for people is what makes healthy churches. Loving, accepting, and forgiving one another are the basis and heart of the true gospel in the kingdom of God.

Caring leadership is not primarily worried about administrative problems, but caring about others and the Lord's flock.

Motive is an important matter, though. So often, our training systems in the body of Christ turn out professionals as readily as a trade school would.

I've seen so many cases of people in the body of Christ who have a personal need to be heard. Concern and regard for those speaking can sometimes wane. The congregation is then viewed as God's channel to bless that leader. This is a frightening approach to leadership, but it appears more often than you would think. Christ's church deserves better. Christ deserves people who lead and teach on the basis of call. Calling is based on concern, high regard, and overall respect for individuals.

You can always tell a true leader because a true leader is willing to undertake tasks he or she isn't good at or duties she or he doesn't necessarily enjoy. I've observed that the leaders who are willing to clean restrooms, straighten chairs, and answer the phones are probably those who ought to be preaching in the church, as servanthood is the basis for all fruitfulness.

4. *God Appoints Leaders*

God places people where they're supposed to be. God chooses people to lead at the right places and at the right time.

There is nothing worse than uncertain leaders in the body of Christ. The church deserves leaders who know that God has placed them in the positions they are carrying out. If He has placed them, you can be sure He will also provide them with the abilities to accomplish the task at hand. Leaders are not to lead "by constraint, but willingly." When leadership moves beyond a vocation or mere hobby into an assignment, the church is safe.

Peter's picture of the church is that the Lord has assigned loving, capable leaders for the believers in every location to guide them successfully through a world that was coming unraveled at an unimaginable pace.

5. *Called by God*

This is a calling that amounts to being entrusted. Peter put it this way: leaders are being entrusted to be examples. This is the primary authority of leaders. It comes from knowing that God has placed them there and has given them instructions.

Leaders do what they do because God has called them and has appointed them to a specific location. This is to be the motive—God's calling, along with the dream to see God's vision accomplished for a particular location. And a leader's attitude is to be that of a servant.

Don't do it because you're greedy. Don't do it to get a salary. Don't lead a particular church to get higher on a pay scale. Churches pay their leaders in order to allow them more worry-free time and freedom to create the highest level of efficiency and effectiveness possible. That's why church leaders are remunerated, for it's a privilege to have time to serve the church.

Those who follow leaders need to recognize that their leaders have been set apart. They have been called by God to serve a function. The salary paid them really is an important issue in the local church.

The care and nurturing of leaders is as vital to the church as is the care the leaders give to the church. All too often, churches burn out their leaders. There is to be a commensurate investment, matching the call that God has placed on a congregation.

I've discovered that congregations usually get back from their pastor and leaders what they invest in them. If they give their pastors and leaders very little time away for replenishment and restoration of their spiritual life, they soon experience weak and worn-out leadership.

I'm very thankful that the leadership of our congregation has been liberal in allowing me study breaks and in recognizing that I do what I do not because of my vocation, but because I'm hearing from God.

Church leadership that is nurtured and cared for by the church itself, that allows the pastor to hear what the Lord is speaking on the basis of his or her appointment and call, is always strong. Peter was concerned that church leadership would not be appreciated and afforded the esteem connected with the word *call*.

On the other hand, leaders also get an opportunity to invest in God's people. I wish that every pastor had the opportunity to pioneer a church. I have, and so have friends of mine. We were fortunate, in the early days of our congregation, to have a team of people who all had the same vision, one motive and one mind. We all wanted to see God create a group of people who would have a deep regard for evangelizing our own local community.

At that time, the Eastside community of Greater Seattle was only about 8 percent churched. My first assistant and I had to risk our paychecks in order to accomplish effective outreach for the care and nurturing of this new church, because we saw this as an investment in God's people. I've noted elsewhere that when leaders have had an opportunity to invest in the people they serve or have been allowed to serve at great personal expense, they are far more fruitful in their effectiveness and their leadership is far more valid.

6. *Nonauthoritarian Leaders*

The church deserves leaders who aren't leading just so they can boss others around. I think it's obnoxious when people take great delight in being authoritative. You know the type. They just can't wait to get people in their home group or class so they can boss them around.

This is the absolute opposite of servant-oriented leadership. Peter anticipated that leaders might be tempted to lord it over those who had been entrusted to them. Possibly, people would use the authority of their position for their own advantage. It's a great temptation. Unfortunately, people are always hurt, and they often question the existence of God when they've been in the hands of a leader who has abused or exploited them in order to gain their own ends.

The problem is that I honestly know about twenty people whose lives I could do a better job of living than they do. I bet you do too. Because of this, the temptation to manipulate or take over is ever-present.

Peter said that if leaders are ever tempted, they need to remember that they have been entrusted with a great treasure. There is nothing closer to God's heart than people. In fact, they are called the "apple of His eye."

The only legitimate authority leaders have in the body of

Christ is example. If you want to have great authority as a leader, then have a great example of a life.

7. *Accountable Leadership*

The church should have leaders who will allow their lives to be examined. It's like living in a fishbowl.

Debbie and I live in a fishbowl. We recognize people all the time when they drive by our house to see where we live. That's okay. That's the reason I try to keep the front yard mowed.

I understand that I must give an account of my life. I must be willing to be accountable to our local council and to our denominational leadership. And I must be willing to have my life scrutinized in such a way that anyone is free to ask whether my life-style is consistent with the statements I make.

This helps to keep leaders very honest. I'll be the first one to say I'm far from perfect. Frankly, I often end up behaving in ways I don't approve of at all, but I'm happy to admit that I'm in a growth process right along with our church. There is no point in being egotistical; our congregation would call me on it. I'm a fellow journeyer, just like you, called by God into the unique and privileged position to lead.

When people want to lead or participate in our congregation, but don't want to be accountable, I get concerned. We, frankly, don't allow it.

Churches across America have leaders who feel they are not accountable. To me this is very frightening. Even in positions like Sunday school superintendents, there are people who work for God, but hide because they believe they are beyond the evaluation of those around them. Christ's church often suffers from leaders who are unwilling to be scrutinized, analyzed, and examined. Ruthless self-analysis is great, but there is nothing like a heart that is open to the input of others.

On occasion, I have said: "When a guy gets angry, he's likely to react and get out of God's will." Now, I have a reputation among our staff for being somewhat of a perfectionist. A couple of times when I've lost my temper, only to find it again, I've said: "Don't do what I do—just do what I say." The staff has not only taped my saying that, but has even made a plaque of it and presented it to me as well.

Saying that, though, doesn't fly, does it? You can't ask people to do what you say if you're not willing to make at least a fair attempt to have your own behavior consistent with your messages. I can't expect others to do what I say if I'm not willing to do it, can I? The church has the right to expect leaders who will not just talk about the process of being a role model, but will be examples as well.

IS CHRISTIANITY REAL?

This section of Scripture will allow us a recapitulation. To all my friends and fellow believers who have been hurt by leaders in the body of Christ, I would like to say: "Yes, Christianity is real, even when we leaders fail." Why do I believe this?

1. Because there are so many leaders who have not failed and are serving Jesus very sacrificially in the body of Christ.

2. The Lord is just as broken and grieved when church leaders hurt His flock as the people themselves are.

3. The Bible realistically told us to anticipate leaders who may use us spitefully, but we are to operate in the gift of wisdom to avoid this.

4. From the section of Scripture we have just read through, Peter has given us a clear outline of how to recognize legitimate leaders. A pattern that is healthy and wholesome is contained in the Word of God. God did not leave us without a plumb line to identify wrongful leadership. He gave us safeguards to prepare us and to protect us from people who would take advantage of our vulnerability to one another.

I see this as a compassionate, precautionary step on the part of God—one that He now expects us to employ with wisdom to keep ourselves safe. But what do I do if I've suffered at the hands of church leaders?

- *Forgive.* By all means forgive—and forgive again.
- *Don't stay subjected to abusive, exploitive leadership.*
- *Take rigorous steps to find a place of worship where the leaders line up with the characteristics Peter outlined.*

Yes, God is very real, even when His leaders fail us. Christianity is vital and alive, even though some leaders use the faith of others to gain their own advantage.

Chapter 14

Moving Beyond Spiritual Naïveté:
Things You Wanted to Know About Satan, but Were Afraid to Ask
(1 Peter 5:5–9)

The last instruction Peter shared with his fellow sufferers was the measures that need to be taken against evil—not just inanimate evil, but evil personified by Satan.

A great deal of spiritual naïveté exists in our culture at present. I've been surprised recently by how often I have encountered people who dabble in the occult—a truly dangerous practice. Certain varieties and brands of New Age and Unitarian beliefs move quite easily into realms of the occult and the demonic, which can seem very innocent on the surface. Paul made it clear that Satan could easily come disguised as an angel of light to fool us. Essentially, these beliefs hold that humans are innately good and that there really is no devil. These premises are not true and prove that we are all susceptible to Satan's deceptions.

The American belief system, by and large, claims that if we don't believe something exists, then it doesn't. This is like saying: "I don't believe there is a wall ahead of me, so I'm going to drive along at 60 m.p.h. I don't see it, so it doesn't exist."

However, my refusal to believe in that wall's existence isn't going to change its reality. My car, blasting into it at 60 m.p.h., will give me a very rude awakening, to be sure.

On the subject of Satan, the Bible very clearly states some vital truths. Satan really is an entity to be reckoned with. His all-consuming desire is to destroy all that God loves and, in his rebellious nature, he has determined that the primary way he will get back at God for kicking him out of heaven is to scar us, if he can. Satan is the true origin of evil in the world, and his diabolic influence is the source of most pain and suffering.

Likewise you younger people, submit yourselves to *your* elders. Yes, all of *you* be submissive to one another, and be clothed with humility, for

> *"God resists the proud,*
> *But gives grace to the humble."*

Therefore humble yourselves under the mighty hand of God, that He may exalt you in due time, casting all your care upon Him, for He cares for you. Be sober, be vigilant; because your adversary the devil walks about like a roaring lion, seeking whom he may devour. Resist him, steadfast in the faith, knowing that the same sufferings are experienced by your brotherhood in the world. (1 Peter 5:5–9)

FACING FACTS

Now, I'm not the kind of guy who sees the devil under every rock. But at times I've had to admit that I have observed a direct attack by Satan.

During the last ski season, the twelve-year-old son of one of our staff members nearly died from a skiing accident. When his skis hit soft snow, he was catapulted through the air and struck a building, suffering severe head injuries.

As I stood in the hospital, praying with his folks, I knew in my heart that although Satan had not actually caused this accident, he did try to snatch that boy's life. Not only was he trying to snatch the boy's life away, but he was also trying to assault and discourage the boy's parents as much as possible, who are two very strong and wonderful believers in Christ.

I was delighted to grab that little guy's hand and pray, "Lord Jesus, we ask You to rebuke Satan and make sure he doesn't snatch this little life or receive any glory!" It felt very sound and good.

Now, not in every instance have I found myself praying in such a way. But I felt in that instance that the enemy would take advantage of our suffering and turn the tables on us if he could.

This pivotal section of Scripture, 1 Peter 5:5–9, deals with moving beyond naïveté about spiritual matters. The apostle Peter was quite concerned that the Christians he was writing to, who had lost their homes, loved ones, possessions, and homeland because of their faith, would be susceptible to demonic attacks when discouraged or facing less-than-optimal circumstances. So he alerted them about this enemy of their souls so that they wouldn't be naïve or become victimized by him. I believe this passage is built around the pivotal statement: "Be sober, be vigilant; because your adversary the devil walks about like a roaring lion, seeking whom he may devour" (1 Peter 5:8).

Peter also gave several specific instructions on how to resist satanic attacks when suffering. There are three times when you have to watch your back for satanic assault or attack:

(1) *When you're having a real "down" time,* when life isn't going as well as you had hoped. You're burned out, worn out, and discouraged.

(2) *When you face a great success.* One of the high points of Jesus' life came when He was baptized in the River Jordan by John the Baptist, and God the Father said: "You are My beloved Son, in whom I am well pleased" (Mark 1:11). Immediately, Jesus was whisked away to the wilderness where Satan challenged Jesus with the three supreme temptations of His life. At points of great victory, we are susceptible to attack by the enemy.

(3) *When you feel neither high nor low.* It's just ho-hum, business as usual.

As you can see, this outline clearly shows that we are to be on the alert at all times. I would add: Be most definitely on the alert when pain and suffering strike.

Evil, which fills the world, and diseases, which attack our bodies, are not explainable without the presence of real, personified evil. For the Christian, any discussion of pain and suffering must also involve a serious discussion about the presence of our enemy, Satan. He deserves the credit for the bulk of the evil and tragedies that happen in the world.

Yet, he is held at bay by God and by the Presence of the Holy Spirit through the church of Jesus Christ. We probably can't fully appreciate or imagine what the presence of real believers means to a world under the dominion of our adversary.

Paul suggested in 1 Thessalonians that the evil that is presently in the world is being restrained; it is not fully unleashed. I've long believed that this is due to the Presence of the Holy Spirit within Christ's church. We think evil and suffering are rampant now, but try to imagine what it would be like without God's people confronting them head-on with the Holy Spirit's help.

It seems, however, that whenever we discuss Satan, we tend toward extremes. Either we pooh-pooh his presence, or we exaggerate his influence. I believe that Satan enjoys our being hung up at either extreme. Of course, he wants us to talk more about him than about Jesus. And, of course, he loves to receive credit for problems and circumstances he didn't create, for Satan is exalted each time his name is mentioned. When the Bible states: "Give *no* place to Satan," it means: Don't give him any visibility or any credit or recognition of *any* kind.

At the other end of the spectrum, Satan is just as delighted when we deny his existence, for now he can go about his work unhindered. After all, if we don't believe the devil is real, this gives him *carte blanche* to wreak a lot of havoc. Neither one of these imbalances is healthy for us.

UNDERSTANDING OUR ADVERSARY

Let's see what the Bible has to say about the devil. In 1 Peter 5, he's described as "a roaring, hungry lion ready to devour us." His strategy against Christians (which is different than for non-Christians) is to neutralize us. This can be accomplished through fatigue, apathy, or somehow making us ineffective for Christ.

In an instrumental way, each of us has the potential to make an impact on at least twenty lives for Jesus each year. Most researchers of evangelism believe that at least 20 percent of the membership of any congregation has evangelistic inclinations.

So, if Satan can neutralize two hundred of us, his strategy can have some negative, long-term effects. As far as he is concerned, it is a great victory for him when he renders a Christian ineffective.

The Bible says that Satan can disqualify us. Paul said that he had to be on his toes, lest the enemy take advantage of him. Paul pummeled his flesh and kept it under check. Paul determined to stay alert, because he knew that one of the enemy's ploys would be to entice him into inconsistent living, which would disqualify his work for Christ.

Satan's only desire is to devour and destroy us, and he works twenty-four hours a day trying to accomplish this. Why? Because he hates everybody and everything God loves. *Because God loves people, Satan hates them.*

Now, if you're a nonbeliever, let me challenge you at this point. Give me a reasonable, logical explanation for the genocide of an entire tribe in the African Sudan. And don't tell me it was because there wasn't enough food to go around. That's utter nonsense, for God created a world that can produce enough food for all the people who inhabit this world. So don't blame it on God, and don't ask why He didn't do anything about it.

Or explain how millions of Cambodians suffered at the hands of the Khmer Rouge. There is no reasonable explanation, except the presence of evil powers and principalities organized under a satanic head to destroy all that God loves.

The Bible states further that Satan is the one who keeps our minds captive and in the dark concerning God's true nature and the free gift of Jesus Christ's salvation, which has been extended to every person on earth. Satan's constant strategy is to distort, to pervert, and to keep our minds and hearts in untruth. He is also the originator of all evil and all diseases.

A rundown of Satan's titles is very insightful. Some of the more notable ones are Lucifer, serpent, tempter, destroyer, accuser, enemy, prince of darkness, prince of the power of the air, and angel of light. The devil is also called the liar and Beelzebub, which is translated as "Lord of the Flies"—another way to say Lord of Filth. Quite fitting, don't you think?

Ezekiel 26 and 28 and Isaiah 14 yield some clues to his biography. These are difficult passages to interpret because they are allegorical or metaphorical explanations of the origins of evil. They are also metaphorical devices to describe how the power brokers of our world participate in Satan's spirit of evil.

It appears that Satan was, in the beginning, the most beautiful angel in all of heaven. As the archangel Lucifer (meaning "morning star"), he had command of all its worshiping hosts. Lucifer had status above all the other angels and God's favor, but, according to the Scriptures, Satan became inflated with pride. This is why 1 Timothy 3 cautions that a new convert should never be a leader in the church, because he or she is susceptible to Satan's sin of pride.

When Lucifer decided he didn't have a big enough slice of the pie, he complained bitterly to God one day: "Hey, God, I'm not getting my fair share. After all, I'm not only the handsomest dude hereabouts, but I'm also very ingenious. You are just trying to keep me down so I won't show You up. But I don't need You anymore, so I'm gonna bust outta here and set up my own kingdom, and I'm gonna take some buddies with me!"

The Bible suggests that he took as many as a third of the angels in heaven with him and immediately set up housekeeping in hell. He planned his campaign and launched his attack on God's prized creation, humans, on Planet Earth.

I think you would have to agree that this guy was not in his right mind. But then, sin and evil are always expressions of insanity. When dealing with the enemy of our souls, we are dealing with irrationality taken to frightening extremes, far beyond any horror movie.

We're talking here about the greatest example of a demented creature. I really believe that pride can lead us into this type of insanity. To me the two are almost synonymous, since pride causes us to lose touch with reality.

When the devil revolted, God forever banished him from heaven and subjugated him to time and space, just as we are. Though we don't know all the facts concerning this matter, we do know a few of them. My personal opinion is that Satan will likewise be destroyed within the realms of time and space.

I don't think he's an eternal being anymore. I think he experienced spiritual death when he was banished from heaven, just as we did when we fell from God's grace. One distinct difference exists, however. There is *no* redemption available for Satan, though there is for us—and this really gripes him. He knew God in a personal way, but defied Him. Satan's ultimate goal was bent on dethroning Christ. The devil is the principal anti-Christ. He's a usurper, a false god, and he cannot be redeemed. He is the perverted imitator of all that is good about God, and the great distorter of all that is right and true.

As the tempter, he uses deceptive ploys to manipulate our imaginations to commit more and more extravagant sins. The nature of sin is that the more you sin, the more you need to sin. As the destroyer, Satan disrupts and breaks our relationships with each other and with Jesus; he destroys our ability to be effective for Jesus. As the prince of the power of the air, he is a usurper who spiritually controls the environs around us, as well as claims illegitimate rule over these realms. He sends sweeping, lying, spiritual mentalities, turning people fearfully or pridefully away from God.

The Bible declares quite strongly in the book of Daniel that the intercession of God's people breaks up, turns aside, and sets to flight the strongholds of control that Satan attempts to set up.

Now, let's stop right here for a moment to set the record straight. Satan is *not* the king. Jesus Christ is the King and Lord over all! Therefore, because Satan is a liar and a usurper, *Jesus has given us the authority to subjugate Lucifer to the will of God by employing Jesus' Name and character*.

While in Germany on a missionary trip, I went for a walk off campus one day and accidentally wound up in the local "red light" district, because I didn't speak German well enough to find out where I was heading. Immediately upon entering this district, I could feel a general filthiness, a garbage-like atmosphere in the air. The area even looked filthy. It was interesting that I could sense the filth, even though I hadn't as yet noticed the pornography shops around me. Why did it feel so filthy? Because Satan loves garbage and is piggish by nature. This experience thoroughly convinced me that there are realms of spiritual influence—good and bad—that one picks up on and senses intuitively.

As the angel of light, 2 Corinthians 11 states, Satan can masquerade as someone impressive and beautiful, who speaks convincingly and tantalizingly. At times, he's very appealing and intelligent. Satan can never create, however, and he will always be a creature as you and I. He can only echo or copy. That's why sin is an aberration and a misemphasis of the truth that God has revealed to us in His Bible.

When Jesus discussed Satan's rule of this world in John 16:11, he said that "the prince of this world now stands condemned" (NIV). Jesus described him further as the ruler of the cosmos (*kosmos* in Greek, which refers to "the universe," loosely translated as "cultures of men").

A true, biblical Christian will always be wary of and suspicious about any political or economic system in the world—even our own in America. These systems can be closely aligned with the satanic spirit that seeks to destroy lives. If you've ever visited a Communist country, you know that government systems can be energized by corporate, political, and geopolitical evils, which all originate with Satan. He is the source of all evil, of all diseases, and he is also the evil one.

How do we deal with him? Why doesn't God snuff out Satan? God has His reasons. He allows Satan to be in this world because God has complete confidence in the Holy Spirit's Presence in the church to keep Satan suppressed until God ends his reign. When empowered by the Holy Spirit, God's people will rout the enemy every time.

If we believers are in tune with the Lord and are at war for Him, we become even stronger believers when the accuser or tempter strikes. Satan's purposes are then thwarted and turned back upon himself! Because the devil is subjugated to God, God uses him to work out His own ends. This planet's fallen state and our redemptive process are so intertwined with this minion from hell that the end of this age will be signaled when Satan is finally destroyed.

Does this mean that we belong to a dualistic faith, a faith that states that good and evil are on even terms, and that God and Satan are merely dueling it out? No, that isn't the case at all. Absolutely not! We do *not* believe in a dualistic faith system as Christians. God is in absolute control. Don't ever forget that. This is the message that Peter desired to get across to us. Evil has been introduced to this realm and is attempting to subvert and to keep this world in its control, but be assured that evil will not succeed.

The great theologian Oscar Cullman once described the nature of this age. He likened the return of the Lord Jesus to the landing of the Allied troops on French soil. It was certain from that point on that victory day was approaching. The landing had been accomplished. The Allied forces were thwarting Hitler's armies everywhere. They were driven back. It was inevitable that Hitler's hordes would be totally conquered; yet, the battle waged on for several months before it actually became reality. Victory Day came when the Allies met in Berlin.

Cullman suggests that the second coming of the Lord Jesus will be the destruction of Satan's kingdom. Meanwhile, God is using His people to seal the fate of evil and suffering on this planet. He has extended healing gifts to His church. He has granted great authority through prayer and intercession. He has established in the heart of every believer a place for empowerment by His Spirit! As Christians, we have to believe that we are having a meaningful impact on the degree and power of evil in this world.

We are not at all under a dualistic system. God is absolutely in control, but the degree of His control over evil very clearly depends on us. That's why Peter stated that we can resist Satan in Jesus' powerful Name; we can cause Satan to step back and his power to be assuaged.

Light and truth in God reign supremely over evil—always have, and always will. We all need to remember that. The Bible doesn't teach us that good and evil are on the same terms. Satan is no match for God Almighty, because he's a mere creature. That's all he will ever be—a creature, just like you and me, although he does have some allies to help him, such as the world systems (the cosmos), our weak flesh (weak wills, that is), the part of us that is the most friendly with this realm, and demons. Talking about demons makes us all a little squeamish. I personally believe in them.

A few years back, a longtime friend shared a story with me I could hardly believe, but knew was true. Joe had been involved in Transcendental Meditation. Upon receiving his *mantra* (chanted Hindu prayer), he pursued this new spiritual experience with great vigor.

This is his story: "Doug, I got to the point where I actually heard voices speaking in my mind, and I heard strange voices come out of my own mouth that I wasn't speaking. I knew I was being lifted to almost superhuman levels when I chanted my mantra. It wasn't me at all anymore, nor my emotions. Then, one day, all at once, I actually saw a flash of light leave my body! That's when it got really scary. This chant seemed to have taken over control of my mind. I didn't know what to do to get rid of it."

Joe became extremely fearful of what was happening to him. Then he encountered a believer, an attorney, in our city. This man, several years older than Joe, shared the gospel with him. As Joe sat in this attorney's office, his newly found friend confronted him with the truth and authority of the gospel of Jesus Christ.

His attorney friend prayed: "Lord Jesus, we just release now Your great power to free Joe from the bondages that have ensnared him."

The power of Jesus freed Joe, and he accepted the Lord. Now, you don't know Joe as I do. He's not a spaced-out kind of individual, but very stable, very sane, and very intelligent. I happen to believe his story, for it appears to be consistent with some of the events that Jesus encountered when He walked the earth, as told in the Gospels.

We can't afford to be unsophisticated about evil in our time. Statisticians suggest that there has never been a time in American history when there has been more interest in the spirit world. This is a very foolish and extremely dangerous interest. In a culture where we sneer at those who believe in the devil, we are more susceptible than ever to all kinds of his spiritual bondages.

Consequently, Peter was quite worried that the people he

was serving would not remain singular in their view of what was happening in the world, even in that day. He reminded them that there were forces outside and within the realm they lived that were of another sphere, an evil sphere. Quantum physics is just beginning to convince the scientific world that there are many strata of reality.

In the midst of suffering it is vitally important that we understand the real presence of Satan, who would destroy us, and to take protective measures. It is vitally important as well that *we stand on our authority in Jesus and resist the devil with our entire arsenal,* realizing that we do have authority over him, for he is real and is bent on destruction.

Not too long ago, a retired missionary from Latin America told me about the high level of demonic manifestations in Latin America. I was startled by his story.

He told me: "In one of the villages in the area where I worked, there was a witch doctor with a larger, bigger demon in him than another witch doctor had. Because he had the biggest demon and more power, he was the chief exorcist in that area. So he went around exorcising the smaller, less powerful demons out of people. Doug, remember that Satan's kingdom is primarily of the rebellious. It is filled with all kinds of renegade angels and demons."

You may laugh in disbelief, but that's the real world out there, and that world is in spiritual chaos. The devil is the motivating evil force, and his kingdom is always in disarray because it is, by nature, rebellious. This is revealed throughout Scripture. This rebellious kingdom can be compared to a motorcycle gang. They may all belong to the same gang, but each member is pretty much on his own and does his own thing.

Satan is also a coward with a wide yellow streak down his back. The Bible states emphatically that Satan will flee immediately if we resist him, and this fact is revealed in several places. James 4 and 1 Peter 5 are two clear examples in which we are told to "resist." Any time the enemy encounters someone who will stand his or her ground and voice the truth of God, he will flee immediately. That's a true promise.

I have written this section with a great deal of trepidation.

The stories shared with you are true. Regardless of our tradition or background, the presence of this evil element in all its forms in our culture and world today is more combative than ever.

Christians cannot afford to be naïve about matters of evil. Neither can we afford to be preoccupied with evil. We must be filled with biblical insight instead.

READY FOR WARFARE

G. K. Chesterton was once asked: "What's the problem with this world?"

Chesterton's reply: "Sir, what is wrong with this world is me."

Remember a story about Peter. One afternoon when Jesus and His disciples were fellowshiping together, Peter said that Jesus was the Son of the Living God. When Jesus announced that He was soon going to be crucified in Jerusalem, be buried, and rise again from the grave, Peter thought it was a bad marketing approach.

If you recall, Jesus became very angry. He turned to Peter and said sharply: "Get behind me, Satan!"

This incident sadly illustrates the fact that we can unwittingly be used as allies in Satan's strategies. Paul gave us another example when he told the church at Corinth that they needed to forgive and restore their fallen leader to his position, cautioning them: "Hey, folks, let's not be ignorant about Satan's devices." Paul was suggesting that we can unwittingly and stupidly fall into the devil's strategies by being unforgiving.

ANALYZING SATAN'S STRATEGIES

Temptation

One strategy the enemy uses for his own advantage is *temptation*. Have you ever been tempted? Of course, we all have been. He stimulates our imagination. We deal with temptation by being sober, by being vigilant, and by continuing the renewing process of our minds.

Deception

Another strategy the enemy uses is *to distort the truth*. When Jesus faced temptation, Satan tried to deceive Him by twisting Scripture. Deception usually entails making something appear true that is actually false, though it may have a kernel of truth in it.

Being vigilant means to be open to the truth. Be on your toes. Be ready to discern what is true. By exposing ourselves to the Word of God, we become discerning individuals, attuned to the truth of God.

Distraction

The third strategy that works to Satan's advantage is *to distract us*. In the parable of the sower, found in Mark 4, God sowed seed (the Word) in the ground (our hearts). In this parable, Satan (represented by the crow) picked the seed out of the ground before it could take root and grow. Don't ever doubt that this doesn't happen on a regular basis. On any Sunday morning, after God's Word has been shared, by the time we get to our cars, God's Word is often snatched away by Satan before being firmly implanted in our hearts. His goal is to distract us before we can make commitments that will allow God's Word to take root in us.

Many distractions come our way. Sometimes one may be television. Sometimes appetites, fears, and anxieties can all be distractions to prevent the Word from taking root in our hearts.

Pride

Still another strategy that Satan employs to get us off the track is *pride*. He is very clever at getting us to succumb to one or more of the forms or attributes of pride, such as self-exaltation, haughtiness, conceit, arrogance, boasting, overconfidence, sanctimony, unreasonable ambition, and self-righteousness.

Christ, by contrast, was free from all worldly pride of appearance, of worldly success, of reputation, of riches or rank, and of kingship. First Peter 5 and other Scriptures make it clear that if Satan can't pull us down in some fashion, he'll try to push us over the edge.

We need to be on constant guard against these satanic tricks, for "God resists the proud/But gives grace to the humble" (1 Peter 5:5).

Defamation

One of the primary ways Satan works against us is to tear down our self-esteem to *defame* us. Some of my friends feel that there is too much talk about self-esteem and self-worth in the church. Often, that rationale is used for fear that we would be influenced too much by psychology.

I disagree with this wholeheartedly. After all, if we don't have self-esteem and self-worth, how are we going to be effective instruments for Jesus and His glory? One of Satan's clear strategies is to wear or tear down the saints, and he'll do it any way he can. In the book of Daniel it is reported to be the work of the antichrist spirit to wear God's image off God's people. What better way to accomplish the destruction of self-esteem than through inferiority complexes, which are the seedbed of his works!

God builds His people up. The gifts of the Holy Spirit raise our esteem and personal worth, both for one another and for ourselves. This satanic strategy often works, causing us to lose touch with reality, giving us spirits filled with timidity rather than the saneness and the enabling power of the Holy Spirit.

OUR COUNTERACTIVE STRATEGIES

Peter provided us with four distinct and effective ways to resist the devil and to deal with his assaults.

Submit to One Another

The first step in resisting the devil is *to submit to one another*. Accountability has a way of reducing the opportunities for Satan's works to take root. Submitting means simply listening with respect to one another. If we don't have people to whom we can listen with respect or to whom we can submit our ideas, visions, and dreams, we are more susceptible to deception.

Be Humble

The second way to resist the devil is with *humility*. In other words, *keep yourself in perspective*. Don't think that you're too good to suffer. Everybody suffers. You aren't the center of the world.

I overheard a very astute observation one day: "If we all had to come together clothed in our humility, most of us would be arrested for indecent exposure!"

"Humble yourselves, therefore, under God's mighty hand, that he may lift you up in due time" (1 Peter 5:6).

Trust God

The third way to beat the devil at his own game is *to trust God*. That is, "cast all your anxieties upon Him, for He cares for you" (1 Peter 5:7, paraphrased). One of the tricks Satan tries to pull on us is to get us to believe that God is not a loving Father, that He doesn't care about us, and that Christ is not capable of protecting us.

Remember when, in the Garden of Eden, Satan approached Eve and said, "Come on, Eve, eat the fruit from the tree in the middle of the garden"?

Eve replied, "No! God told us not to."

But Satan said, "Aw, come on, eat it. The only reason God doesn't want you to eat it is because He's jealous. He doesn't want any competition, because He knows you'll be as wise as He is then. Don't you know that yet? Go ahead. Eat it, Eve."

By uttering these lies about God, the devil libeled and slandered God. That's one of his aims: to keep us from trusting God. He keeps us from trusting God by perverting His image in our lives.

If you should hear this kind of talk when you're experiencing difficult times, recognize it for what it is—a satanic attack.

The true story that follows will thrill your whole being! About a year ago, a young Nigerian prince of the Islamic religion accepted Christ. When he returned to his village and shared the story of his conversion with his father (the king), his father personally ordered and oversaw the execution of his own son by machete! At the king's order, this young prince was taken outside the village and literally hacked to death by his fellow tribesmen.

As the tribe walked back to their village, the young prince stood up, *totally recovered,* and caught up with them! The tribe was absolutely terrified! By the time they all reached the village, not a mark could be found on the prince, let alone severed arms and legs they had witnessed just a short time before!

This entire tribe of former Muslims now belongs to an evangelical church of believers in Africa. This true story is told to show that we can trust God with the outcome of our lives.

One of my favorite books by J. B. Phillips is titled *Your God Is Too Small!* In it he talked about the distortions we have of God's image.

Phillips illustrated several of our wrong beliefs about God that undermine our ability to trust Him. He outlined some of the misconceptions with humorous little titles. For example, he said that we sometimes view God as a resident policeman or a tyrannical parent. He's a "grand old man" or an escape artist. Or He's a jack-in-the-box, for you never know when He's going to pop up. He may even be seen by some, according to Phillips, as the Chairman of the Board or the Great Disappointer or a narcissist on the silver screen. We may simply see God as a mystical vision or Santa Claus in heaven, ready to give us all that we request. All these false images of God have a way of attacking us.

Often, these images are associated with parental images. Often also, adult children of alcoholics have a very difficult time perceiving God as a father. Or victims of abuse have trouble believing that God would desire only good for them. These are all the seedbeds in which evil takes root and attacks God's rightful image in our hearts and lives.

Obviously, we can't go back and rewrite our history, but one of Satan's tactics is to get us to relive over and over the evil assaults in our pasts. The positive step we can take to rid ourselves of reliving past hurts and assaults is to move on responsibly from this moment with the life we have ahead of us. With some effort on our part, we can rebuild and redevelop our imagination about God by dealing with our thoughts about what He is really like.

Right at the heart of our belief system there has to be trust in God. The impacts of disease and suffering are greatly minimized when this preparation is undertaken in our hearts.

Resist and Stand Firm

The fourth tool is to *resist Satan and stand firm in the faith by avoiding self-pity*. Remember that everyone in the world suffers—not just you.

Another of Satan's ploys is to have us believe that we're getting a raw deal. Self-pity says, "I'm suffering more than anyone else." It attacks our trust in God, as well as distorts and weakens our confidence in Him.

Resisting Satan means simply that we stand our ground; stop all self-pity; stand strong; and stand firm! Note that Peter didn't tell us to yell louder or shout louder, because louder is not necessarily better or more effective. He just said to *resist Satan* and to *stand steadfast,* knowing that the same sufferings are experienced by your fellow believers throughout the world.

Resisting Satan requires a sober and vigilant mind. Alert minds are better able to spot the point of attack and to resist with conviction.

Our tendency to think that we're a "special case" is quite common. In fact, it's part of our human condition that we think we're an exception to the rules or in an extraordinary situation. None of us is. We all suffer. We all face the reality of evil in this world.

REVIEW

Let's review some of the simple truths we have learned in this chapter about the presence of evil and suffering in the world, and what we can do about it.

1. We have learned that Satan does, in fact, exist, along with his minion demons.
2. We found that evil and suffering in this world are energized by a personality called Satan.
3. We have learned that Christianity is *not* a dualistic faith. God and Satan are *not* on equal terms.
4. We have learned that Satan lies about and slanders God.
5. We have been warned about the dangers of naïveté toward the spirit world of Satan.
6. We have learned that one of Satan's great strategies is to catch us in the snare of self-pity.
7. We have learned that we can trust God with the outcome of our lives.
8. We have learned that we can resist Satan and win. We don't give in to him!

Conclusion
(1 Peter 5:10–14)

Is Christianity real when it doesn't work?

That all depends, doesn't it? It depends on what we mean by "work." Does it mean that Christianity is assuring us a painless and problem-free life? It doesn't work that way. So I guess the answer would be no. If, however, we believe that living in Christ (and He in us) gives us an indomitable spirit, courage, and a quality of life, then pain and suffering, in fact, cause Christianity to thrive, and we become overcomers in the process.

We've journeyed through the heart of a fellow sufferer: the apostle Peter. Scholars believe it wasn't too long after finishing the books of 1 and 2 Peter that he was sentenced to death by Nero, the depraved Roman emperor. Because Peter felt in his mind that he was unworthy, he refused to be crucified in the same manner as his Lord Jesus had been.

It is generally believed that within months of writing these two books Peter was crucified, at his own request, upside down in about A.D. 64, the end of an illustrious ministry on earth and the end of a life fervently devoted and dedicated to the glory of God.

Is Christianity real when it doesn't work? I think Peter would say it was a moot question. Christianity always works. A life lived in Christ is always successful.

I had breakfast one morning with my good friend Chris, who lives in our neighborhood, just a short distance from us.

In 1989, Chris's wife, Karen, died of cancer. Nevertheless, Chris and their two kids have continued to live strongly in the Lord.

We have tried in the past few months to connect regularly for breakfast or a cup of coffee, here and there. Chris called me one morning at 9:00 A.M., rousing me out of bed. It was a Saturday morning, so I had allowed myself to sleep in, as I needed all the rest I could snatch to get me in shape for three services on Sunday. Besides, I was writing this book until 2:00 A.M. that morning!

Debbie answered the phone and called to me, "Doug, how about breakfast with Chris?"

I kind of moaned something, got up, exercised on my stationary bike, showered, and was only five minutes late meeting him.

We had a great time discussing how the Lord had been working in both of our lives that week. Chris is a negotiator for a large corporation and is a tough man, accustomed to facing the pressures and rigors of business life.

He shared with me a humorous anecdote about the kinds of Christmas cards he had received. They were one of two types: that Karen was having the greatest time in heaven anyone could ever imagine, or that this would be the worst Christmas Chris and the kids ever had, and the card sender wanted to reach out to him.

Leaning toward me, he said, "Doug, I feel really guilty about this, but I'm not sad about Karen anymore. Is there something wrong with me? Am I callous?"

When Debbie and I had prayed with Karen in her last hour, we could sense the joy and anticipation Karen had about meeting her Lord. Her heart had been well prepared to meet this suffering. She and Chris had talked extensively about the issue of death and had grappled repeatedly with the agonies presented them by chemotherapy, radiation therapy, bone marrow transplants, and every effort to keep Karen alive.

"No, Chris, there's nothing wrong with you," I said. I know how well prepared you and Karen were for this suffering. And I know that, for you, death was in perspective, because your heart was prepared to handle real life after she was gone. There's no need to feel guilty."

Leaning back and heaving a big sigh of relief, he said, "Whew! I was really wondering. That phrase you used, 'prepared to handle real life,' caught my heart. Thanks, Doug. That makes me feel better."

Is Christianity real when it doesn't work? I suppose it is real only if you're living a real life.

I think what Peter wanted to leave as a legacy for the believers he loved and shepherded was that they would be able to prepare their hearts to face suffering.

We've already stated, over and over again, the certainty that all Christians will suffer. But it is our heart's preparation that allows Christians to meet and to deal with pain, disease, and suffering differently from the way non-Christians do. And, for us, Christianity isn't a credo, a way of life that works for us. *It works within us, around us, and through us as we commit and entrust every facet of our lives to Christ!*

As I sat at breakfast with Chris, cutting my blueberry pecan pancakes into bite-sized pieces, my heart rejoiced through and through. Our dear friends, Chris and Karen, were evidence to me that all Debbie and I believed was indeed real!

As we walked out the restaurant door and headed for Chris's car, I turned to him and remarked, "Isn't it great that all we believe in and hope for is more real than real itself?"

We both laughed and headed on home to face another week.

But may the God of all grace, who called us to His eternal glory by Christ Jesus, after you have suffered a while, perfect, establish, strengthen, and settle *you*. To Him *be* the glory and the dominion forever and ever. Amen. By Silvanus, our faithful brother as I consider him, I have written to you briefly, exhorting and testifying that this is the true grace of God in which you stand. She who is in Babylon, elect together with *you*, greets you; and *so does* Mark my son. Greet one another with a kiss of love. Peace to you all who are in Christ Jesus. Amen. (1 Peter 5:10–14)

Bibliography

Barclay, William. *Daily Study Bible: New Testament*. Vol. 14, *The Letters of James and Peter*. Philadelphia: Westminster John Knox, 1976.

_____. *The Master's Men*. Nashville: Abingdon Press, 1976.

Beker, J. Christiaan. *Suffering and Hope: The Biblical Vision and the Human Predicament*. Philadelphia: Fortress Press, 1987.

Bennis, Warren. *On Becoming a Leader*. Reading, MA: Addison-Wesley, 1989.

Bennis, Warren, and Burt Nanus. *Leaders: The Strategies of Taking Charge*. New York: Harper & Row, 1985.

Breese, David. *Satan's Ten Most Believable Lies*. Chicago: Moody Press, 1987.

Cedar, Paul. *The Communicator's Commentary: James, I & II Peter, Jude*. Edited by Lloyd J. Ogilvie. Waco, TX: Word Books, 1984.

Coles, R. "The Inexplicable Prayers of Ruby Bridges." *Christianity Today* 29 (August 9, 1985): 17–20.

Collins, Gary. *The Magnificent Mind*. Waco: Word Books, 1985.

Elliot, Elizabeth. *On Asking God Why*. Old Tappan, NJ: Revell Books, 1989.

Ellul, Jacques. *Money and Power*. Translated by LaVonne Neff. Downers Grove, IL: Inter-Varsity Press, 1984.

_____. *The Presence of the Kingdom*. Colorado Springs, CO: Helmes and Howard, 1989.

_____. *The Subversion of Christianity*. Translated by Geoffrey W. Bromiley. Grand Rapids, MI: Eerdmans, 1986.

Frankl, Victor. *The Unconscious God*. New York: Simon & Shuster, 1976.

Graham, Billy. *Facing Death and the Life After.* Waco: Word Books, 1982.

_____. *Till Armageddon: A Perspective on Suffering.* Waco: Word Books, 1984.

Hammarskjöld, Däg. *Markings.* New York: Ballantine Books, 1985.

Ladd, George. *A Theology of the New Testament.* Grand Rapids, MI: Eerdmans, 1974.

Lewis, C. S. *The Problem of Pain.* New York: Macmillan, 1978.

_____. *The Screwtape Letters.* New York: Macmillan, 1982.

_____. *The Visionary Christian.* New York: Macmillan, 1984.

Michener, James. *The Source.* New York: Ballantine Books, 1965.

Nicoll, W. Robertson, ed. *Expositor's Greek New Testament.* 5 vols. Grand Rapids, MI: Eerdmans, 1952.

Nouwen, Henri. *With Open Hands.* New York: Ballantine, 1985.

Ogilvie, Lloyd J. *Twelve Steps to Living Without Fear.* Waco: Word Publishers, 1987.

Phillips, J. B. *The Newborn Christian.* New York: Macmillan, 1984.

_____. *Your God Is Too Small.* New York: Macmillan, 1961.

Seamands, David. *Healing for Damaged Emotions.* Wheaton, IL: Victor Books, 1981.

Sproul, R. C. *The Holiness of God.* Wheaton, IL: Tyndale, n.d.

_____. *Surprised by Suffering.* Wheaton, IL: Tyndale, 1989.

Tenney, Merrill, ed. *The Zondervan Pictorial Encyclopedia of the Bible.* 5 vols. Grand Rapids, MI: Zondervan Press, 1974.

Thielicke, Helmut. *How to Believe Again.* Translated by H. George Anderson. Philadelphia: Fortress Press, 1972.

Tournier, Paul. *Creative Suffering.* San Francisco: Harper & Row, 1981.

The Whole Person in a Broken World. San Francisco: Harper & Row, 1981.

Williams, Redford. *The Trusting Heart.* New York: Time Books, 1989.

Yancey, Philip. *Where Is God When It Hurts?* Grand Rapids, MI: Zondervan Press, 1977.